Student Companion to
George
ORWELL

Recent Titles in
Student Companions to Classic Writers

Student Companion to Nathaniel Hawthorne
Melissa McFarland Pennell
Student Companion to Charles Dickens
Ruth Glancy

Student Companion to
George ORWELL

Mitzi M. Brunsdale

Student Companions to Classic Writers

Greenwood Press
Westport, Connecticut • London

Library of Congress Cataloging-in-Publication Data

Brunsdale, Mitzi.
    Student companion to George Orwell / Mitzi M. Brunsdale.
       p. cm.—(Student companions to classic writers, ISSN 1522–7979)
    Includes bibliographical references and index.
    ISBN 0–313–30637–0 (alk. paper)
    1. Orwell, George, 1903–1950—Criticism and interpretation. 2. Orwell, George,
1903–1950—Examinations—Study guides. I. Title. II. Series.
    PR6029.R8 Z5895   2000
    828′.91209—dc21   99–049690

British Library Cataloguing in Publication Data is available.

Library of Congress Catalog Card Number Number: 99–049690
ISBN: 0–313–30637–0
ISSN: 1522–7979

First published in 2000

Greenwood Press, 88 Post Road West, Westport, CT 06881
An imprint of Greenwood Publishing Group, Inc.
www.greenwood.com

Printed in the United States of America

The paper used in this book complies with the
Permanent Paper Standard issued by the National
Information Standards Organization (Z39.48–1984).

10 9 8 7 6 5 4 3 2 1

Cover photo of George Orwell © Bettmann/CORBIS.

In memoriam:
Jack Landwehr

Master teacher,
Generous colleague,
Sagacious chairman,
Dear, dear friend—

requiescat in pace.

Contents

Series Foreword

This series has been designed to meet the needs of students and general readers for accessible literary criticism on the American and world writers most frequently studied and read in the secondary school, community college, and four-year college classrooms. Unlike other works of literary criticism that are written for the specialist and graduate student, or that feature a variety of reprinted scholarly essays on sometimes obscure aspects of the writer's work, the Student Companions to Classic Writers series is carefully crafted to examine each writer's major works fully and in a systematic way, at the level of the non-specialist and general reader. The objective is to enable the reader to gain a deeper understanding of the work and to apply critical thinking skills to the act of reading. The proven format for the volumes in this series was developed by an advisory board of teachers and librarians for a successful series published by Greenwood Press, Critical Companions to Popular Contemporary Writers. Responding to their request for easy-to-use and yet challenging literary criticism for students and adult library patrons, Greenwood Press developed a systematic format that is not intimidating but helps the reader to develop the ability to analyze literature.

How does this work? Each volume in the Student Companions to Classic Writers series is written by a subject specialist, an academic who understands students' needs for basic and yet challenging examination of the writer's canon. Each volume begins with a biographical chapter, drawn from published sources, biographies, and autobiographies, that relates the writer's life to his or her work. The next chapter examines the writer's literary heritage, tracing the literary influences of other writers on that writer and explaining and discussing the literary genres into which the writer's work falls. Each of the following chapters examines a major work by the writer, those works most frequently read and studied by high school and college students. Depending on the writer's canon, generally between four and eight major works are examined, each in an individual chapter. The discussion of each work is organized into separate sections on plot development, character development, and major themes. Literary devices and style, narrative point of view, and historical setting are also discussed in turn if pertinent to the work. Each chapter concludes with an alternate critical perspective from which to read the work, such as a psychological or feminist criticism. The critical theory is defined briefly in easy, comprehensible language for the student. Looking at the literature from the point of view of a particular critical approach will help the reader to understand and apply critical theory to the act of reading and analyzing literature.

Of particular value in each volume is the bibliography, which includes a complete bibliography of the writer's works, a selected bibliography of biographical and critical works suitable for students, and lists of reviews of each work examined in the companion, both from the time the literature was originally published and from contemporary sources, all of which will be helpful to readers, teachers, and librarians who would like to consult additional sources.

As a source of literary criticism for the student or for the general reader, this series will help the reader to gain understanding of the writer's work and skill in critical reading.

Preface

George Orwell believed that a writer's subjects were determined by his times. If he had lived before the Industrial Revolution, he wrote in 1935, he might have happily settled down as a vicar in a rural England that still revered its old truths and traditions—the comforts of the countryside, the decency of fellow human beings, the certitude of knowing good from evil— and he might have written gently descriptive works about that peaceful world (*CEJL* 1:1–7). But Orwell lived in the brutal first half of the twentieth century, when soulless machines—locomotives and automobiles, mines, mills and factories, munitions and armaments—and the profiteers they enriched, changed England and the world forever. Despite his natural inclination to satisfy his writer's ego, his sense of beauty, and his urge to set the truth out for posterity, impulses that he believed motivate every writer, Orwell's times forced him to defend freedom by writing from political purpose. For him, liberty meant telling the truth, the objective truth which people usually don't want to hear. Starting in 1936, with many of his countrymen misled by Soviet communism, he relentlessly attacked totalitarianism, especially the Soviet variety, even though in those days criticizing any government whose propaganda described it as socialist was like spitting on the tablecloth (Wain 31). In the process, Orwell turned political writing into an art.

It cost him dearly. Already gravely ill in 1946, he began his most demanding work, *Nineteen Eighty-Four*, the novel that turned "Orwell," his pen name, into "Orwellian," today a description of totalitarian terror. He compared his demon-driven struggle of writing to a long painful illness, which he also knew a great deal about. By the time he completed *Nineteen Eighty-Four*, his life was nearly spent, but the value of his dark vision and its paradoxically bright message was just beginning to be appreciated. Orwell saw things as they really are, but he also insisted that just one ordinary individual who tells the truth can offer humanity the hope it needs to go on. Today the publication of Peter Davison's twenty-volume *Complete Works of George Orwell* testifies to Orwell's vast worldwide influence as a truthteller, revealing "an eccentric, cussed, contrary, incurably English personality," the "unmistakable Orwell voice of defiant unvarnished honesty, of the plain man bluntly telling things as they are" (James 74).

Orwell is chiefly known for his only perfectly composed book, *Animal Farm*, a parable about the inevitable perversion of lofty political ideals, and for *Nineteen Eighty-Four*, which has stood for a half century as a stark beacon against the purposes and tactics of totalitarianism. "Those famous, world-changing novels are just the bark"; "Orwell's journalism is the tree" (James 78), and his reputation has swung with the pendulum of pragmatic politics. Throughout his life, Orwell poured out essays, articles, and hundreds of reviews pointing out that almost all the popular political "emperors" of his day really wore no clothes. His left-wing intellectual contemporaries scorned him for it, but when he died in 1950, during the Cold War, he was eulogized for his denunciation of Stalin's Big Brotherism. By the year 1984, Western governments were seeking détente with Stalin's softer-appearing successors, and literary critics, conveniently ignoring the voices of dissidents like Solzhenitsyn from under the rubble of the Soviet Union's Gulag and psychiatric prison hospitals, hastened to rejoice that the horrifying dystopia of *Nineteen Eighty-Four* had never come to pass.

In 1996, discrediting rumors began to circulate that in 1949 Orwell had kept a private "Big Brother" dossier of about one hundred thirty persons he believed to be "crypto-Communists and fellow-travelers." He also had passed on thirty-five names still not released by the British government to a semisecret British Foreign Office counterpropaganda department, but even though he had been attacked constantly by the leftist intelligentsia, this was no personal vendetta; Orwell intended to continue his fight against totalitarianism from beyond the grave. Despite predictable leftist howls of outrage, time has proved that in almost all cases Orwell's warnings about totalitarianism were on target, couched in a brilliantly clear style impossible to forget. Through his works, Orwell continues to battle hypocrisy, deceit, and lies with the deadly weapon of truth, "old fashioned, empirical truth" (Ash 14).

In the same spirit, I have discussed Orwell's works chronologically in the setting of his violent times—and ours. Orwell's own words always speak best, so I have used excerpts from his journalism in their historical context for to-day's young readers. Citations below are from the most accessible paperback versions of Orwell's works and from *The Collected Essays, Journalism and Letters of George Orwell,* far more widely available than the definitive, voluminous, and necessarily expensive *Complete Works.* In today's violent and hypocritical world we need Orwell's sanity, his common sense, above all his scrupulous in-tellectual honesty, more than ever before.

My profound thanks to Dale Nelson, my colleague and friend, who pro-vided valuable research and insights for a book he ought to have written; to Anne Jones, for helping me through the dark summer of 1998 and finding me Rex; to Dr. Carrie Wood and the Oncology Section of the University of Min-nesota Veterinary Teaching Hospital, and Dr. Dean Gushwa and the staff of Valley Veterinary Hospital, for giving Duke back to me; to Dr. Del Hlavinka, for providing invaluable medical information about tuberculosis; and to John—always with love.

1

Becoming Orwell

Because George Orwell lived during the turbulent first half of the twentieth century, he witnessed some of the most wrenching upheavals that shaped the modern world. From the age of five or six, he said, he knew he would be a writer, and so as an adult he threw himself into extreme experiences like poverty and war, observing and chronicling and making his own sense of them with a unique combination of compassion and integrity. Eventually he taught himself to tap into the prestigious ancestry of political satire in England to analyze the social shifts taking place in his century, so that much of his writing resembles fictionalized sociological tracts (Astier 292).

Eric Arthur Blair was born on June 25, 1903, the second child and only son of an Anglo-Indian family in Motahari, Bengal, about four hundred miles northwest of Calcutta. Eric's father, Richard Walmesley Blair, a Sub-Deputy Opium Agent, First Class, in His Majesty's Bengal Civil Service, was forty-six when Eric was born. Eric's mother, Ida Mabel Limouzin, was half her husband's age, an attractive recently-jilted former governess who had grown up in Moulmein, Burma, and married Richard Blair on the rebound in 1896. Although Ida was accustomed to the difficulties of living in a remote tropical country and coped well with them, she followed a common English colonial practice and left India in 1904 with one-year-old Eric and his six-year-old sister Marjorie, so that the children could be educated in England. Except for a 1907 three-month furlough in England which resulted in the birth of Eric's sister

Avril, Mr. Blair stayed in India to serve out the seven years until his retirement, inspecting Indian opium crops the British sold to China.

During his formative early childhood, Eric grew up fatherless and often sick with a runny nose and cough. Otherwise he was comfortable enough living at Henley-on-Thames, a quiet market town in Oxfordshire. With a maid to help with the household chores, his mother made a happy home for them in "Ermadale," a roomy house she named for "ERic" and "MArjorie." The house was about a mile from the river, a pleasant area for watching barges and canoeing under the old stone arches of the town's bridge, down through gentle hills and lush green meadows. Orwell always loved the peaceful Thames Valley, and he frequently wrote about the happiest times of his childhood there, fishing from a grassy bank "with the rod in my hands . . . the smell of wild peppermint fit to knock you down . . . and I was happy as a tinker" (*CA* 70).

Itinerant tinkers in highly class-conscious Edwardian England were generally regarded as a subspecies only slightly more palatable than out-and-out criminals. Orwell much later recalled that before he was six, his principal heroes were working-class people who did interesting things—farmhands, fishermen, bricklayers, plumbers—but it was not long, he said, before he was forbidden to play with the plumber's children (*RWP* 125). Mrs. Blair would have felt duty-bound to preserve her children from contact with their lower-class contemporaries whose speech patterns marked them as "common" as clearly as a sign around the neck. Parents of Mrs. Blair's station usually felt that at such a linguistically susceptible age, lower-class usage might be transmitted like measles or chicken pox and damage their children for life.

As a youngster, Eric did not have many friends. He detested the genteel little parties with middle-class area children that he and Marjorie were allowed to attend, and Marjorie and her friends, older by those few years which make so much difference to children, barely tolerated Eric anyhow. Rowdy older boys, including Humphrey Dakin who ten years later married Marjorie, often reduced "stinking little Eric," as they cruelly called him (Shelden 18), to tears. Like many lonely children, Eric invented an imaginary companion for himself and took refuge in books. When he was eight, *Gulliver's Travels*, Jonathan Swift's satiric dissection of his world's social ills, appeared among Eric's birthday presents, and it made an impression on him he never forgot. Not long before he died, Orwell praised the "inexhaustible" fascination of *Gulliver's Travels* and observed that he had reread at least part of it during every year of his life (*CEJL* 4:220).

Besides reading, young Eric was already writing. At four or five, he composed a little poem about a tiger, which his mother proudly wrote down for him. For many years he did not realize how deeply his mother loved him, and while his gift for words allowed him to escape from often brutal childhood humiliations, the comfort he found in reading did not ease his growing feelings of inadequacy. Mrs. Blair had good books in their home, but she preferred socializing to reading. Many of her friends were "progressives," members of the socialist Fabian Society and even a few suffragettes. Conversations Eric overheard between his mother and her friends seem to have left him believing that "the hatefulness—above all the physical unattractiveness—of men in women's eyes" seemed to be an established fact (Shelden 22). By the time that Mr. Blair reappeared in Eric's life in 1912, an aloof elderly stranger home from India, sizable seeds of doubt about his own worth had taken root in his personality.

The Blair children attended a small day school in Henley as youngsters, but they, like all middle-class children whose parents could wangle it, went away to single-sex boarding schools at eight or so. Mrs. Blair saw to it that Eric was accepted at a preparatory school renowned for placing its graduates in prestigious public schools like Eton and Harrow, and in September 1911, Eric entered St. Cyprian's, located near Eastbourne in Sussex, about sixty miles south of London. From the very start he hated everything about the place, especially Mr. and Mrs. Wilkes, its headmaster and mistress, and almost all of his fellow students. According to his searing posthumous autobiographical essay, "Such, Such Were the Joys," his loathing for St. Cyprian's and everything it did to him in his five years there seems to have increased until he died.

The "joys" of Eric's school days left deep scars. As Orwell knew, discussing England means discussing education, and discussing English education is impossible without discussing class (Gross 10). The Blairs, living on a retired civil servant's relatively modest fixed income, had to scrimp ingeniously to educate their children in the style they considered proper. St. Cyprian's yearly fee was about £180 per year, roughly a third of Mr. Blair's yearly pension, but Eric was bright enough for the Blairs to cut a deal for half-price fees with Headmaster Wilkes and his wife, known familiarly to the boys of St. Cyprian's as "Sambo" and "Flip." The idea was that once Eric won a scholarship to Eton or Harrow, his achievement could be advertised to attract more high-paying students. At age eleven, Orwell maintained, Flip and Sambo began openly to rub his nose in his comparative poverty, refusing to give him the spending money his parents sent. They even denied him the birthday cakes which other students could have, because, as Mrs. Wilkes openly proclaimed, a boy like Eric, attending on the Wilkes' bounty, should not enjoy such things. Eric's schoolmates could hardly have failed to notice that Mrs. Wilkes humiliated him both in public and in private, or that he received the canings, deserved and otherwise, from the headmaster, and as boys do, they made the most of his unhappiness. The British class system was such a subtle "instrument of discomfort" (Gross 10) that Orwell later insisted that sending a child to school among wealthier fellows was the greatest cruelty one could inflict (*KAF* 41).

How much Orwell exaggerated the ordeal of his days at St. Cyprian's is debatable. Several published memoirs by "Old St. Cyprianites" seem to indicate that life there might not have been quite so horrid as Orwell painted it. Cyril Connolly, one of Orwell's few school friends, felt that the Wilkeses tried to do their best, given the standards of the times. Mrs. Wilkes, however, seems to have been the real authority in the school, and she could be malignantly capricious. Her former student David Ogilvy, later a successful advertising executive, described her in his autobiography as "satanic," carrying "the art of castration to extraordinary perfection . . . [and playing] games of emotional cat-and-mouse against every boy in the school" (Ogilvy 15).

In spite of Flip and Sambo and the boys, Eric Blair was writing. To build character, St. Cyprian's boasted a Cadet Corps, and after the outbreak of World War I in August 1914, the students were treated to battlefield tales from visiting Old Boys. Nineteen of St. Cyprian's Old Boys were killed or were missing during the first two years of the war, and eleven-year-old Eric Blair, caught up in the patriotic fervor that was sweeping England's youth to oblivion, responded with a poem titled "Awake! Young Men of England," his first published work, appearing in his hometown newspaper.

Eric's few other bright moments at St. Cyprian's came because of his likable drawing and geography master, Mr. Sillar, who despite Mrs. Wilkes' disparagement would sometimes take the boys on expeditions to catch butterflies. Eric, though, enjoyed best his holidays at Shiplake, where his family lived between 1912 and 1915, and in the summer of 1914 he became friendly with the three Buddicom children who lived nearby. Both the oldest, Jacintha, then thirteen to Eric's eleven, and Eric's younger sister Avril, recalled that Eric always seemed perfectly happy there (Buddicom 13). Eric and Prosper Buddicom created ferocious concoctions that disgusted the girls, like a homemade whiskey still that blew up on the stove while the Blairs' cook was napping, causing her to quit. Eric and Jacintha spent hours talking and reading together, and she believed that he "was always going to write; not just as an author, always a FAMOUS AUTHOR, in capitals" (Gross 2).

First, though, he had to finish his education. Studying furiously to fulfill his parents' promise to Sambo and Flip, Eric at thirteen first won a scholarship to Wellington College, where he spent the January to March term of 1917. He then received a scholarship to Eton, where he entered in May, just shy of his fourteenth birthday.

Eton, which has always granted its students considerable freedom, proved considerably more pleasant for Eric than St. Cyprian's. Eton's nine-hundred-odd "Oppidans" (students whose parents footed the bill) lodged in Windsor, while the seventy subsidized King's Scholars, including Eric, lived in the ancient college itself, where after his first year he had a room of his own. Beatings by the Sixth Form boys, who functioned as judges, jurors, and executors of the school's justice, were frequent, but the pressure to "swot" for all-important examinations was off. Despite his brilliance, Eric's academic career at Eton was mediocre because he took advantage of his new liberation and read almost exclusively what interested him.

During Eric's first months at Eton, his growing tendency to rebel against the norms of his class was bolstered by a pervasive disillusionment far removed from the jaunty patriotism of "Awake! Young Men of England." In a war that cost a total of ten million lives, too many of England's young men had died useless deaths in the trenches, and too many returned shell-shocked or embittered by the monstrous follies of the graybeards safe at home who had sent them there. By 1917, the whole British Army was demoralized, and so was most of the home front. Eton, one of the traditional alma maters of British leaders, suffered horribly. When the war ended on November 11, 1918, 1157 Old Etonians had been killed, as though a plague had wiped out the whole population of the school (Shelden 63).

By that time, as Orwell later recalled, the war had almost ceased to affect Eton's ever-hungry adolescents, tormented by the bad wartime food made immeasurably worse by rationing (*CEJL* 1:537), and they simply tuned out the patriotic stories and what doomed young officer Wilfrid Owen called "the old lie," that it is sweet and fitting to die for one's country. As a member of Eton's Officer Training Corps, Eric preferred the signaling section, where during training exercises he could sit under a tree by himself thinking the long, long youthful thoughts sparked in him by the rebellious poet Shelley, the *fin de siècle* decadent Ernest Dowson, and the laconic elegiac poet A. E. Housman.

Eric was also beginning to notice that girls might be more than childhood playmates. While he was at Eton, his parents moved again, this time to a flat at Notting Hill Gate, and they arranged for him to spend much of his holiday time with the Buddicoms. Proximity to the bubbly, bright, and two-years-older Jacintha had the natural effect; fifteen-year-old Eric was soon smitten, though their mutual attraction never progressed beyond a non-kissing flirtation. It did result in a flurry of poetic creativity on Eric's part, including a rather daring poem characterizing Jacintha as "The Pagan," and a sonnet which opens with the lines, "Our minds are married, but we are too young/For wedlock by the customs of this age" (Buddicom 87). Aside from adolescent poetry and the satiric stories and poems Eric contributed to Eton's literary magazines, however, his public school career was undistinguished. In the 1920 summer examinations, he was 117th of 140, although he distinguished himself during Eton's peculiar "Wall Game," a violent muddy football-less scrimmage.

By December 20, 1921, when Eric Blair left Eton, he had become a young man. He had stretched up nearly to his adult height of six feet three inches and had taken up smoking, an especially unhealthy habit, considering his weak lungs and two bad bouts of pneumonia in 1918 and 1921. The reasons behind his first choice of career seem cloudy. Some family friends claimed that Mrs. Blair pushed him toward a civil service career in Burma, where her mother and other relatives still lived, and one of Eric's friends at Eton thought Eric harbored romantic notions about the Far East (Shelden 1991: 80). On the other hand, Jacintha Buddicom believed that Eric was a born scholar who lived for books and had his heart set on going to Oxford. She had heard Mrs. Buddicom and Mrs. Blair often deploring old Mr. Blair's unshakable refusal to consider anything for Eric but a career in the "Indian Civil," which Jacintha felt hurt Eric deeply. Jacintha's brother Prosper, who didn't care for books at all, was destined for Oxford, while Eric, who she felt would have appreciated a chance at Oxford was forbidden it by his father (Gross 4–5).

In June 1922, Eric Blair took his examinations for the Imperial Police, and on October 27 he sailed for Burma, one of the least desirable postings in the Far East. The lush imagery of Kipling's poem "The Road to Mandalay," one of Orwell's lifelong favorites, may have raised his hopes for a tropical paradise, but when Blair disembarked at Rangoon on November 22, its brutal realities must have nearly overwhelmed him with horror and disgust (Gross 20).

Burma was daily growing more dangerous for the few Europeans who lived there. When Eric Blair began his career in the Imperial police, Burma was seething with nationalistic fervor. It had the highest crime rate and some of the worst political unrest in the British Empire, and just before his arrival, an Imperial policeman had his nose cut off by rioting knife-wielding monks (Gross 21), while the morale and standards of conduct of the Europeans there had sunk to lamentable levels.

In all, Blair spent about four and a half years in seven different Burmese cities. He hated to leave Jacintha, but evidently she did not return his affection, since she answered only the first of several letters in which he poured out his loneliness and misery. In his first weeks there, he also began the elementary lessons in Burmese required of new personnel and eventually became fluent in the language. His assignments followed the standard pattern of the times, moving him into positions of increasing authority where he had ample opportunity to observe the mixed-race, open, and classless Burmese society with its ancient tradition of sexual equality and emphasis on individual dignity (Gross 22). To his dismay, Blair also witnessed the casual cruelty with which the Europeans treated the Burmese, whom they mostly considered subhuman.

At first, Blair seemed to share the Europeans' anti-Burmese sentiments, but Burmese Dr. Maung Htin Aung, who had been one of the rebellious Rangoon university students who provoked Blair into lashing viciously out at them on a train, declared that Blair put aside his prejudices and soon began to hate his role as a British Imperial policeman (Gross 22). In 1926, Blair, now fluent in Burmese, was posted to Moulmein, where his anger and frustration built up to fever pitch. His outraged observations of the inhumanity that then pervaded British Imperial service eventually resulted in two of his most famous essays, "A Hanging" and "Shooting an Elephant," published in 1931 and 1936 respectively. From then until he left Burma, Blair sought out both white and non-white friendless, poor, defeated, and downtrodden human beings, and his experiences with them became the basis for his first novel, *Burmese Days* (1934). Dr. Aung believed that if Blair had stayed longer in Burma, he and the Burmese would surely have become friends, and if he "had been Orwell, not Blair," he might have helped to change English opinion about Burmese nationalism (Gross 29). Staying on, though, became impossible for Blair. By mid-1927 he was sicker in soul than body as he recuperated from a serious case of dengue fever. He concluded that the Empire was enslaving its masters and turning him into a monstrous brute. On July 14, he sailed for England, unable ever to forget the faces of the human beings the British imperial system had forced him to punish so harshly.

On the way home, Blair left his ship at Marseilles, where he watched a street protest against the execution of the anarchists Sacco and Vanzetti in the United States. Blair found himself greatly relieved to be able to tell a fellow Englishman on the street that the two might be innocent. This taste of free speech foreshadowed the first big turning point in his life, because when he reached England, already "half-determined" to quit his job in the Imperial Police, "one whiff of English air" made up his mind (*RWP* 137–38). As soon as he reached his parents' new home at Southwold, a resort town on the Suffolk coast, he declared he wanted to go on a family vacation to Cornwall for a month, and there, according to Avril, he told them that what he really wanted to do was write. Mrs. Blair was saddened, but Mr. Blair was disappointed and outraged that Eric was rejecting tradition, not to mention sacrificing considerable pay for sick leave by insisting on resigning effective January 1, 1928.

By ending his civil service career and refusing support from his parents, Eric Blair was escaping not only the imperialism that had sickened him but any other form of "man's dominion over man" (*RWP* 138). Like several characters in his novels, he then seems to have made it his goal to fail, reasoning that by accepting himself as the failure he thought he was, he could find a certain honor in not giving in to values he thought were false. Convinced of his own worthlessness and brandishing his desire to battle injustice like a terrible swift literary sword, Blair, nearly penniless, set out on a two-and-a-half-year descent into destitution that resulted in his first book-length publication, the autobiographical *Down and Out in Paris and London* (1933). From this point on, he habitually wore the scruffy corduroys of the working class, apparently oblivious to their clash with his posh Eton accent.

In the fall of 1927, even though he was far from well and suffering badly from England's damp cold after the tropical climate of Burma, Blair moved into an unheated London flat, which he used until the following spring as a base for expeditions into the city's tramp subculture. To distract from his Eton accent, he camouflaged himself in worn-out dungarees and shabby jacket and smudged his face. He spent nights in crowded "spikes," dormitories attached to local workhouses where the poor shared their meager food and tobacco with him, told him their stories about better and mostly worse times, and exposed him to their illnesses, almost certainly a factor in Orwell's struggles against lung disease. Back in his flat, he warmed his hands over candle flames to record his experiences until horrified friends gave him a small oil stove (Shelden 1991: 119). Blair was never really "down and out," since he could always have called on his family; but he was not "slumming" either, because he cared deeply about the unfortunate people for whom he was preparing to speak.

After he spent a winter observing London's slums firsthand, Blair left for Paris, where his aunt Nellie Limouzin lived "in sin" with her French lover. Blair settled into the grubby little Rue du Pot de Fer, which despite its sleaziness was located in what Ernest Hemingway called the "best" (meaning the most typical) part of the Latin Quarter (Gross 40–41). Blair's tenement was in the middle of a walking-distance area bounded by the Sorbonne, the splendid Jardin des Plantes, the Jardin du Luxembourg, and the Montparnasse cafes, allowing him to experience the seedy side of the city while remaining within range of its more pleasant areas, not to mention the escape route Aunt Nellie offered. Blair refused to take that easy way out, though, even when he fell dangerously ill in March with severe bronchitis or possibly pneumonia. After a gruesome hospital stay followed by near starvation that May, he found a job as a hotel *plongeur* (dishwasher), episodes that appeared in *Down and Out in Paris and London.* Despite all the ugliness that Blair sought and found before he returned to England at Christmas of 1929, he held onto his trademark high-spirited zest. He delighted in aspects of life other people might find intensely disgusting (Gross 49) and wove them into an unforgettable portrait of the poverty just beneath the surfaces of two of Europe's most glittering capitals.

Already during the summer of 1929 in Paris, Blair had written two novels, three stories, and several articles (Gross 40), now lost. He had offered articles to various English magazines that November and December, and his literary luck turned when Max Plowman, editor of the illustrious British journal *Adelphi,* accepted an article on tramps, eventually published as "The Spike." When Blair came back to England, he became a regular reviewer for *Adelphi* and struck up lasting friendships with Plowman and his coeditor and bankroller Sir

Richard Rees. For the next two years, Blair lived with his parents at Southwold even though he detested the resort area. He spent the summer of 1931 with migrant workers picking hops in Kent, a physically painful job he eventually worked into his 1935 novel, *A Clergyman's Daughter.*

Blair's closest friend in the early 1930s was Brenda Salkeld, a vicar's daughter who taught physical education at a girls' school in Southwold. They shared walks, went horseback riding, and talked books endlessly. Some time in 1930 he proposed, but Brenda refused, commenting later that she and Eric had begun as friends, but she soon realized marriage would have been impossible because his writing would always come first and he would be impossible to live with. Their relationship soon modulated into an affectionate friendship (Shelden 1991: 143–44).

Blair's literary efforts were proceeding slowly. *Modern Youth* lost several stories he submitted before they went out of business, but in October 1931, *The New Statesman* published his article "Hop-picking," and that December, after acquiring a literary agent, Leonard Moore, Blair submitted the manuscript of *Down and Out in Paris and London* to T. S. Eliot at Faber and Faber. Eliot's rejection in February 1932 so depressed Blair that he wanted to destroy the book, but Moore thought he might still be able to place it. In April, Blair took a teaching job at The Hawthorns, a small day school he thoroughly detested after two months. He recorded those unhappy memories in *A Clergyman's Daughter.* He also carried on a torrid, mostly out-of-doors romance with Eleanor Jaques, whom he had known at Southwold, though Eleanor, too, soon realized that for Blair, writing had to come first. That August, Victor Gollancz, a fervently Socialist publisher, offered Blair a contract for *Down and Out in Paris and London* with a welcome forty-pound advance, and on November 19, Blair chose a pen name for its publication: George Orwell.

Down and Out in Paris and London appeared in January 1933 to good reviews. Orwell had already finished the first hundred pages of *Burmese Days,* and by the end of February, Moore had negotiated the American publication of *Down and Out.* During a teaching job he took at Exbridge that spring, Orwell enjoyed a few more chilly outdoor trysts with Eleanor—all that his limited budget would allow—before she dropped him in July. After he finished *Burmese Days* in December, he wrote to Brenda fervently praising James Joyce's *Ulysses* for its frank portrayal of sexuality and the fearful despair of modern times, the topics Orwell himself most wanted to address in fiction. He had a near fatal attack of pneumonia just before Christmas, but he came home from the hospital on January 8, 1934, with an idea he turned into *A Clergyman's Daughter.* He completed that novel the following October while dickering with the U.S. publishers Harper and Row over *Burmese Days,* since Americans found that anti-imperialist book more palatable than the British did. At the same time, Orwell was trying to persuade Harper and Row to commission him to do a short biography of Mark Twain, but they declined. Orwell moved to London on October 20, living for a time above Francis Westrope's Booklover's Corner, where Orwell worked until 1936.

With Orwell, new living space usually meant a new book project. His writing was gaining momentum, because shortly after settling in with the Westropes, he started his next novel, *Keep the Aspidistra Flying* and wrote a few poems that appeared in *Adelphi*. After requesting changes in *A Clergyman's Daughter*, Gollancz published it on March 11, 1935, and since *Burmese Days* sold a respectable three thousand copies in America, Gollancz agreed to bring it out that June.

Orwell's personal life was beginning to look up, too. Buoyed by his modest literary success—he was making about £ 200 a year from his writing—Orwell moved to a flat in Hampstead Heath and promptly fell head over heels in love with Eileen O'Shaughnessy, then living in London with her brother Laurence, a rising young lung specialist, and his wife Gwen, also a physician. Orwell proposed to Eileen almost immediately, and though she initially turned him down, they saw one another frequently that summer. In addition, when *Burmese Days* came out, Orwell's old school chum Cyril Connolly gave it a good review in *The New Statesman*, and they renewed their friendship after a fourteen-year hiatus.

In spite of these improvements in his personal and literary circumstances, Orwell was disturbed by the growing tension in Europe, where fascism was flexing its muscles. In 1935 Germany repudiated the Treaty of Versailles and Italy invaded helpless Ethiopia. Though the conservative-led National Government remained in power, massive British unemployment caused many British voters to swing to the Left. The British Communist Party, the Independent Labour Party (ILP), and the Socialist League all demanded that the working class unite against international fascism and the National Government at home, though the British Labour Party opposed communist involvement—with good reason. In August 1935, the Seventh Comintern (session of the International Communist Party) stressed the clandestine "Popular Front" concept, an infiltration tactic based on the ancient story of the Trojan horse (Johnson 323–44).

As the power of fascism and the influence of its equally sinister opponent, communism, mounted in 1935, Orwell became increasingly concerned with the international political scene, which he felt was approaching disaster. Through Gordon Comstock, the hero of *Keep the Aspidistra Flying*, Orwell eerily predicted "the humming of the aeroplanes and the crash of the bombs . . . squadron after squadron darkening the sky like gnats" (*KAF* 21). While writing this novel, Orwell was trying to thrash out his own political position, eventually concluding that socialism alone could successfully oppose fascism, which he considered an extended form of capitalism.

Accordingly, in January 1936, Orwell's interests shifted from literature to politics. Soon after he brought the manuscript of *Keep the Aspidistra Flying* to Gollancz, Gollancz offered him £ 500 to research and write a book on unemployment in England's severely depressed North, possibly for consideration by Gollancz' large Left Book Club. The money would allow Orwell to marry Eileen and buy the little shop at Wallingford that they had in mind, so he quit his bookstore job and headed north, covering the one hundred miles between Coventry and Manchester in buses and on foot. He arrived at the village of Wigan on January 30 and promptly rented a room above a tripe shop to see life there at its very worst.

Orwell spent about two months in the North, as short a stay as possible (Gross 55–56). Aside from the tripe shop which he vividly described in *The Road to Wigan Pier*, his introductions from ILP officials provided him some fairly decent lodgings, and he also visited his sister Marjorie and her family at Leeds. Orwell went down into the mines where because of his height he knocked his head severely against a beam and strained his legs and back muscles so badly he had to spend several days in bed. He attended some political meetings where the Communist-led heckling and violence disgusted him, but after visiting the miserable homes of miners and unemployed workers, Orwell came away in March sickened and saddened, and determined to tell the world about it all.

On April 1, 1936, Orwell moved in at "The Stores," Wallingford, in Hertfordshire, the same month Gollancz published *Keep the Aspidistra Flying*, which received indifferent reviews. Undaunted, Orwell opened a little grocery, started one of his most famous essays, "Shooting an Elephant," and married Eileen on June 9 in an Anglican ceremony in the village church, because he wanted to honor traditional English values. By early October he had finished *The Road to Wigan Pier*, its first half a harrowing glimpse into the harsh lives of impoverished Northern workers and their families, and its second half so unorthodox an exploration of socialism that Gollancz had to swallow hard to publish it the next March, adding a note in which he disavowed Orwell's position. By that time, however, Orwell's passion for justice had led him far beyond Victor Gollancz and the Left Book Club. Hostilities had broken out in Spain between the left-wing government and mutining right-wing generals under Francisco Franco, and on December 23, Orwell left for Barcelona, an introduction from the ILP in his pocket and the willingness to fight for his beliefs burning in his heart.

The Spanish Civil War pitted Fascist leaders Hitler and Mussolini, who supplied men and armament to their proxies, the Nationalists led by Franco, against Stalin, who contributed three thousand specialists and advisers, vast amounts of equipment, and an enormous Communist propaganda effort to Stalin's proxies, the left-wing Republicans, who initially were mainly comprised of Popular Front fighters, anarchists, and Communists. About 40,000 foreigners, including 2500 British and 2500 Americans, fought for the Republican side. The British suffered an estimated 543 killed and 1762 wounded (Johnson 330)—among the latter, George Orwell.

Although he had originally intended to report the war as a journalist and then had thought about enlisting in the Communist-sponsored International Brigade, upon arriving in Barcelona on December 30, 1936, Orwell decided to fight under the auspices of POUM (the letters represent the Spanish phrase for the Workers' Party of Marxist Unification), because he realized that POUM was resisting Communist social and political counterrevolutionary activities. Orwell believed POUM's cause was worth fighting for (Gross 66). After about a week, he reached the Aragon front and stayed in its rat-infested trenches for four months. During that glacial February in the mountains, he received two pieces of good news: *The Road to Wigan Pier* had been chosen by the 40,000–member Left Book Club, a larger audience than Orwell had ever had before, and Eileen was in Barcelona, working for John McNair in the POUM Executive Office. In March she even visited Orwell at the ILP frontline position near Monte Trazo.

Orwell and Eileen had had high ideals when they came to Spain, but those ideals were shattered when they were caught up in hostilities between factions of the Republican side of the Civil War. Most of the European Left uncritically supported the Soviet-led Communists, believing Stalin a lesser evil than Hitler, but POUM members opposed the terroristic tactics the Communists were using to destroy opponents of their orthodox Popular Front (Gross 64). During May, the Communists purged POUM members from the Republican government, taking over the Interior Ministry and all important police and parliamentary posts, just as Stalin was purging his former revolutionary associates and anyone else in the Soviet Union he believed to be a threat. Stalinist propagandists branded the POUM as "Trotskyist" and spread the word that POUM was Franco's "Fifth Column." Back in Barcelona in early May, Orwell helped defend POUM's headquarters, then returned to the front, and ten days later was shot in the throat. He spent the next two weeks in a Lerida hospital and then went back to a Barcelona sanatorium to recuperate.

Orwell was released on June 16, two days after Orlov, the Communist head of the Spanish NKVD (secret police), had ordered POUM leaders arrested. The NKVD took the POUM chief Andrés Nin and his lieutenants to Barcelona's former convent of St. Ursula, known as the "Dachau of Republican Spain," where Nin, Orwell's model for Emanuel Goldstein in *Nineteen Eighty-Four*, chose death under torture rather than making a false confession (Johnson 334). Thousands of POUM members were executed or tortured to death in Spanish Communist prisons, and since the Spanish NKVD described both Orwell and Eileen as "known Trotskyists," they had to flee for their lives. After their friend Georges Kopp was arrested, Orwell took to the streets disguised as a tramp, but he daringly visited Kopp in jail several times. Finally on June 23, Orwell and Eileen, her nerves battered, escaped to France.

The costs of the Spanish Civil War were enormous. A total of nearly 200,000 people were killed, 25,000 died of starvation, 130,000 were murdered or shot behind the lines. Half a million Spaniards fled into exile, more than half never to return (Johnson 339). For Orwell, one of very few major European writers to denounce Communist brutality in Spain, his experience there marked a crucial watershed in his life and career. Until 1937, "Orwell saw the world struggle as between Left and Right, with the goodwill and the good arguments on the side of the Left. . . . After 1937, he saw it in terms of democracy *versus* totalitarianism, and he no longer cared whether the totalitarianism called itself Left or Right" (Gross 79). The Spanish experience changed his outlook forever.

The Spanish police confiscated Orwell's diaries, but almost immediately on reaching England, he began to write about the POUM martyrs. He tried to place his article, "Eyewitness in Barcelona," with *The New Statesman*, but his provocative view that the Republican leftist government was using barbaric fascist methods to achieve socialist aims (Shelden 1991: 277) was unacceptable to *The New Statesman*'s editor Kingsley Martin, who like most left-wing intellectuals categorically refused to link communism with fascism. Martin also rejected Orwell's reviews of books dealing with the Spanish Civil War. While Franco waged his war of attrition in Spain, Orwell was preparing his own anticommunist barrage, *Homage to Catalonia*. He had great difficulty finding a publisher, but the book finally appeared in April 1938. Its sales were the most dismal of all of Orwell's books in his lifetime.

Orwell was exhausted that fall, and his doctors recommended a warmer climate and rest, which Eileen badly needed, too. On September 2 they sailed for Morocco where they stayed until the following March despite bad housing, the culture shock of living amid an impoverished Arab population, and a severe intestinal illness. That fall as he watched Stalin cynically cut off support to his one-time cohorts in Spain, Orwell ridiculed the Soviet show trials in articles and reviews (Gross 118). He began a new novel, *Coming Up for Air*, a book full of disgust and despair at the failure of the European intelligentsia to realize the dangers that he saw looming desperately close.

Barcelona fell to Franco's forces on January 28, 1939; Madrid surrendered two months later, at the same time that Hitler renounced Germany's 1934 treaty with Poland. Orwell returned to Southwold, where in spite of his own severe chest illness and his father's terminal cancer, they managed at last to reconcile their differences. Just before Mr. Blair died on June 28, Gollancz published *Coming Up for Air*, which sold well. Orwell then felt himself at loose ends, trying to establish a direction for his literary efforts by examining the ways in which other writers, especially Charles Dickens, had proceeded (Shelden 1991: 315). Orwell was also contemplating a long novel projected as "The Quick and the Dead," but he never started it. Aggravating his general disgust with English policies, police descended on his home at Wallingford and confiscated books from his library. On September 1, 1939, when Hitler defied the Anglo-French appeasement policy and sent his Panzers roaring into Poland, Orwell might have felt less dismay than relief. Orwell's spirits rallied during World War II, partly because he found any kind of action preferable to waiting, and partly because the war was eventually won through the efforts of the ordinary men Orwell always celebrated.

Not much happened militarily during the "Phoney War" of the 1939–40 winter. Germany was readying its spring *Blitzkrieg*, and Orwell drifted along at Wallingford, tending his garden and writing book reviews while Eileen worked for the government Censorship Department at Whitehall in London. He was roused that spring when Nazi forces conquered Norway in April, swept through Holland and Belgium, and in May drove the British army to the beaches at Dunkirk, where Eileen's beloved brother Dr. Laurence O'Shaughnessy was killed. France surrendered in June and most of Britain believed that invasion was imminent. Orwell moved into a flat near Baker Street and, too ill for regular service, became a sergeant in the Fifth London Home Guard Battalion. At the same time, he was producing dozens of reviews and essays for seven different periodicals, including the left-wing British *Tribune*. Because of his hectic pace, he abandoned his habit of methodically hand-revising his work and composed single drafts directly at the typewriter.

Orwell was reminded of the bombardment in Barcelona when Hitler's furious blitz descended on London, and he responded with *The Lion and the Unicorn*, a long essay paying tribute to the loyalty of ordinary British folk and indicting what he called their "House of Lords" leadership (Shelden 1991: 338). Except for *The Road to Wigan Pier*, *The Lion and the Unicorn* became Orwell's best-selling work to that date. That December, the prestigious U.S. *Partisan Review* invited Orwell to write "London Letters," which he kept up until 1946, and he also began a series of broadcasts for the BBC.

In the spring of 1941, Orwell had discovered that his work was being censored (Shelden 1991: 340). In spite of his unhappiness at this governmental policy, he accepted a full-time job not long afterward with the Indian Section of the BBC's Empire Service, making propaganda broadcasts to indoctrinate

Indians with "cultural imperialism," an agenda he eventually found he could not support. Because of his dedication to the war effort, Orwell tried his best with this job, but it was office drudgery of the worst sort for him, because he was passionately dedicated to Indian liberation. He even asked the BBC engineers to shut off the transmission power for his program, but they refused (Gross 93).

By the next spring, the threat of a Nazi invasion had largely dissipated and the sense of urgency lifted from British shoulders, leaving a dank sense of frustrated expectancy. Orwell concluded that his efforts at the BBC were futile (Shelden 1991: 347) because of continual official censorship. Eileen, now working at the Ministry of Food, was absorbed in her own career as an antidote for her grief. Around this time, Orwell had several brief affairs with young women who worked at the BBC, an indication of his loneliness and perhaps a hint of the depression that may have accompanied his physical deterioration. His friend and BBC colleague William Empson observed that during this period, Orwell himself "stank, and evidently knew it. . . . It was the rotting lungs that you could smell . . . a sweetish smell of decay" (Gross 97).

In September 1943, in what Churchill called the "end of the beginning" of the war, Orwell had had enough. He resigned from the BBC, took on the literary editorship of the *Tribune* which he retained until 1945, and launched a project he had been thinking about since Spain, a kind of "parable" about "the gramophone mind" of Soviet Communism (Shelden 1991: 365)—*Animal Farm*, which he finished the next April. Rejected by Gollancz and several other publishers, *Animal Farm* was published by Fredric Warburg at the close of World War II. It received immediate and astonishing acclaim.

Orwell had never been busier than he was during the last two years of the war. Besides all of his writing, he was producing regular "As I Please" columns for the *Tribune,* reviewing for the *Observer* and the *Manchester Evening News,* and assembling another volume of essays, and he and Eileen were bombed out of their Mortimer Crescent apartment.

Despite the war, this might have been one of the happiest times of Orwell's life, with literary success finally close at hand and his home life stabilizing. Believing that he was sterile, Orwell had decided he and Eileen should adopt a baby. The child they named Richard Horatio Blair was born May 14, 1944, and Eileen left her job to care for him. They both adored the child, but Orwell left the *Tribune* in February 1945 to become a war correspondent for the *Observer,* while Eileen took Richard to the home of her brother's widow, Dr. Gwen O'Shaughnessy, near Newcastle. Shortly after Orwell arrived in Paris, suffering from another bad case of bronchitis, tragic news reached him. Eileen had died on the operating table; she was thirty-nine.

After Eileen's death, Orwell plunged himself into work—in 1945 he published over 130 articles and reviews—and he acquired "Barnhill," a rambling, dilapidated old house in the remote Scottish Hebrides. He also proposed fruitlessly to several women, hoping to find someone to share his life and care for Richard. One was Sonia Brownell, an attractive blonde editorial assistant with whom he had a brief fling.

Orwell's health dramatically declined during the harrowing winter of 1946, when heating and decent food were virtually unobtainable in England. In April 1947, he packed up his son and Susan Watson, the baby's nanny, and left for Barnhill, where no one had lived since 1934. Orwell freed himself from his contractual obligations to Victor Gollancz so that the project that would become his masterpiece *Nineteen Eighty-Four*, a scathing denunciation of totalitarianism, could be published by the firm of Secker and Warburg. Driving himself brutally, Orwell managed to complete the manuscript in December 1948, continually coughing up blood and near collapse.

During the brief remainder of his life, *Nineteen Eighty-Four* became a bestseller in both Britain and America. Ironically, Orwell was simultaneously at the height of his literary fame and at the verge of death. New antibiotic treatments for tuberculosis were just being developed, and Orwell underwent streptomycin therapy in 1948 and 1949, but in his weakened condition he could not tolerate its grueling side effects. After a lifetime of abusing his weak lungs with tobacco, rough living conditions, and a strenuous work routine, Orwell's strength was almost exhausted.

In the spring of 1949 he met Sonia Brownell again. She was on the rebound from a failed affair with a French philosopher, and Orwell needed someone with publishing experience to look after his literary estate. This time she accepted his proposal and bought herself an engagement ring at his expense in early September. Friends who attended their hospital wedding ceremony on October 13 felt that Orwell seemed happy with plans for moving to a Swiss sanatorium and was full of enthusiasm for a new book he wanted to write, but on January 21, 1950, four days before he and Sonia were to leave for Switzerland, George Orwell died alone at forty-six in University Hospital, London.

Orwell's wealthy friend David Astor arranged the traditional Anglican funeral Orwell had wanted, and he was buried near the Astor estate in Oxfordshire, in the beautiful Thames Valley he had always loved. Another friend who shared many of Orwell's opinions, Malcolm Muggeridge, wryly noted in his diary that dying on Lenin's birthday and being buried by David Astor represented the whole range of Orwell's life (Bright-Holmes 175). According to Muggeridge, Orwell's funeral was "a rather melancholy, chilly affair, the congregation largely jewish [*sic*] and almost entirely unbelievers," with Eileen's family showing the only genuine grief and the pallbearers looking "like Molotov's bodyguard" (Wolfe 227).

Orwell's will directed that no biography of him should be undertaken. For all the literary success that came almost too late, for all the furor Orwell's staunch anticommunism caused among left-wing intellectuals, for all his wrath at injustice and his devastating satires of totalitarianism, Malcolm Muggeridge spoke for many of his friends who remembered him "exactly like Don Quixote, very lean and egoistic and honest and foolish, a veritable Knight of the Woeful Countenance" (Wolfe 227): "Not merely the most courteous, kindly and lovable man I have known, but as the one of all my friends with whom, if I could today, I would choose to spend an evening" (Gross 132).

His Only Real Education

George Orwell always wrote from his own experience. He encountered life's unfairness very early and took refuge in books, as many unhappy children did before the advent of television and computer games. The more he read, the more angry he became at injustice and the more he yearned for the happiness and security traditional English values like decency, integrity, and compassion offered. As he grew up, he also continually sought out dangerous experiences to test himself, and gradually he built the single, simple theme of all his work: that one man, even if he knows he is doomed, must fight as hard as he can against unjust collective human forces that try to dehumanize and strangle him, so that in his own heart and soul he can regain the peace he knew as a cherished child. Orwell waged his lifelong battle against injustice with both deeds and words, and the words he read often contributed significantly to those he wrote.

One slim clue from Eric Blair's first four years suggests a childhood source for the odd mixture of anger and nostalgia that animated most of his adult writing. Eric's mother kept a diary in 1905, the year after she returned from India with one-year-old Eric and his older sister Marjorie, and she noted on February 11 that "Baby" (Eric) called everything "beastly." Most toddlers probably could not have come up with that term on their own, suggesting that Mrs. Blair's initial unfavorable reaction to England strongly influenced her son (Crick 7–8).

Orwell's lush evocations of the tropics in *Burmese Days,* the most powerful descriptive passages he ever wrote, may reflect happy memories of India, either his own infantile unconscious ones or, more likely, his mother's. In India, the Blairs had enjoyed a good-sized bungalow with large gardens, and a houseful of native servants freed Mrs. Blair to dote upon her little boy.

Living in the cold, gray, rainy climate of England, with no father at home until Eric had been at boarding school for a year, a new baby sister to occupy Mrs. Blair, now making do with only one daily maid, and his older sister Marjorie away at school, must have seemed increasingly "beastly" and unfair to young Eric. He probably felt neglected, resentful, isolated, and misunderstood; and he had a hard time making friends among the few children whose families were acceptable to his mother. From the age of two, he suffered continually from a runny nose, coughs, and a wheezy chest; and when he went to school he was far too shy to let his mother, whom he adored, know how miserable he was. In "a sweeping, unprovable, Orwellian sort of generalization," such youthful problems may be classic symptoms of a future writing career, "that classic way of avenging oneself for an unhappy childhood" (Stansky and Abrahams 1972: 16).

The books young Eric gobbled up fueled his desire to write. When he was five, Mrs. Blair enrolled him at "Sunnylands," a day school run by Anglican nuns where Marjorie was already an unstoppable reader. Eric quickly learned to read and shared Marjorie's books, soon devouring anything in print he could find. The books, good and bad, that Eric Blair read while he was at Sunnylands, St. Cyprian's, and Eton and during his lonely years in Burma became his guiding lights—a hodgepodge of children's books, popular contemporary novels, eminent Victorian and Edwardian fiction and drama, and masterpieces of world literature. Among the twelve writers Orwell named in 1940 as his favorites—Shakespeare, Swift, Fielding, Dickens, Charles Reade, Samuel Butler, Zola, Flaubert, James Joyce, T. S. Eliot and D. H. Lawrence (*CEJL* 2:24)—Orwell as an adult most often praised Jonathan Swift for *Gulliver's Travels*, the towering eighteenth-century satire that made a singularly long-lasting impact on him. He had received it (probably in an expurgated children's version) for his eighth birthday, and he claimed in a BBC "Imaginary Interview" with Jonathan Swift he broadcast in 1942, it had lived with him ever since (Crick 20 n.9). Overall, the influence on George Orwell of young Eric Blair's voracious reading far outweighed the effect of most of what he read after 1927, the beginning of his own literary career. His early reading also remained so vital to his creative life that in his last years he produced distinguished literary essays about Swift, Dickens, and his other favorite authors he had first encountered as a boy.

A generation earlier, Victorian parents stuffed their children with uplifting evangelical reading material, but by the outbreak of World War I, even youngsters Eric's age were seeking out their own books, mainly geared toward secular entertainment (Sutherland 122). Even before entering St. Cyprian's, Eric had been devouring relatively sophisticated boys' adventure stories like R. M. Ballantyne's *The Coral Island*, a popular fable of British imperialism where three adventurous teenaged British colonists are rescued by a heroic English missionary from "savages" breathtakingly bent on "wholesale murder" (Sutherland 147), and Mark Twain's *Tom Sawyer*, the quintessentially American yarn of a rule-defying young hero who successfully and hilariously defies authority by mingling with outcasts from polite society. Both books celebrated independence and self-reliance, which Eric Blair always respected.

At St. Cyprian's, Eric's reading proved a welcome escape from the psychological abuse he was enduring. He enjoyed the Edwardian equivalents of comic books, working-class Britain's gory "penny dreadfuls," originally luridly illustrated eight-page rehashes of middle-class staples like Dickens' novels. By Eric's time the dreadfuls had supplanted most of the mayhem with adventure and eventually they produced a worldwide revolution in popular art (Sutherland 497–98). Orwell also read the evangelical *The Boys' Own Paper*, published as an antidote to the dreadfuls. *The Boys' Own Paper* supplied "pure and entertaining reading" celebrating adventure, mystery, sport, and public school life, indelibly stamping generations of British "lads" of all classes (Sutherland 19).

Eric's youthful companion Jacintha Buddicom recalled that she and Eric immediately shared their love of reading. They liked ghost stories like Poe's "Premature Burial" and James' "The Turn of the Screw" so well that she was surprised Orwell never wrote any. She also believed that the inspiration for his mature masterpieces *Animal Farm* and *Nineteen Eighty-Four* came from works they read together as children, including Beatrix Potter's bittersweet fable, *Pigling Bland* (1913), which they both adored. Little white Pigling Bland, thrust out of his loving home too young, meets the unfriendly world head on, rescues a winsome porker maiden from captivity, and escapes from wicked Farmer Piperson into "peaceful green valleys" like Orwell's favorite countryside around Henley "where little white cottages nestled in gardens and orchards" (77).

Eric was so fascinated with the Buddicoms' copy of H. G. Wells' long essay, *Modern Utopia* (1905), an outgrowth of Wells' interest in T. H. Huxley's evolutionary theories, that the Buddicoms finally gave it to him. This was the first of Wells' books that intoxicated young Eric. Before the turn of the century, Wells had unleashed his vivid, free-wheeling style on a large imaginative body of "scientific romance" that laid the foundation for twentieth-century science fiction (Sutherland 666). Soon, though, Wells gradually began to reveal his exasperation with the futility of human life. Once he had read Sir Thomas More's sixteenth-century *Utopia*, whose Greek name means "Nowhere," an ironic work describing a perfect society that flawed humanity will never achieve, Wells "saw that he, he only and no other, was actually the Man Who Could See in a Country of the Blind. Life at once became clear to him and it was *Utopia* that had showed him the way" (Ford 117). Wells used this notion, from Plato's "Allegory of the Cave," as the title story of a 1911 fiction collection.

The Time Traveller [*sic*] of Wells' *The Time Machine* (1895) encounters two parallel human societies in the far future, one made up of gentle artistic decadents and the other of technology-oriented underground predators who emerge at night to prey on the artists, a pessimistic image of the gulf between England's ineffectual *fin de siècle* esthetes and the brutish 1890s urban proletariat. In *When the Sleeper Wakes* (1899), Wells' first dystopia (a portrait of a future society gone hopelessly wrong), a "sleeper" named Graham wakes after two hundred years to a world of Marxist contradiction. The capitalistic world-state oppresses the proletariat by depriving them of technology, and Graham leads a serfs' revolt which inevitably fails. These novels foreshadowed Wells' increasingly socialist interest in political and social themes, where his guesses about future societies are all "negative, satirical, gloomy" (Seymour-Smith 218). *Modern Utopia* shows Wells as a gloomy dreamer suffering from a sense of social inferiority despite the glittering future in which he wanted so badly to believe. Wells "did not believe in Utopias. But he felt guilty about the pessimism which his imagination generated" (Seymour-Smith 218). Writing before the era of mass production, Wells prophesied Science triumphant, glorying in its invincible offspring, the Machine. Before Wells died in 1946, he saw many of his predictions come horrifyingly true in the era of Prosperity at Any Price—as many of George Orwell's have done.

While attending St. Cyprian's, Eric Blair felt gloomy, pessimistic, and guilty, especially at the end of vacations, when he had to leave his friends, the Buddicom children, and return to the dangerously unpredictable mood swings of Mrs. Wilkes, who intimidated him and probably caused permanent damage to his self-image and his attitude toward women. In his posthumous memoir, *Such, Such Were the Joys*, he claimed the huge and lasting lesson of his boyhood taught him that in the world he lived in, it was impossible for him to be good (*CEJL* 4:334).

If Eric couldn't feel that he was "good," however, Eric could still read, and he found a fellow admirer of Wells' novels, Cyril Connolly, who became the only lifelong friend Eric made at St. Cyprian's. Connolly shared Eric's hatred for the place. Much later he recalled that he, Cyril, had made his mark at St. Cyprian's by pretending to be "the gay, generous, rebellious Irishman," but he knew Eric was the true [rebel]. Tall, pale, with flaccid cheeks, large spatulate fingers, and supercilious voice, he was one of those boys "who seem born old . . . he thought for himself . . . and rejected not only St. [Cyprian's] but the war, the Empire, Kipling, Sussex, and Character" (Connolly 43). Connolly grew up to be a genuine man of English letters, "an ironic pessimist of the civilized Irish variety [and] an authoritative historian of the educated sensibility of his age"

(Seymour-Smith 302). When he and Eric Blair met as schoolboys, though, Cyril was a pug-nosed little fellow about Eric's age with tiny blue eyes and a thick brow whose family was not much better off than Eric's. The two of them read everything from boys' magazines and Sherlock Holmes mysteries to the weighty Victorian social philosophy of Thomas Carlyle, the Victorian social problem novels of Dickens, and Shakespeare's mighty tragedies, but they were especially struck by Wells' *The Country of the Blind*, which they repeatedly "stole" from each other.

Writing in 1936, English critic Ford Madox Ford declared *The Country of the Blind* was "magnificent . . . a book that prophesied so far ahead that it is still modern" (Ford 110–11). Wells used Plato's image of humanity lying chained in a cave, spellbound by flickering shadows of reality. A few brave souls escape, experience the real world, and return to try to free their fellows, who ridicule them as liars and reject the freedom they offer. Seeing himself as one of those escapees who was trying to teach the rest of humanity about his progressive social views, Wells joined the socialist Fabian Society in 1903, but he left the group after a well-publicized clash with fellow Fabian George Bernard Shaw. Wells tried hard to combine his belief in socialism with the hope that humanity could gradually perfect itself through evolution and scientific innovation, but his fiction shows that he could not quite convince himself. By 1914, Edwardian England knew Wells as a leading proponent of socialism, world government, free thought, and free love, fiercely opposed to many comfortable English traditions and moral principles. Looking back in 1940, Orwell still considered Wells the most influential novelist of his time and tellingly described his boyhood infatuation with Wells' novels in terms of his own unhappiness. He felt his boyhood world was filled with pedants, clergy, and golfing enthusiasts, with employers and parents distorting their children's professional and sexual lives, and with deadly-dull teachers snickering over their bits of Latin. Then he discovered Wells and found him marvelous. Orwell loved Wells because he wrote science fiction about inhabitants of other planets and of ocean depths, and because Wells was certain that the future would not be what respectable people thought it was going to be (*CEJL* 2:144).

Eric's rebellious reading at St. Cyprian's also included other "popular" and "progressive" authors. He and Connolly incurred Mrs. Wilkes' wrath by surreptitiously reading popular author Compton Mackenzie's daring *Sinister Street* (1913–14), which titillated their adolescent sensibilities with such purplish passages as "The sensuousness of her abandonment drugged all but the sweet present and the poignant ecstasy of possession" (*CEJL* 4:422; Shelden 456 n.7). Eric also borrowed Thackeray's tamer *Vanity Fair* (1848) from Mrs. Wilkes' personal library, and there discovered a powerful combination of English satire descended from Fielding and moral severity from seventeenth-century Puritan author John Bunyan. Eric also happily encountered that re-doubtable Victorian rebel Samuel Butler, who mercilessly satirized the hypocrisy of his time in his superbly eccentric novel, *The Way of All Flesh* (1903). This novel so devastatingly demolished the popular idealistic view of the Victorian family that it has been called the most savagely comprehensive critique of Victorian ideology to be found in fiction (Sutherland 663).

More conservative influences came from two of the most popular literary voices of Eric's boyhood, whose work Orwell explored much later in penetrating critical essays. Kipling's realistic stories presented simple masculine situations, like army life, as well as portraying British imperialism, fair play, public school solidarity and loyalty, self-reliance, and paternalism in animal fables like *The Jungle Books* (1894, 1895). Another of Orwell's perennial favorites, Charles Dickens, whose harrowing boyhood descent into poverty when his family went bankrupt far outstripped the financial strains of Eric's childhood, was Victorian England's best paid novelist. Dickens' reform-minded British social problem novels like *Oliver Twist* (1836) and the scathing social satire *Bleak House* (1852–53) exposed young Eric Blair to a "striking use of imagery, rhetoric and dramatic device [which] advanced fiction technically to the threshold of modernism" (Sutherland 186).

Other authors that stimulated Eric's mind at St. Cyprian's included G. K. Chesterton, the "cheery and beery" author of the Father Brown mysteries (Seymour-Smith 222), and P. G. Wodehouse, whose farcical fantasies about the inane aristocrat Bertie Wooster and his unflappable valet Jeeves flayed England's Edwardian effete aristocracy lounge-lizards. Eric also initially admired the plays of George Bernard Shaw, the witty, controversial Fabian dramatist of ideas and considerable theatrical skill, but as an adult he found Shaw's ideas disappointing. Eric also felt let down by the popular but shallow fiction of John Galsworthy. Orwell later wrote a penetrating essay on Wodehouse, but he never analyzed Shaw's works or Galsworthy's.

When fourteen-year-old Eric Blair arrived at Eton in the midst of the Great War, he astonished his less well-read, mostly sports-oriented schoolmates with his unusual ability to quote literary progressive writers like Wells, Shaw, Chesterton, and Butler, though doing so probably increased his social isolation. At Eton, as at St. Cyprian's, he had very little spending money, but he discovered lending libraries offering nearly everything from popular youth magazines to serious adult fiction. In his 1939 novel, *Coming Up for Air*, Orwell gave his own teenage reading list to his autobiographical hero George Bowling (*CA* 143, 141). Looking back at his adolescent self, the fictional Bowling insisted that all these books so exactly suited the stage of development he had reached, that they seemed to have been created especially for him (*CA* 141). This almost random reading, largely books not well-known today, strengthened social concerns for Eric that later became central to Orwell's fiction.

Eric found a strong satiric humor, often combined with sympathetic views of poverty, in the fiction of Barry Pain, England's leading comic writer in the first years of the twentieth century, as well as in the humor of Canadian Stephen Leacock and the quirky work of American short story writer O. Henry. He also found sexual frankness, daringly explicit for its time, in Elinor Glyn's *Three Weeks* (1907) and George Moore's *Esther Waters* (1894), a consciously naturalistic derivative of Zola. Eric also enjoyed macabre ghost stories by Oliver Onions and W. W. Jacobs, like *The Monkey's Paw* (1902), and he absorbed the liberal-idealist philosophy in May Sinclair's art novel, *The Divine Fire* (1904), Silas Hocking's children's fiction, and the London novels of cockney author William Pett Ridge, who listed his recreation in *Who's Who* as "roaming east of Aldgate and south" (Sutherland 537), then one of the British capital's most notorious slums. Popular American Socialist Jack London also prowled the slums. *The Iron Heel* (1907), a future fantasy that terrifyingly anticipates fascism, and *People of the Abyss* (1903), written after London saw the horrors of London's East End for himself, both impressed Eric profoundly.

Several aspects of Blair/Orwell's life intriguingly paralleled London's. Before their early deaths, London's at forty, Orwell's at forty-six, each man deliberately sought life-threatening experiences and subsequently incorporated them into powerfully realistic fiction. London, born in 1876 to a free-love-preaching charlatan and a depressed spiritualist, claimed, "I never had a boyhood and I seem to be hunting for that lost boyhood" (Watson 105). Orwell's young self, thrust at eight a generation later into the harsh injustice of St. Cyprian's, already seemed old: "His 'eyes of a child', even when literally a child, saw further than other children's" (Gross 11). London and Orwell both educated themselves through a broad range of reading; each consciously vowed to become a writer; each man went out tramping in English slums to learn about the misery of the poor, and both preached revolutionary socialism as the only means of helping them. Both men died as widely read popular authors, but they each paid a fatal physical price for their success and neither enjoyed many rewards for his success. No one knows whether the boy Eric Blair knew about London's deliberate voluntary embrace of poverty and its relation to the passionate prose of *People of the Abyss*, or when the notion of emulating London's slum-crawling came to Eric Blair, but London's outrage at injustice and his powerful adventure stories strongly appealed to Eric's writer's soul.

A typical boyish thirst for exotic, dangerous adventure probably also inspired Eric's interest in both Stevenson's *New Arabian Nights*, whose "Suicide Club" Eric chose as his "Glorious Fourth" oration at Eton, and London's *The Call of the Wild*, but the latter book, the story of a noble dog kidnapped and sold into sadistic bondage in Alaska, must have reinforced his deep-seated hatred of injustice. That hatred festered for a long time, but young Eric did not wallow completely in pessimism. He "got stuck" (or bored) halfway through Thomas Hardy's gloomy novels, and Ibsen's plays, much celebrated by Eric's idol Shaw, gave Eric only the impression that it was "always raining in Norway" (*CA* 143).

Eric's long interest in D. H. Lawrence, who in 1917 was arguably as infamous in England for scandalously eloping with his professor's German wife as he was for his Oedipal third novel, *Sons and Lovers* (1913), began with "Love on the Farm," a poem which Eric came upon by accident. Written from a girl's point of view, the poem insists that her sexual satisfaction depends on surrendering her personality to her lover, "drown[ing] against him" in "sweet fire," dying and "find[ing] death good." Adolescent Eric Blair was "completely overcome"—though in the heat of the moment he forgot to note the author's name (Stansky and Abrahams 1972: 121). The powerful earthy imagery of "Love on the Farm" probably inspired Eric's October 1918 love poem to Jacintha Buddicom, "The Pagan," praising "naked souls alive and free" and the sonnet he wrote to her two months later, where he conceived of her as Juliet to his Romeo and protested the stifling "customs of this age" (Shelden 1991: 66). Jacintha, a little older than Eric, did not take his Lawrentian efforts very seriously.

Orwell in later years often defended his liking for Oscar Wilde's *The Picture of Dorian Gray* (1891), which he called "a good bad book" that he read while at Eton (Woodcock 110). Wilde's parable of Gay Nineties decadence portrays an artist whose handsome self-portrait supernaturally turns uglier as the artist himself gradually becomes corrupt. The fascination of putting on a disguise and diving into the lower depths of his society may have spurred Orwell to submerge himself in the slums of London and Paris.

Both at Eton and afterwards, Eric tended to avoid the other "new" authors then experimenting with fictional theory and form, like Virginia Woolf and Wyndham Lewis. In his teens, Eric was probably not ready for Woolf's stream of consciousness technique or even the full blast of Lawrence's "highly charged, seismic relationships between men and women" (Stansky and Abrahams 1972: 120).

Instead, Eric plunged back into books he already knew well, like *The Way of All Flesh* and Shaw's *Androcles and the Lion*. He was deeply impressed by George Gissing's naturalistic social problem novels, which derived mainly from Scottish philosopher Thomas Carlyle's clarion calls for social reform. Presenting a deterministic view of human beings as victims of largely uncontrollable forces like economics and heredity, George Gissing produced third-generation social problem novels dealing with working-class life. *Demos* (1886) pits a young proletarian socialist against an aesthetic aristocrat, showcasing Gissing's disillusioned political views and presenting a wide spectrum of socialist positions from populism to intellectualism. *The Odd Women* (1893) ferociously probes the dilemma of the many "superfluous" genteel women abounding in Victorian society, who had little or no choice except marriage to escape from dehumanizing poverty. Gissing's masterpiece, *New Grub Street* (1891), stingingly indicted the Victorian literary establishment. Its impoverished hero, novelist Edwin Reardon, is destroyed by toiling for Mudie's Circulating Library, the only literary work he can get. Mudie's throttled the creativity of the impoverished writers they hired by forcing them to celebrate its often censorious middle-class values.

Like Gissing, the naturalistic novelist Arnold Bennett modeled much of his fiction on the French writers Maupassant, Flaubert, and Zola. Bennett's *The Old Wives' Tale* (1908) and his *Clayhanger* trilogy (1910–15) were set in the Midlands, illuminating extraordinary elements in dull characters and everyday life. Bennett's simple vocabulary, highly disciplined objectivity, and extensive naturalistic description accurately mirror "the relative amounts of joy and sorrow that enter into the average human life" and give *The Old Wives' Tale* "its chief strength, the incomparable strength of literal and fearless truth" (Cooper 229). Orwell later called Bennett a "giant" of the pre-World War I generation (*CEJL* 2:199), and the "literal and fearless truth" of Bennett's literary message was a formative influence on his own writing (Woodcock 315).

In his teens Eric was also ripe for infatuation with the tersely elegant, cynical, elegiac verse of A. E. Housman, then at the height of his popularity, who occasionally came down from Cambridge to lecture to Eton's Literary Society. Connolly, who accompanied Eric to Eton, commented just after the poet's death in 1936 that Housman appealed "especially to adolescence and adolescence is a period when one's reaction to a writer is dictated by what one is looking for rather than what is there" (Stansky and Abrahams 1972: 121). By seventeen Eric Blair had memorized all the poems in Housman's *A Shropshire Lad*, admiring there, he later said, gratification of his own self-pity, "the 'nobody loves me feeling,' " a "bitter, defiant paganism, a conviction that life is short and the gods are against you," and an "unvarying sexual pessimism" because the girl always died or married somebody else (*CEJL* 1:504). This seemed great wisdom, the grown-up Orwell thought, to boys pent up in all-male public schools like Eton and conditioned to think of women as "something unattainable" (Shelden 1991: 65).

Disillusionment, scepticism, and antinomianism, the notion that old British virtues like thrift and patriotism had become useless, became popular catchwords during the bitter aftermath of World War I, in which a grand total of ten million soldiers died. The patriotic fervor that had inspired young Eric's poem "Awake! Young Men of England" cost Eton dearly, and their courage

—13 won the Victoria Cross, 548 won the Distinguished Service Order, and 744 won the Military Cross—was largely wasted. Eric Blair's own confidence in Britain's leadership was badly shaken, too. Had he been able to go on to Oxford, a university education might have broadened his outlook and set him upon a different path in life, but as things were, the novels he came across at St.Cyprian's and Eton became his only real education, an education that he, like George Bowling, gave himself.

During several depressing monsoon seasons in Burma he read classics like Tolstoy's sweeping Napoleonic novel *War and Peace,* Poe's haunting ghost stories and mysteries, and Mark Twain's hilarious tales and sketches. He also read Joseph Conrad's finely wrought novels of primitive exotic landscapes and European adventurers trapped by their romantic fatalism, probably an influence on Orwell's first novel, *Burmese Days.*

Conrad's novels, which he consistently built around solitary heroes who are alienated or isolated by chance or choice, fall into two groups, the first dealing with the question of his hero's physical self-possession, like Jim of *Lord Jim* (1900) and Kurtz of *Heart of Darkness* (1902). Kurtz personifies the evils of colonialism, which doomed Europeans with inner weaknesses to panic and abandon. Conrad's next three books, his so-called political novels, still deal with new ways in which a man may fatally lose full possession of himself. This group culminated with *Under Western Eyes* (1910), a book Orwell knew well. It pioneered the political detective novel in English and was one of Conrad's most significant explorations of revolution, its causes, its excesses, and its betrayal. The decision of its hero Razumov to pry himself away from humanity proves self-destructive, but through him, Conrad achieves profound psychological depth by using subtle narrative devices—placement of crucial images, sudden shifts in narrative, a large symbolic scene which pulls together various elements of the plot, and ironic comments which suggest another dimension to the story (Karl 212). Several of Conrad's literary devices strongly influenced modern novel writers, including Orwell, especially the use of shifting points of view to round out characters' motivations, extensive flashbacks which both create suspense and ensure insight into the psychological pattern which produced the crisis or the decision, and the use of unconventional symbols to provide illumination through a metaphysical dimension. Conrad's popular *Victory* (1915), mentioned by George Bowling as having a linear narrative, a celebration of the value of work to human life, and a new clarity of style, all joined in the story of a man who "masters his destiny" as none of Conrad's earlier protagonists had been able to do. In Conrad's lonely heroes, estranged from home, betrayed by self or fellows, Eric Blair probably recognized a reflection of his role as an Imperial policeman, the role that Burma taught him to despise.

An unusual combination of contemporary British authors—the Victorian Samuel Butler, the popular W. Somerset Maugham, and the scandalous D. H. Lawrence— also powerfully impressed Blair in Burma (Stansky and Abrahams 1972: 208). Samuel Butler's *Notebooks,* full of Butler's unconventional Darwinism, savaged the idealism and false consciousness underpinning the self-satisfaction of the Victorian bourgeoisie (Sutherland 96). The *Notebooks* also offer young writers a stylistic guide that "reads uncannily like Orwell at his most characteristic, off-hand, and assured" (Stansky and Abrahams 1972: 209):

I never knew a writer yet who took the smallest pains with his style and was at the same time readable. Plato's having had seventy shies at one sentence is quite enough to explain to me why I dislike him. A man may, and ought to, take a great deal of pains to write clearly, tersely, and euphoniously: he will write many a sentence three or four times over—to do much more than this is worse than not rewriting at all. (quoted in Stansky and Abrahams 1972: 209–10)

Another sardonic observer of human life was W. Somerset Maugham, whose most famous novel, *Of Human Bondage,* appeared in 1915. In its bleak, hostile autobiographical world, the hero finally manages to cast off all of his constricting traditional inherited beliefs. Unlike Butler, though, Maugham went to great pains to achieve his unadorned, highly readable, seemingly casual style, and eventually, so did Orwell.

Vastly different from the clear, stripped-down style with ironic twists that characterizes Orwell's best work, like Maugham's, was the passionate prose of D. H. Lawrence, the only "modern" author Eric Blair read in Burma, where he absorbed *Women in Love* (1920) and Lawrence's brilliant 1914 short fiction collection *The Prussian Officer and Other Stories.* The obsessive repetitiousness with which Lawrence voiced his most antibourgeois and anticapitalistic passions in *Women in Love* may have encouraged the strident preachy tone of Orwell's 1936 *Keep the Aspidistra Flying,* whose inescapable subject, like that of Lawrence's unsettling short story "The Rocking-Horse Winner," is money, money, money. *Women in Love* (1920), Lawrence said, contains "the results in one's soul of the [First World] war" (quoted in Walker 1596) and embodies Lawrence's belief that Western civilization can no longer respond to the individual's most urgent needs because industrialism has destroyed the traditional order of society. In the passionate relationship of Birkin and Ursula, two of the main characters of *Women in Love,* Lawrence did hint at the possibility of the redeeming power of sexual fulfillment, but he describes their quest for wholeness of being as "a wandering to nowhere . . . away from the world's somewheres [*sic*]" (quoted in Walker 1596)—and "nowhere" is the translation for "utopia."

Once Eric Blair came back from Burma and launched his writing career, his reading time dwindled away. A few works, though, captured his attention, strengthened his already formidable hatred of injustice and his nostalgia for solid old traditional English values now forever lost, and contributed significantly to his literary development. While he was working at the Westropes' London bookshop in 1934–35, he insisted to his good-natured sometime lover Kay Ekevoll that she should read "Dickens and Conrad and . . . repair lack of knowledge of the great tradition before tackling the moderns, like Lawrence and Joyce" (Crick 168, 431 n.21).

James Joyce's *Ulysses* (1922) particularly captivated Orwell. *Ulysses* is a stunning combination of symbolism and realism heavily seasoned with naturalism, celebrating life by retelling the ancient myth of Odysseus wandering the Mediterranean after the Trojan War in the modern terms of a decent, ordinary, threatened Jewish "outsider" who roams the streets of turn-of-the-century Dublin on one unforgettable Bloomsday. When Orwell was courting Brenda Salkeld in 1933, he insisted that she read *Ulysses*, because everything about it fascinated him—its experiments with style and structure, its sexual frankness, its combination of earthy realism with intellectual concerns, and especially Joyce's ability to get into the mind of a common man and convey it convincingly to his readers, something Orwell felt most intellectual writers could not do. He believed that Joyce's protaganist Bloom interested him because "he is an ordinary uncultivated man described from within by someone who can also stand outside him and see him from another angle" (*CEJL* 1:128). Orwell deliberately adopted this dual fictional perspective to bring two worlds that are normally far apart "into intimate contact" (Shelden 1991: 180), juxtaposing his own perspective with those of the tramps and the poor he portrayed in *Down and Out in Paris and London*.

The next spring, when Orwell was working on *A Clergyman's Daughter*, he reread *Ulysses*, but he now found it gave him an inferiority complex. Realizing that he and Joyce had entirely different talents, Orwell nevertheless attempted his one foray into the avant-garde, a chapter of *A Clergyman's Daughter* loosely following Joyce's surrealistic "Nighttown" section of *Ulysses*. Neither Orwell nor his readers particularly liked this experiment, but even then, Orwell had still not quite gotten *Ulysses* out of his system. He ironically alluded to it in *Keep the Aspidistra Flying*, making his autobiographical hero Gordon Comstock toil fruitlessly at a would-be verse masterpiece describing a day's wandering through London.

Around the time Eric Blair took the pen name name "George Orwell," he became acquainted with Aldous Huxley's *Brave New World* (1930), which featured a harrowing future society. *Brave New World* was heavily indebted to Evgeny Zamiatin's *We,* which Orwell did not read until the mid-1940s

(Shelden 1991: 50 and Woodcock 209) and which Huxley for some reason pretended never to have read at all (Seymour-Smith 289). Just after World War I, Huxley had rapidly made a serious reputation as a satirical novelist and essayist, incorporating ideas from a wide range of fields to his caustic views of society. Through several novels, Huxley's recurrent theme insisted that twentieth century egocentricity and ignorance of any reality beyond the self ensures a pointless and sordid existence. In his best known work, *Brave New World*, wholeness is totally negated by the centrally administered, scientifically controlled future world government which Huxley dated as "A.F. 632," referring to a society that begins "After Ford," after Henry Ford's implementation of modern industrial assembly-line methods. The dehumanized inhabitants of Huxley's World State fall into five groups genetically predestined for different levels of work. The State controls them all with drugs and technological devices. In this dystopia, art and religion are considered threats to World Peace. Stubborn nonconformists are forcibly removed to a remote island, and one of them, Huxley's hero John the Savage, is initially attracted to, then repulsed by the vulgarity and horror of his world (Richardson 47). By 1946, Huxley had decided that the hopelessness of the quest for wholeness was the novel's most serious defect, but *Brave New World* is generally considered "one of the great modern denunciations of the evils that grow out of the uncritical belief in progress, of an acceptance without discrimination of all, good or bad, that the machine age may have to offer" (Woodcock 48). By the 1930s, George Orwell, too, had had considerable firsthand experience of those injustices.

During the six and a half months in 1938–39 that Orwell spent in Morocco recuperating from the wounds, physical and psychic, that he had received in Spain and the chest ailment now suspected to be tuberculosis, he was also suffering from dysentery brought on by bad water, distressed by the poverty of the local Arabs, and unable to shake off his conviction that the next world war would soon explode. While he was working on *Coming Up for Air*, he and Eileen took refuge in reading Dickens' novels—*Our Mutual Friend*, which Eileen had brought from England, and the early novels *Barnaby Rudge* and *Martin Chuzzlewit*. All three novels deal with the miseries of England's poor and argue for dramatic social changes.

Immediately after returning to England to attend his dying father, Orwell wrote one of his longest essays, explaining his reasons for believing Dickens' novels still mattered (*CEJL* 1:460–92). Even though he recognized Dickens' literary limitations. Orwell celebrated Dickens' appeal, which Orwell believed depended on the universal emotional appeal of the concept of brotherhood. According to Orwell, the code Dickens voiced was both in his time and Orwell's, still believed in, even by people who violated it (quoted in Shelden 1991: 313–34). Orwell felt that Dickens' ability to touch all kinds of people made him a radical, not a conservative writer. Orwell himself was trying to emulate Dickens' simple moral criticism of society, one Orwell felt might prove more revolutionary than trendy "politico-economic criticism." In addition, Orwell was constantly aware of the face behind the pages of Dickens' work, a face that might well have been a face Orwell himself felt he should have had: a laughing face, with a little anger, but one free of triumph and evil motives, the face of a man that always finds himself struggling against something, but who carries on his fight openly without ever being afraid; a type hated by all the "smelly little orthodoxies" which Orwell felt were contending in his time for human souls (*CEJL* 1:460).

During his wartime work with the British Broadcasting Company, Orwell had ample opportunity to encounter "smelly little orthodoxies"—and some bigger ones. In the early 1940s, Orwell met Arthur Koestler, who became his close friend. Koestler, a Hungarian who settled in England, had seen firsthand how orthodox Soviet Communism disposed of its most fervent revolutionaries. Koestler's first novel, *The Gladiators* (translated from Hungarian in 1939), sympathetically treats the ancient Roman slaves' revolt led by Spartacus in twentieth-century terms. *Darkness at Noon* (translated from German in 1940), his finest novel, was one of the first exposés of the true nature of Stalin's rule in the Soviet Union. Koestler's protagonist Rubashov had helped bring about the 1917 "Glorious Workers' Revolution," but he becomes a rebel, not a victim, an old-guard Communist fully aware he is about to be liquidated by Stalin, who has betrayed the Communist ideal. Rubashov attains an ultimate spiritual freedom even while he contemplates his inevitable fate. Koestler's matter-of-fact message is harrowing and psychologically convincing, although most English left-wing intellectuals did not pay any attention to it while Stalin was their ally against the Nazis.

Koestler's influential *Horizon* essay "The Yogi and the Commissar" (1942), also intrigued Orwell. Orwell himself had experienced Soviet deviousness in Catalonia, where the idealistic Marxist POUM members Orwell supported were savagely betrayed and hunted down by Soviet-led Spanish Communists. Orwell agreed wholeheartedly with Koestler that a power-hungry totalitarian regime would always corrupt revolutionary ideals. When the Labour Party came to power in England at the end of the war, Orwell hoped for peaceful changes in British society, but he warned in his essay, "Catastrophic Gradualism," that great dangers lurked just as dangerously in the aimless leadership of practical men as in the dictatorial rule of power-crazed ideologues. Subsequently he used some of Koestler's ideas to attack the allure of the "commissar mentality" among English left-wing writers and politicians. Orwell, however, did not allow his friendship with Koestler or his sympathy with Koestler's anti-Soviet views to affect the uncompromising honesty with which he reviewed Koestler's books—and everyone else's. When Orwell observed in print that Koestler's *Arrival and Departure* (1943) was really a tract, not a satisfactory novel, Koestler accepted the verdict as proof that Orwell applied the same strict standards to his friends' work as he did to his own, but Koestler also had to admit, "I don't think George ever knew what makes other people tick, because what made him tick was very different from what made most other people tick" (Wadhams 169–70).

By the time he began work on *Nineteen Eighty-Four*, Orwell had also been profoundly affected by an important dystopic work that had mysteriously emerged from the Soviet Union, Evgeny Zamiatin's *We* (1920; tr. 1925), which Orwell first read in the mid-1940s. Zamiatin had been the moving spirit behind the Serapion Brothers, a 1920s literary group that at first wanted to interpret the revolution only in an individual, not in a collective, way and were therefore condemned by Stalinists, who believed artistic expression should be reduced to a dreary homogenized least common denominator. Zamiatin believed that "Real literature can be created only by madmen, hermits, heretics, dreamers, rebels, and sceptics, not by diligent and trustworthy functionaries" (Seymour-Smith 1059), a position bound to rattle Soviet bureaucrats. His satiric masterpiece *We* was probably spirited out of the Soviet Union by Stalin's secret police and was translated into Czech without Zamiatin's knowledge. The Soviet government seized on the translation as provocation and threw the author into impoverished exile in Paris. *We*, one of the most powerful modern dystopian novels, was intolerable to the Soviets primarily because it declares that the United State [*sic*] of 2600 is bent on destroying history, freedom, and individualism. Its overt reference to citizens of the State not by name but as "numbers" was far too close to actual practice in the U.S.S.R. for the Soviets' comfort, since *zek*, Russian for "number," is the generic term by which prisoners were known in Stalin's vast prison system, the Gulag Archipelago. At the end of *We*, its hero D503 leads an abortive revolution and is crushed by the authorities and forced to undergo the surgical removal of his imagination, an unholy foreshadowing of the Soviet mental hospital prisons of the 1970s and 1980s.

Upon discovering *We* at the same time he was beginning work on *Nineteen Eighty-Four*, Orwell reviewed it for the *Tribune*. Unlike Huxley, Orwell freely acknowledged his debts to *We* (Woodcock 213), which both resembles and differs from his own dystopic view in *Nineteen Eighty-Four*. For Orwell, the most appalling aspects of the world Zamiatin postulated in *We* were its satanic quality and the tendency to revert to more primitive cultural forms which seemed to Orwell to be integral to totalitarianism, colored by the ancient sinister civilizations based on slavery (*CEJL* 4:485–86). Orwell also clearly saw that Zamiatin had intuitively grasped totalitarianism's black irrationality: human sacrifice, sadism as its own end, and adoration of a Leader who endowed himself with divine attributes (*CEJL* 4:74–75).

Just prior to beginning *Nineteen-Eighty Four*, Orwell also encountered James Burnham's Machiavellian work, *The Managerial Revolution* (1940), "which theorized a tripartite division of the world, each unit ruled by a 'self-elected oligarchy' "(Crick 342). In 1946, while he was starting *Nineteen Eighty-Four*, Orwell insisted that this view of the world would probably result in an unconquerable form of government that would constantly wage cold war upon its neighbors (*CEJL* 4:8–10). Orwell used Burnham's chilly vision as the basis for the malignant three-nation world order of *Nineteen Eighty-Four.*

Orwell's difficult life and his works share a general reputation for pessimism. Even Eileen sometimes found his bleak outlook on humanity and its future appalling (Wadhams 66–67), and some of it probably derived from the naturalistic reading which seemed to influence him most in his youth and from having his warnings about Soviet totalitarianism largely ignored until the publication of *Animal Farm.* The unhappy fate of the revolutionary beasts in Orwell's *Animal Farm* and the destruction of *Nineteen Eighty*-Four's protagonist Winston Smith seem to argue for not just pessimism but obsessiveness, even masochism (Seymour-Smith 300). This view, however, fails to take into account Orwell's hope in ordinary humanity (the "proles" in *Nineteen Eighty-Four*), the traditional values of common sense and decency that he never abandoned, and his relentless anger at injustice.

The same kind of righteous anger fueled the one novel that seems to have educated Orwell best. Throughout his life Orwell returned again and again to Jonathan Swift's *Gulliver's Travels* (1726–27), one of the world's masterpieces of satiric fantasy fiction, the genre Orwell chose for his masterpieces, *Animal Farm* and *Nineteen Eighty-Four.* In Lemuel Gulliver's four journeys, Swift ferociously targeted several ills of his society by creating imaginary cultures like Lilliput, which allowed him to assault individual and political pretentiousness, and Brobdingnag, the land of giants, where he attacked human grossness. In his final journey, Gulliver met the noble equine Houyhnhnms, superior in every way to the wretched humanoid Yahoos who disgusted Gulliver so much that when he returned to England he spurned his wife and felt comfortable only with his horses.

As a thinker in the Age of Reason, Gulliver saw the ideal of rational man as perfect, but when Yahoo-like humanity fell short of his ideal, he swore off mankind as hopeless. Beyond social satire, though, *Gulliver's Travels* may be read as a novel of incomplete initiation. Travel broadened Gulliver's outlook and changed him, but it failed to teach him one of life's most important lessons—that valuing reason to the extreme of denying emotion makes living as dull, as predictable, as boring as a scientific experiment. In other words, Swift, bitterly disillusioned with human institutions, mocked Gulliver's naïve optimistic faith in Progress as a product of human reason. Swift was profoundly sympathetic to human beings as individuals, so he struck out angrily in *Gulliver's Travels* against the societal human failings which caused so much discontent and misery. Late in his life in an "Imaginary Interview" with Dean Swift, Orwell commented that he couldn't resist feeling Swift had "laid it on a bit too thick . . . too hard on humanity, and in your own country" (quoted in Shelden 1991: 454 n.14).

On the whole, plumbing the depths to which materialistic and technological progress had plunged humanity left Orwell with a Swiftian outrage against any institution which sacrificed human decency to Progress, and debased human emotion into societally leveled "correctness." In their last, most powerful works, Swift and Orwell both revealed the same paradoxical attitude toward their fellow human beings. On the personal level, both men maintained close friendships, because when they saw people as individuals, they generously accepted their failings and praised their goodness. When people joined into groups, though, both Swift and Orwell loathed and satirized the human mob tendency for the more powerful to oppress the weak and outsiders. Orwell's reading had broadened his youthful anger at being victimized into his recognition that the lower classes of his society suffered just as unjustly as he had, and the experiences he sought out in slums, mines, and the rat-infested trenches of the Aragon front intensified his determination to make their suffering public. Orwell's life work included critical and polemical essays and the several heavily autobiographical literary genres he explored, from the documentaries *Down and Out in Paris and London, The Road to Wigan Pier*, and *Homage to Catalonia*, through realistic novels with social themes like *Burmese Days, A Clergyman's Daughter, Keep the Aspidistra Flying*, and *Coming Up for Air*, and finally his masterpieces, the satiric fable *Animal Farm* and the satiric dystopia *Nineteen Eighty-Four*. In all of these, he insisted that only individual effort, even if it is doomed to fail, can combat social injustice. Orwell called the capacity to achieve that individual effort the "crystal spirit." Of all admirable human qualities, the "crystal spirit" always mattered most to him, and he never ceased to celebrate it in prose as clean and clear and honest as that spirit itself. Very few writers have done it better.

3

Getting Ready to Write: *Down and Out in Paris and London*

HISTORICAL SETTING

During the Roaring Twenties, an enormous gulf existed between the rarefied world of the Western wealthy and the sordid world of the poor that lay, mostly ignored, just beneath it. France and Italy pressured Germany for impossible war reparations, paving the way for another global conflagration. Russia turned Communist in 1917, breaking off three hundred years of autocratic tsarist rule and igniting large-scale social and economic changes which Socialists worldwide hoped would improve the lives of Russia's poor. Even though prosperity seemed to outweigh poverty in Britain, the British economic and social structures and attitudes were deteriorating. Prior to World War I, the great British industries born in the Industrial Revolution— textiles and clothing, iron and steel, coal and engineering—had served the nation well, as did the British service industries—finance, insurance, trading and transport—and their enormous overseas investments. Debts from the First World War, however, were aggravated by extensive stagnation in the very British industries and regions—Wales and the North—that had powered nineteenth-century industrialization, resulting in mass unemployment and embitterment (Supple 320, 323–24). The situation in Britain when Orwell returned from Burma had become so bad that the civil or class war Marx advocated was a distinct possibility. The Lord Chancellor himself proposed using British army troops to put down uprisings (Johnson 38 n.120).

Britain's problems reflected an enormous European cultural transformation. Unsettling new theories by Marx, Freud, and Einstein all forced people to realize that their comfortable world was falling to pieces. Marx insisted that class war was inevitable and that the workers should become collective dictators by force if necessary. Freud suggested that people's actions were the result of unconscious sexual urges impossible then to discuss in mixed company. Einstein's mathematical theories, when filtered down into popular reading material, shook the very foundations of scientific thought. Those physical perceptions that had shaped man's ideas about time and space, right and wrong, law and justice, and the nature of societal behavior could no longer be trusted, and now ordinary people, not understanding any of these theories completely, felt a confusing mixture of exhilaration and dismay (Johnson 11).

This mammoth cultural upheaval spilled over into the lives of ordinary British citizens just when millions of war veterans were beginning to return home, expecting the British government to fulfill its promise to "make Britain a fit country for heroes to live in" (Arnstein 273). At the same time, escalating inflation and a bad slump in international trade dramatically escalated British unemployment. The rich stayed comfortable, while the poor endured growing miseries brought on by socioeconomic injustices.

Such unfairness shocked Orwell deeply. He decided to share the dreadful living conditions of the poor and teach himself to write so that he could tell the world about them. He tramped around London during the winter of 1928 and again in 1930–1931 and in between, during the last three months of 1929, he lived and worked in a Parisian slum. These experiences provided the raw material for *Down and Out in Paris and London*, which Eric Blair began in 1930. It was finally published on January 9, 1933, launching his literary career as "George Orwell."

All of Orwell's works seem to lie somewhere between fact and fiction, and so whether *Down and Out in Paris and London* should be classified as fiction or autobiography used to be debatable. In 1989, however, a newly discovered first edition of *Down and Out* Orwell annotated as a gift for Brenda Salkeld proved that he based these sketches firmly on close observation of fact, rearranging some events and adjusting certain details. Orwell also noted there that his descriptions of his Paris comrade Boris, his own three days of starvation, and his short career as a *plongeur* (dishwasher), were all as accurate as he possibly could make them (Shelden 1991: 132). Hence Orwell intended *Down and Out in Paris and London* to be understood as very thinly veiled autobiography—but this autobiography is also a work of art.

Orwell stated elsewhere that almost all of the incidents he described in *Down and Out in Paris and London* really took place, but that he rearranged them. On the surface, *Down and Out in Paris and London* does appear to be merely a straightforward re-creation of Orwell's experiences in Paris and London over a four- to five-month period. When Orwell shaped his experiences into *Down and Out in Paris and London* (it took him about three years) however, he placed descriptions of the time he spent in Paris before those of the time he spent tramping in London and roughly balanced them, which was not true in real life. By doing so, he achieved a "consistent, symmetrical, and ordered narrative" (Hammond 81).

PLOT

In his famous *Aspects of the Novel*, E. M. Forster carefully distinguished between "story" and "plot." According to Forster, "story" means an author's simple chronological arrangement of events, while "plot" is more complicated, being the "story" plus the motivation behind each of its events. In this sense, *Down and Out in Paris and London* is virtually plotless, a deficiency Orwell later acknowledged in most of his early fiction. Not at all a conventional novel, *Down and Out in Paris and London* is Orwell's detached documentary exposition of the lives of desperately poor people. Orwell's minimal story line, narrated in the first person, so closely reflects his own experiences, except for chronology, that any discussion of the book necessitates reference to its author's life at the time he described.

At the beginning of *Down and Out in Paris and London*, Orwell plunges into the middle of his young anonymous English narrator's experiences in the squalid ironically-named "Rue du Coq d'Or" (Street of the Golden Rooster), in reality the more prosaically titled Rue du Pot de Fer (Street of the Iron Pot). The narrator then relates being robbed by an Italian scoundrel (in reality a female Parisian prostitute), which forces him into a few weeks of solitary gut-grinding poverty. He meets Boris, a penniless White (noncommunist) Russian refugee with a big heart and grandiose ambitions. Pooling their minimal resources, he and Boris nearly starve, but eventually find menial jobs in a luxurious Paris hotel. Later, they take jobs at a trendy new restaurant, the Auberge de Jehan Cottard, but working there proves unendurable. The narrator appeals to an English friend to find him a job at home, a transparent device which links the Paris half with the London half of the book.

The job in England is supposed to involve supervising a mentally retarded boy, but upon the narrator's arrival in England he discovers that his prospective employers have gone abroad for a month, leaving him stranded with only a few shillings in his pockets. Determined to brave it out since he was sure no one could starve to death in London, he trades in some of his clothes for ragged ones and during the days he roams London's streets. He spends his nights either outdoors or in various flophouses, meeting a broad assortment of British tramps, learning their language and customs, and directly experiencing the injustices the world inflicts on the destitute. Near the close of the narrator's experiences in Paris and again at the end of his experiences in London, Orwell steps out of his narrator's role to comment on the wider issues of socioeconomic injustice which afflict the poor in France and England.

THEMATIC ISSUES

Often the term "theme" is confused with "topic." The "topic" or "thematic issue" of a literary work is the one- or two-word answer to "What is this story about?" Orwell's topic of *Down and Out in Paris and London* is simply "poverty." However, "theme" is a far more complicated matter. It is the author's statement of his position on his topic, the central or dominating idea of the work, an abstract concept which the author presents in concrete terms through his characters, their actions, and his choices of imagery. "Theme" is expressed as a complete sentence which usually ties together many abstract issues or concerns into a coherent whole. Statements of the theme of a complex work often differ in detail between thoughtful readers. The theme of *Down and Out in Paris and London* might be expressed as, "Poverty in early twentieth-century Europe results from oppression of some people by groups of others, like capitalists and the upper class, in a system which tries to but cannot completely destroy the basic human decency of an individual so long as he resists with all his might." Issues which contribute to the theme of *Down and Out in Paris and London* are poverty, the condition of being poor, social injustices like capitalism and the British and European class systems, self-revelation, and individual responsibility.

Orwell revealed the topic, theme, and intention of *Down and Out in Paris and London* through the successive titles he gave the book. He called his first version "Days in London and Paris," indicating he intended a simple documentary account of his experiences. When the manuscript was finally accepted for publication, however, Orwell favored the title "The Lady Poverty" or "Lady Poverty," from a poem by Alice Meynell: "The Lady Poverty was fair/But she hath lost her looks of late" (*CEJL* 1:85). His Socialist publisher, Victor Gollancz, preferred "Confessions of a Down and Out in London and Paris." As a first-time author eager to be published, Orwell tactfully compromised on "The Confessions of a Dishwasher," since he felt he would much rather be called a dishwasher than a down and out (Shelden 1991: 163), but just before publication Gollancz changed the title to *Down and Out in Paris and London*. Orwell swallowed hard for the sake of sales.

The titles Orwell preferred, "Lady Poverty" and "Confessions of a Dishwasher," spell out his topics: poverty and self-revelation. They also suggest two aspects of the autobiographical aspect of the theme of his first book. By embracing "Lady Poverty" he rejected the corrupt money-hungry Imperial system and tried to make amends for serving it. If he accepted failure and poverty and made the best of a bad lot, as he later wrote, he could live successfully by a different set of rules, his own (*CEJL* 4:344). "Confessions" shows that he wryly intended to reveal himself relentlessly, and that he felt he could cleanse himself by doing so.

Although social unrest in Britain had calmed down somewhat by the time Orwell was gathering material for *Down and Out in Paris and London*, neither the Conservatives nor the Labour Party, which first came to power in 1924, seemed to want to do anything about the widening gulf between the British rich and poor which struck Orwell so keenly. For *Down and Out in Paris and London*, Orwell chose a telling epigraph, a quotation an author uses as his keynote, from Chaucer: "O scathful harm, condition of poverte!" Orwell had learned that poverty removes the poor from ordinary standards of behavior and forces them to evolve their own codes of conduct which mainstream society usually finds unacceptable. In *Down and Out in Paris and London*, he demonstrated that the poor, like the rich, almost always mask their real selves to appear more important, more capable, more of everything desirable than they are. The difference between the mask-wearing rich and the mask-wearing poor, according to Orwell, was that the rich usually get by with wearing their masks, while the masks the poor adopt usually contribute to their sad downward spiral to oblivion.

Orwell relentlessly depicted the physical suffering of the poor in *Down and Out in Paris and London*. One of the most harrowing episodes begins with his bout of pneumonia in a horrifying Paris public hospital, where he faced a close brush with death in a dark, filthy, nightmarish ward with antiquated medical treatments "from which patients rarely escaped alive" (Shelden 1991: 129). A few months later, after his money had oozed away, he went a desperate three days without food, which he described as "an ugly experience. . . . Hunger reduces one to an utterly spineless, brainless condition . . . as though one had been turned into a jellyfish" (*Down and Out* 38).

Even after he pawned his overcoat for food, the work he found was nearly as bad as the pangs of hunger. He worked as a *plongeur* (dishwasher) in the hellish bowels of the "*Hotel X*," one of the dozen most luxurious hotels in Paris. To one side of its imposing classical facade the *chef du personnel* led him through a "rathole" service entrance and down winding stairs into "dark labyrinthine" subterranean passageways, to a "tiny underground den" so low the extremely tall Orwell could not stand upright, in a temperature about 110 degrees Fahrenheit (*Down and Out* 55–56). During an average day, *plongeurs* like Orwell walked an average of fifteen miles, and he soon discovered that during the peak hours of his 7 A.M. to 9:15 P.M. shift, the heat might rise as high as 130 degrees.

After five or six weeks of near-total fatigue, lured by empty promises of more money and better working conditions, he and Boris left the Hotel X for the newly opened Auberge de Jehan Cottard. It was a thoroughly bad small restaurant that proved chic, picturesque, expensive, and so filthy that the perpetually blocked sink was coated with grease, raw meat lay on the garbage-strewn floor, and rats gnawed on ham left unattended on the kitchen counter (*Down and Out* 113). All of these horrid things, of course, went unnoticed by the rich who patronized the place.

The experiences Orwell shared with the London poor were different, but just as physically draining as those he had in Paris. He called England a very good country "if you're not poor" (*Down and Out* 125), cleaner, drearier, quieter than Paris, with people that were better dressed, milder in disposition, and more homogeneous, with less drunkenness and more idling, than the volatile mixture of Europeans he had encountered in the Rue du Coq d'Or (*Down and Out* 134). For Orwell, the smoky bistro and the frenetic sweatshop characterized the Paris he knew. The ubiquitous tea urn and the Labour Exchange, where unemployed men congregated in fruitless quests for work, typified London for him.

Despite being an Englishman, Orwell mercilessly exposed England's lack of compassion for the homeless. To protect its middle class from a permanent presence of tramps, British laws had established "casual wards" or "spikes" at local workhouses. A tramp could stay only one night per month in a given spike, so he spent his days wandering from spike to spike. Beds cost at least seven pence per night, and if a tramp didn't have that much, he faced a grim list of alternatives. In Paris, tramps could sleep in parks, but sleeping outdoors in London's public places, as Orwell himself had done, was forbidden by law. For two pence, tramps could have the Hangover, sleeping outdoors sitting up, draped over ropes cut promptly at 5 A.M. Four pence bought the Coffin, a wooden box crawling with insects and topped with a tarpaulin. If a tramp did have the wherewithal, common housing included the strictly disciplined Rowton Houses, with individual cubicles and decent bathrooms, which cost one shilling; and the Salvation Army facilities, which supplied clean beds at seven to eight pence that stank, Orwell claimed, "of prison and charity." He preferred dirty common lodging houses which cost seven pence or a shilling, but provided warm kitchens and a semblance of social life. In the late 1920s, about 15,000 Londoners used these nightly (*Down and Out* 208–10).

For Orwell, the emotional oppression of the poor was even worse than their physical ordeals. The hardships of Britain's lower classes proved the bitter truth that money was now "the grand test of virtue" (*Down and Out* 174). Those who had it reveled in the glittering surface worlds of glamorous European capitals and congratulated themselves for doing so. Those who didn't have money did the exhausting dirty work that kept those places going, slaving until they were too worn out to continue. Public assistance in Paris and London at that time was virtually nonexistent, and charitable organizations like churches and the Salvation Army tended to humiliate and thus dehumanize the poor still further.

Their emotional stresses were even worse. In the Paris hotel *cafeteries* at meal time, two-hour bursts of crazed activity, the four large *plongeurs* who worked in this murky equipment-stuffed twenty-by-seven-foot cellar kept deliriously colliding with each other, causing inescapable and vicious quarrels. Lower than the low, *plongeurs* did the kind of job women would have done, Orwell said, if women had been strong enough. At the Auberge de Jehan Cottard, he became so exhausted that he shamelessly bullied the poor old woman who did the cooking.

The London street people endured a different kind of psychological abuse. One of the characters in *Down and Out in Paris in London* was an impoverished "screever" (sidewalk artist) who had once studied at the Sorbonne. Now reduced to trying to support a wife and six children on chalk sidewalk art, the man told Orwell that interference was the bane of the existence of poor people like himself. Once an outraged churchwarden "or something" had chased the screever away from his painstaking copy of Botticelli's nude Venus, violently denouncing it as an "obscenity outside God's holy house" (*Down and Out* 171).

Orwell's passionate desire to understand and reveal the causes and effects of social injustice drove him to cut himself off from his family and even his country, so that he could experience poverty for himself. When he took up residence in Paris, he had only the little money he had saved from Burma, and it soon disappeared. Earlier in London he had spent only a few days at a time in the shadowy society of the tramps, but by going to Paris, he was almost completely separating himself from his native culture and its language. In doing so, he could see not only the poor, but himself more clearly.

One of Orwell's lasting preoccupations was the psychological damage that socioeconomic pressures create by forcing individuals to distort their images of themselves. From living among the poor in Paris, Orwell painfully learned to look behind the masks that the injustices of modern society forced individuals and groups to wear, like the one he had worn as an Imperial policeman in Burma. When he did so, he was shocked. He had expected poverty to be squalid and boring, but the Rue du Pot de Fer surprised him. Existence there proved extraordinarily complicated, with a hypocritical secrecy that revolted him most of all. A poor man, he realized, has to tell expensive lies to keep up appearances—smuggling clothes so neighbors won't see that he is selling them at a secondhand shop, or fleeing panic-stricken from a bakery rather than admitting he can't afford the extra two centimes for a decent loaf of bread. Such deceptions drive the poor farther and farther into hopelessness; by being driven to such deceptions himself, Orwell learned to recognize not only their destructively false self-images but to discern his own, which he tried to abandon forever.

Facing up to responsibility for one's actions, attitudes, and positions can be the occasion for considerable personal growth. Not all the survival techniques necessary to the poor that Orwell learned in Paris and London were negative. In *Down and Out in Paris and London* he faithfully recorded the astonishing camaraderie of the starving when he and Boris were down to their last twenty-five centimes. He characteristically saw another side to the harrowing fatigue of the *plongeurs*, too: even they had their pride, because they would keep on working, although it might kill them. This for Orwell proved that pride in personal capacities can sustain an individual, even one trapped in the most demeaning situations. Even more important, he realized that poverty had one enormous redeeming feature: it annihilated the future by freeing the individual from worry. It had one great consolation, too, that was nearly a pleasure: he had reached the bottom—and he could manage it. Being "down and out," Orwell wrote in his first book, freed him from a lot of anxiety (*Down and Out* 20–21).

CHARACTER DEVELOPMENT

With the exception of himself as first-person narrator, all of the characters Orwell presented in *Down and Out in Paris and London* are grotesques, like most of Dickens' slum dwellers. For dingy local color, Orwell included thumbnail portraits of flat characters (stereotypes) like the screaming Parisian *hotelière* of the first pages of *Down and Out in Paris and London* and her tenants, who, despite her repeated warnings, squash bedbugs on the wallpaper. He was so intrigued with the way that poverty turns human beings into "eccentrics" who have abandoned the attempt to be normal or decent and exist in solitary, half-deranged ruts (*Down and Out* 7), that he created some unforgettable vignettes, like his sketch of the Rougiers, a couple who had not taken off their clothes for four years and lived by palming off sealed packets of scenic postcards as pornography to tourists wanting a taste of "gay Paree" (*Down and Out* 7–8). Another was Charlie, an innocent-looking young runaway from a wealthy family. Charlie's favorite topic was his theory of love, which led to his strange, decadent little tale of sex and sadism about a violent rape he supposedly committed in an exotic red-draped subterranean chamber (*Down and Out* 10–15), an experimental Oscar-Wildeish episode that Orwell seems never to have repeated.

Charlie also provided Orwell with what the writer called a "good" story for the end of the Paris section of *Down and Out in Paris and London*. Roucelle, an elderly cat-food-eating Parisian miser, did himself in through a get-rich-quick scheme involving cocaine. Roucelle became entangled with a young Jew who had a plan for smuggling the drug into Paris, but the Jew double-crossed him, and Roucelle lost his money and died, it was rumored, of a broken heart (*Down and Out* 122–25). Despite this story's slightly anti-Semitic tinge, a fairly common tendency in European fiction of the 1920s and 1930s, Orwell deftly and economically brought Roucelle to decrepit life.

The most true to life character in the Paris portion of *Down and Out in Paris and London* is Boris, Orwell's boastful Russian friend. The generous Boris constantly offered to help Orwell by appealing to well-off former mistresses and old army buddies, but Boris's schemes always fell through. Boris's inflated ideas and his impractical tendency to promise more than he could deliver more than once landed them both in worse difficulties, as in the episode where Boris told Orwell a purported Communist secret society might buy Orwell's articles on English politics. The supposed Communists first pretended to buy Orwell's writings for the magnificent sum of one hundred fifty francs (Orwell was living on six francs a day), then bilked him out of it all plus five more francs Orwell could ill afford to lose (*Down and Out* 44–50). With eternal optimism, Boris kept claiming that nothing was easier to get than money (*Down and Out* 29), but his connections mostly evaporated, leaving him in the most abject despair, a victim of his own self-deception.

For the London sections of *Down and Out in Paris and London*, Orwell wrote brief glimpses of the eccentric poor, but being English himself, he seems to have more sympathy with the London tramps than he did with the Parisian slum dwellers. Most middle-class English people looked down on the Irish, but Orwell made a point of describing several Irishmen compassionately, like the old Irishman who whistled to a blind bullfinch in a cage (*Down and Out* 139). Orwell also described in detail the multiple ailments of another ancient Irishman who had been on the road for fifteen years, from scalp eczema to flat feet with several other physical problems in between. Even though he smelt very unpleasant, Orwell said, the man was kind to him and showed him how to get tea and buns from humiliatingly pious women missionaries for a minimal amount of pretended prayer (*Down and Out* 139–40).

Orwell's closest friend among English tramps was Bozo, a crippled beggar who also did sidewalk art. Orwell admired Bozo's courage in standing up to adversity and holding onto his spiritual independence and described Bozo without a shred of sentimentality as an "exceptional man." Bozo had no future but begging and a lonely death in a workhouse, but he had managed to keep his mind functioning and so nothing, Orwell said, could make the man relinquish his human decency. Bozo might be hungry and cold and homeless, but as long as he could think and read and watch for meteors, he had the freedom of his own mind. This was the kind of individual courage and self-respect Orwell most admired (*Down and Out* 160–68).

STYLISTIC AND LITERARY DEVICES

By seeking out unpleasant experiences like slum living for artistic as well as moral reasons, Orwell displayed in his life and his first book one of the major trends of Modernism, a loosely-defined literary movement which broke with traditional forms and techniques of expression around the start of World War I. At this time a flurry of autobiographical stories known technically as "*Künstlerromane*" ("artist-novels") appeared, portraying young men struggling to turn themselves into literary artists and telling their stories in naturalistic, even shocking language: James Joyce's *A Portrait of the Artist as a Young Man*, D. H. Lawrence's *Sons and Lovers*, the German poet Rainer Maria Rilke's *The Notebooks of Malte Laurids Brigge*, Thomas Mann's "Tonio Kröger," Kafka's "The Hunger Artist," and others.

Twentieth-century *Künstlerromane* share an intriguing underlying structure, the pattern of tribal initiation found in all human societies from primitive cultures to contemporary Western fraternal organizations like the Masons or the Elks. As Eric Blair taught himself to write, he unconsciously reenacted that mythic pattern of initiation and then recorded his experiences, especially the crucial "ordeal" stage of that process, as lightly fictionalized autobiography in *Down and Out in Paris and London*.

Primitive peoples initiate a young man into adulthood by having him recreate the suffering, death, and rebirth of the tribal god. This process generally has five stages. In the first, the candidate is separated from his family, sometimes voluntarily and sometimes stolen by older men masquerading as "gods," and taken into a dark forest which symbolizes death. In the second phase, he is kept secluded in a special hut, symbolic of the womb, where supernatural forces threaten him with destruction before he is taught the sacred traditions of the tribe (Eliade 198). The third stage, either on or near sacred ground or at the place of seclusion, features a physical initiation, the "ordeal," symbolizing the suffering and death necessary to mystical rebirth. The fourth phase, usually continuous with the third, often features the revelation of sacred objects and involves long circuitous trips which retrace routes originally blazed by mythical beings . During this stage, the initiate receives many more symbols of rebirth. He receives a new name, he is treated as a young child, and he learns a new language (Eliade 199). Finally, the candidate, now declared an adult, returns to his original group. To show that he has outgrown his mother's apron strings, he either actually or seemingly rejects her and dominates women in general (Eckert 163–67).

Eric Blair experienced this five-stage growth process, lightly fictionalizing it in *Down and Out in Paris and London*, and by doing so, he turned himself into George Orwell. The first stage of his initiation into artisthood was his total separation from his family, his home, and England, which he demonstrated by beginning *Down and Out in Paris and London* with scenes and stories of Parisian, not the English, slums. Instead of starving in Paris, he could have appealed to his aunt Nellie Limouzin, who lived there, just as he could have called on his parents to avoid sleeping in the tuberculosis-ridden London spikes, but he chose not to. The second phase, seclusion, was the lonely period when he was weak and sick, trying to write in his bug-ridden Paris room while he learned the traditions of being poor, pawning his possessions to stay alive while he minutely observed his surroundings and the eccentric people around him. The third phase, the ordeal, was the three days of near-starvation which followed his horrifying hospitalization with pneumonia. He emerged with a heightened sense of comradeship with the poor and a renewed determination to survive so that he could tell the world about their suffering.

The fourth phase of Orwell's initiation, his initial steps in his new life, brought him back to England. In the London slums, his Eton accent stamped him as an inexperienced newcomer, and he had to learn a new language, the jargon of the streets, the most effective techniques of begging, and the hierarchies of vagrant life. In 1927–28, his earliest attempts at putting his experiences into fictional form were not terribly impressive, in part because he had not yet mastered the language of the slums. His friend Ruth Pitter recalled that "He used to put in a fair number of rude words . . . and we had to correct the spelling. I would have thought an Old Etonian knew every word there was and a few more. He certainly couldn't spell the London rude words" (quoted in Crick 425 n.8). Eventually, though, by associating with the destitute, Blair assimilated their "rude words" in both English and French. He even devoted all of Chapter 32 of *Down and Out in Paris and London* to a glossary of English street language, though many terms then considered unacceptable had to be edited out before the book could be published.

For Eric Blair's tramping excursions in London, he had a special ragged costume he put on at friends' flats, and he always took a name different from his own. Depressed over having lost several stories when *Modern Youth* went bankrupt, he tried to get himself arrested just prior to Christmas 1931, calling himself "Edward Burton," perhaps echoing the British explorer "who went native to reach Mecca" (Crick 135, 147). Later, when Gollancz was readying *Down and Out* for publication, he suggested Blair use the pseudonym "X." Blair didn't care for "X," but commented to his agent Leonard Moore, "a name I always use when tramping etc. is P. S. Burton . . . but what about Kenneth Miles, George Orwell, H. Lewis Allways. I rather favour George Orwell" (*CEJL* 1, 106).

In taking a new name, Blair was deliberately remaking his life. A librarian in Leeds, where Blair visited his sister Marjorie in early 1932, noted that Blair seemed "in the process of rearranging himself" (quoted in Crick 427 n.1). He had always disliked the name "Eric," and "George" was England's dragon-slaying patron saint, the "Orwell" was one of his favorite British rivers, and the combination "George Orwell" "had a manly, English, indeed country-sounding ring with perhaps an undercurrent of industry in the buried ore" (Crick 147). Even though he continued to publish reviews and articles as "Eric Blair" until 1934 and retained that name throughout his life for all legal purposes, he adopted "George Orwell" as his new literary self: "In effect, the writer 'Eric Blair' died with the first good review of *Down and Out*" (Shelden 1991: 165).

In the final stage of his initiation, Orwell plunged into the London literary scene where he really belonged. He also treated the women in his life with a curious mixture of desire and rejection, an attitude that appears in his treatment of most of the female characters in his later books. So far as is known, he always was devoted to his mother, but he found her rented retirement home, her frequent bridge guests, and the whole cozy Southwold seaside resort area intolerable. For his parents, the presence of an unconventional and unemployed son, a mostly rejected would-be writer who had himself rejected his father's lifestyle, made for uncomfortable family relations, and the racial prejudices of the elder Blairs' social circle of retired Anglo-Indian civil servants, according to Eric's sister Avril, rubbed their son raw (Crick 123). Avril herself made a decent living from operating The Copper Kettle in Southwold, a genteel "Ye Olde Tea Shoppe," which later in *A Clergyman's Daughter* Orwell rather cruelly lampooned as a favorite hangout of gossipy little old ladies cooing over lapdogs, proving that one of the dangers of having a novelist as a friend or worse, a relative, is that it offers him a tempting source of raw material (Shelden 1991: 139). Orwell also was romantically attracted to several young women, but he had no money to court them. All of these women felt that Orwell's writing definitely came first with him.

As Orwell passed through the stages of his artistic growth, he gradually revised *Down and Out in Paris and London* from his first raw collection of sketches into an organic whole, divided roughly into two halves, the twenty-three sections on his Parisian experiences and the fifteen dealing with those in London. In each half he first plunges his readers into a seamy slum and vividly brings the eccentrics there to life through stories they purportedly told him. Orwell recalled in later life that when he was about sixteen, he had discovered the joy words could give him and he wanted "to write enormous naturalistic novels and unhappy endings, full of detailed descriptions and arresting similes, and also full of purple [sexually suggestive] passages in which words were used partly for the sake of their sound" (*CEJL* 1:3). About ten years later, he packed *Down and Out in Paris and London* full of naturalistic description, sparing no unsavory detail in documenting his smelly, squalid surroundings in terms that assault all the senses: shrieking women, noisy children chasing garbage, reeking refuse carts, and flophouses full of humanity unwashed for weeks on end.

By using exact, if distasteful detail, Orwell was able to make his readers share the effects of living on bread and margarine, with bugs falling into the last liter of milk, and cheap lung-scorching tobacco the only way to endure three weeks without a bath. The words Orwell chose—everyday language in a deceptively simple style—allowed him to force his readers to see that the self-pity and boredom of poverty threatened human dignity: "someone who has lived even a week on bread and margarine," he wrote in *Down and Out in Paris and London*, "is not a man any longer, only a belly with a few accessory organs" (*Down and Out* 19).

Orwell also could not resist including in each half of *Down and Out in Paris and London* one section in which he set forth his opinions about poverty and his views on solving the problems which cause it. In Chapter 22, inspired by having toiled in a Paris hotel himself, he develops the concept that the life of a *plongeur* is really slavery, and furthermore it is useless slavery. The affluent classes do not recognize that workers are human beings, because they fear what the poor might do were they not enslaved (*Down and Out* 118). In Chapter 36, Orwell reflected on the inaccurate negative image of all English tramps as criminals and blackguards, and suggested that the evils of their lives, hunger, the lack of women, and enforced idleness, might be wiped out by providing meaningful work for them (*Down and Out* 205–57), so that they could support themselves and their families. In both cases, Orwell pointed to a great need for reorganization of society through recognizing its lowest members as individuals, not just helpless wretches who had to live in a squalid underworld the well-to-do mostly ignored.

During 1933, *Down and Out in Paris and London* gave Orwell his first modest literary success. The first reviews were generally good, very much better than he had expected, though the book sold less than two thousand copies. The noted critic C. Day Lewis complimented Orwell's "clarity and good sense," the *Times Literary Supplement* favorably compared Orwell's eccentric characters to Dickens,' and *Time and Tide* (11 February 1933) perceptively declared that not only George Orwell's experiences were interesting, Orwell himself was of interest.

ALTERNATIVE CRITICAL PERSPECTIVE: SOCIALISM

By espousing the cause of the unfortunate in *Down and Out in Paris and London,* Orwell separated himself from the "upper-lower-middle class" conservative beliefs of his family and his class, but even though the vehemently socialistic Victor Gollancz published the book, Orwell's views were by no means mainstream socialistic, if indeed such a thing existed in 1930s England. Orwell claimed in *The Road to Wigan Pier* (1937) that at seventeen or eighteen he had been "both a snob and a revolutionary" who sympathized with the poor through books like London's *People of the Abyss,* but he also said that as a youth he had neither understood what socialism really was nor could he see the working class as human beings, because he couldn't stand their accents and their "habitual rudeness" (*RWP* 141–43). His experiences in Paris and London dramatically changed those attitudes forever.

Though he never accepted any conventional definition of socialism, Orwell's experiences in London and Paris did teach him that the poor were indeed human beings, one of the few concepts that all of the various tribes of socialists could agree about. Socialism had arisen in the nineteenth century to challenge the sanctity of private property, advocating its use for public welfare. In response to the societal abuses produced by industrialization, a wide spectrum of theories about social reorganization sprang up, and at first the terms "socialism" and "communism" were almost interchangeable. Early British "utopian" reformers like Robert Owen (1771–1858) had briefly tried to set up model communities and establish fair working conditions. This notion was revived by the Fabian Society, which started in 1884 and was backed forcefully by George Bernard Shaw and Sidney and Beatrice Webb. The Fabians, among whom Orwell's mother had several friends, helped to found the British Labour Party in 1900. They repudiated both utopian schemes and Marxist insistence on class struggle, believing instead in infiltrating existing governmental structures and parliamentarily wearing down their opposition as the ancient Roman general Fabius Cunctator had worn down and eventually defeated the Carthaginians' great leader Hannibal.

Orwell's *Down and Out in Paris and London,* though political only in the most general sense, could be read from several socialist points of view. Most obvious would be a Wellsian utopian socialist reading, based on Orwell's call at the close of the book for government establishment of small farms run by the workhouses, farms on which the British indigent could grow their own food. Orwell believed that if the tramp represented labor to the workhouse and the workhouse represented food to the tramp, the tramp could settle down and become respectable.

Orwell's loosely-defined socialism in *Down and Out*, however, would have had nothing to do with "Christian socialism," a religious concern for the welfare of the lower classes first advocated in the nineteenth century by Charles Kingsley and F. D. Maurice and responsible, in Orwell's view, for such banes of English tramping life as the Salvation Army. In *Down and Out* Orwell reserved some of his most scathing condemnation for hymn-singing missionaries whose enforced price of handed-out meals was attendance at religious services with a gaggle of old women who reminded Orwell of "boiling-fowl" (*Down and Out* 182–83). For Orwell, genuine charity never debased the people who needed it. The best example of it in *Down and Out* is a self-effacingly embarrassed young clergyman who avoided any thanks and thus, as one tramp remarked, would never be "a——bishop" (*Down and Out* 185).

A socialist reading of *Down and Out in Paris and London* would also stress Orwell's belief that the match-selling and busking of the poor were simply legalized crimes (*Down and Out* 172). Like nineteenth-century social critic Thomas Carlyle, Orwell felt nothing set a beggar in a different class from other people or gave others the right to despise him (*Down and Out* 172). Further, Orwell believed that the only reason beggars were despised was that their work failed to produce a decent living. In the socialist view, government ought to step in, divest the wealthy of their excess goods, and use the confiscated funds to make the lives of the poor better. In *Down and Out*, however, Orwell did not go that far, preferring individual effort as far as possible to bureaucratic interference. This may have been the basis for Orwell's early and lasting ambivalence about Shaw's Fabianism. As a youth, Orwell had admired Shaw's ability to "debunk" the ideals of the monied establishment, but even then he realized that Shaw, whom he called "Carlyle and water," had some peculiar ideas that probably would not work out in practice (*CEJL* 1:125).

Any socialist reading of *Down and Out in Paris and London* should consider Orwell's extreme individualism, his utter refusal to be pinned down to any convenient political label. By concentrating on the individuals who showed him that the poor are indeed human and insisting on basing his accounts of "Lady Poverty" on his own intimate experience, Orwell was demanding that his readers uphold with him the norms of human decency. For Orwell, any socialist reading of *Down and Out in London and Paris* had to rest on the worth of the individual, never the group. For Orwell, each man, not his government, had to determine his own destiny.

4

Settling Down and Writing Books: *Burmese Days, A Clergyman's Daughter, Keep the Aspidistra Flying*

With the publication of *Down and Out in Paris and London* in January 1933, George Orwell became a writer. He quickly wrote out his apprenticeship in his first three novels, completing *Burmese Days* that December; *A Clergyman's Daughter* in early October, 1934; and *Keep the Aspidistra Flying* in December, 1935. In each of these novels, he attacked a different dehumanizing collective force—imperialism in *Burmese Days,* the British class system in *A Clergyman's Daughter*, and capitalism in *Keep the Aspidistra Flying.*

BURMESE DAYS

Eric Blair left England for Burma as an unhappy nineteen-year-old on October 27, 1922, and he returned to England an embittered man on July 14, 1927. That exile changed the course of his life, because below its surface lurks a speculative " 'shadow' story . . . of Blair the writer-in-embryo" (Stansky and Abrahams 1972: 205). In Burma, Blair seems to have been trying ineffectually to smother the desire to write which he had had since he was five years old, even using a copy of *Adelphi*, a literary journal he would have liked to contribute to, for jungle target practice (Stansky and Abrahams, 1972: 206–7). He was reading the works of Maugham and D. H. Lawrence when he began *Burmese Days*, which he wrote mostly at night while teaching at the

Hawthorns, in a dismal London suburb he called one of the most godforsaken places he had ever seen.

HISTORICAL SETTING

In 1922, Imperial policemen stationed in Burma received hardship bonuses because of the country's seething crime rate, the highest in the British Empire. Over the previous decade, murder cases in Burma had doubled, and in some areas, the homicide rate was six times higher than Chicago's in the Al Capone era (Shelden 1991: 82). The major problem was native *dacoit* gangs, who were night-prowling thieves, rapists, and murderers.

Political instability was also mounting. In 1885, the British had arbitrarily made Burma a province of India, a country with which the Burmese had no cultural ties. This act bitterly galled the Burmese, especially when India, but not Burma, received dyarchy status in 1919, a shared-rule system which allowed natives a greater voice in the British-dominated government. Burmese Buddhist monks then called for boycotts of British goods and organized student strikes, forcing the British to prepare for open rebellion.

By 1923 the situation was so volatile that the British extended dyarchy to Burma. Natives over eighteen could now elect three-fourths of their national legislature. They also now elected Burmese ministers who supervised local government, education, health, agriculture, excise, and public works. The catch was that the British still controlled the Burmese government by appointing those ministers in charge of law and order, revenue and finance (Stansky and Abrahams 1972: 171–72). Burmese police constables were always led by English officers, a grave irritant for the Burmese, who were thus held accountable to Western concepts of law and order quite different from their own more flexible usage. In practice, Burmese magistrates judged less on Anglo-Saxon principles of right and wrong than on compromises through which both sides might hope to gain some satisfaction. Oriental customs officially repugnant to Westerners, like blatant bribery, also flourished in Burma.

PLOT

Burmese Days is a straightforward twenty-five-chapter chronological narrative covering a few months in the mid-1920s in the small Burmese town of Kyauktada. Its major conflict pits British imperialism against Burmese self-determination. Under the dyarchy reforms, the British governor commanded each exclusively European Club in Burma to admit one or two senior Burmese officials to their membership (Gross 26). Orwell pungently called these clubs "the real seat of the British power, the Nirvana for which native officials and millionaires pine in vain" (*BD* 17). The European Club in Kyauktada prided itself on never having admitted an Oriental to membership.

A scheming, corrupt Burmese magistrate, U Po Kyin, wants to be the token native in the Kyauktada European Club. He engineers a concerted campaign of slander against Dr. Veraswami, a decent and humble Indian physician whom the Europeans tolerate, to keep him from being chosen instead. Veraswami is the friend of John Flory, Orwell's protagonist, a thirty-five-year-old English timber merchant. Flory, who has a bruise-colored birthmark stretching halfway down his left cheek, is scorned as a "bolshie" (Bolshevik) by the hate-filled Ellis and the other five whisky-swilling Europeans in Kyauktada because of that friendship and because Flory is sympathetic to the Burmese and other nonwhites. Flory also has a mercenary native mistress, Ma Hla May.

Orwell's secondary story line introduces Elizabeth, a husband-hunting young Englishwoman, to Flory. Elizabeth ensnares him easily, but her aunt learns that Lt. Verrall, a British army officer sent to Kyauktada in case of a native uprising, is an "Honourable," a younger son of the nobility, "rare as dodos in Burma." She turns Elizabeth against "that drunken wretch Flory whose pay was barely seven hundred rupees a month" (*BD* 195). Elizabeth then uses Ma Hla May, who is furious because Flory jettisons her for Elizabeth, as a pretext to dump Flory so she can try to land Verrall, a "tough and martial rabbit" (*BD* 184).

After U Po Kyin disgraces Veraswami and the doctor is abandoned by all the Europeans including Flory, who gives in to social pressure and his own cowardice, U Po Kyin realizes his life's ambition of election to the European Club, unaware that his self-effacing wife Ma Kyin had unobtrusively planted the successful strategy in his head. Flory, in an agony of self-disgust, shoots first his dog, then himself, the first of Orwell's protagonists to fall victim to a combination of psychological insecurity and societal rejection. Elizabeth, spurned by Verrall, marries Deputy Commissioner Macgregor and "fills with complete success" the role she has been cut out for from the start, that of a hardened, selfish, cruel "burra memsahib" (*BD* 287), the Indian term for the wife of a British Imperial official who brutally exploits her position.

CHARACTER DEVELOPMENT

John Flory is both physically and emotionally disfigured by his birthmark, which symbolizes his alienation from his fellow Europeans. Flory's haggard face reflects his—and Orwell's— soul-sickness at belonging to the British ruling class and supporting the Imperial system he knows is corrupt. Flory's trouble, like his birthmark, began before his birth, because his parents, like Orwell's, belonged to Britain's lower-upper-middle class. His "difference" targeted him with cruel jokes at a cheap third-rate public school, from which he emerged at twenty in most respects "a barbarous young lout" who nonetheless hid "certain possibilities" of decency (*BD* 65) in a world that mocked them and him. After fifteen lonely years of numbing himself with whisky and mechanical sex with native women, Flory detests the "slimy white man's burden humbug"(*BD* 39) and cynically concludes that the white men are in Burma simply to rob the natives.

Although Flory recognized corruption as integral to British imperialism, his birthmark also signals an incapacitating inner flaw, his self-pitying lack of "the small spark of courage" (*BD* 63) to act on principles he knew in his heart were right. Like Blair aboard the ship bringing him to Mandalay, watching in horror as a Britisher savagely kicked a helpless coolie, Flory keeps still; but his secret revolt poisons him, like a hidden disease. "You see louts fresh from school kicking greyhaired [*sic*] servants. The time comes when you burn with hatred of your own countrymen" (*BD* 69).

Burma was Flory's university, where he learned not to set himself up against public opinion. He deliberately makes himself suffer to shut out the pain from outside (*BD* 64), preferring self-inflicted pain, which to some extent he can manage, to uncontrollable pain forced on him by others. He aches continually because he has no one to share the exotic Burmese landscape with him—no one but his cocker spaniel Flo (the name as a truncated version of "Flory" shows how deeply inferior he felt). The rest of Flory's years of exile stretch out before him, "lonely, eventless, corrupting" (*BD* 66).

Flory's sense of inadequacy dooms his relationships. He befriends Dr. Veraswami, but not wholeheartedly, because fear of being ridiculed by the other Europeans forces Flory to insult the Hindu physician in public. When Flory "rescues" just-arrived Elizabeth from a relatively harmless water buffalo, something seems "to thaw and grow warm in him" (*BD* 80). He wants to share his fondness for Burma and the Burmese with her, but his feelings of inadequacy make him wait too long. Elizabeth, shallow and predatory, throws him over for the arrogant and sadistic Verrall. By the time Flory musters his courage to help the Burmese, to defend his friend Dr. Veraswami, and to propose to Elizabeth after Verrall jilts her, Flory realizes it is all tragically too late.

Orwell also made the self-serving Elizabeth a representative product of the brief time in one's life when he felt a person's character is fixed forever (*BD* 90). After two terms—all her parents could afford—of rubbing elbows with the rich in a snobbish English girls' school, she identified everything that was cheap, shabby, and laborious, "from a pair of stockings to a human soul," as "bad," and everything expensive, elegant, and aristocratic as "good" (*BD* 90). Elizabeth's hatred of art and her snobbish rejection of the beauty of Burmese culture make her a far less appealing character and more of an outcast from genuine humanity than Flory is. Eventually her amorality will turn her into either a "scraggy old boiling-fowl" or a "meditative snake" (*BD* 206, 95), Orwell's images for expatriate Englishwomen like Elizabeth's mercenary aunt. Flory dies by his own hand, but Elizabeth survives, momentarily triumphant, by marrying Mr. Macgregor, sire of nine illegitimate half-Burmese children.

Like Orwell, Flory dismissed his fellow Europeans as "dull boozing witless porkers," whose stupid self-satisfaction was backed up by a quarter of a million British army bayonets (*BD* 29, 69). Orwell strewed despicable minor European characters throughout *Burmese Days*, ranging from the relatively mild Westfield, who believes that too much law and order has "done in" the Raj (*BD* 32) to the fanatically brutal Ellis whose physical assault on a native parallels an attack Orwell himself, goaded by rebellious native students, had committed in a Burmese train station (*BD* 242, Gross 24).

In *Burmese Days*, Orwell generally sketched the "brown" characters (Flory's adjective for southeast Asians, as opposed to "black," the adjective the other Europeans use) compassionately. He generally treated the native servants' manipulation of their masters with wry humor, though he reserved biting satire for the grasping Ma Hla May. For the obscenely obese U Po Kyin, master of Oriental intrigue, Orwell unleashed his already powerful insight into the criminally bureaucratic mind, playing it against the practicality of the one person U Po Kyin subconsciously acknowledges as his superior, the person who to biased European eyes ironically seems a virtual nonentity—Kyin's wife.

THEMATIC ISSUES: DISILLUSION WITH IMPERIALISM

Burmese Days "can be fully understood only in relation to Orwell himself: his complex personality, his deeply ingrained sense of failure, his sense of alienation, his Anglo-Indian background" (Hammond 93), which all came together in his disillusion with British imperialism. The novel reveals Orwell's disgust with the Imperial system as incompatible with human decency. Its theme may be stated thus: that the desire for wealth and power which drove both the Empire and those individuals, both British and native, who could most thoroughly compromise their principles to succeed materially would cause them to lose their humanity and their souls. Those like meek Dr. Veraswami who choose friendship over personal advantage pay a heavy price—a second- or third-class life devoid of intellectual companionship. The self-serving actions of women like Elizabeth and her aunt reveal Orwell's disgust with women who value material gain over genuine emotion.

STYLISTIC AND LITERARY DEVICES

Orwell's authorial intrusions into the narrative of *Burmese Days*, like the general observations he wove into *Down and Out in Paris and London*, illustrate the tough literary feat of simultaneously conveying two perspectives, a technique he used throughout his fiction. In his earlier book, Orwell participated in the action as a tramp, but he also functioned as a sophisticated and articulate narrator, revealing the realities of poverty to his middle-class readers (Shelden 1991: 137). In *Burmese Days*, he parallels the sad specifics of Flory's decline and fall with keen commentary on colonial attitudes, helping readers blur the line between failed individuals like Flory and themselves. This shows up British imperialism as far more personally debasing to the masters than to the natives they dominate.

From reading D. H. Lawrence, Orwell learned about the powerful "sense of place": intense descriptive nature passages that express physical presences and nuances of emotional response. Orwell achieved lushly evocative, descriptive passages in *Burmese Days*, but afterwards he used description only sparingly, like some exotic spice. Perhaps because he might have been trying too hard to achieve Lawrentian effects in *Burmese Days,* Orwell also had Lawrentian difficulties with pace, awkward dialogue, and wordiness. On the other hand, Orwell had also read and savored Maugham's stripped-down prose and Samuel Butler's advocacy of "common, simple straightforwardness" (quoted in Stansky and Abrahams 1972: 209). This helped Orwell produce marvelously cutting phrases like Mrs. Leckersteen's "delicate, saurian hands" (*BD* 97), a step toward Orwell's major stylistic achievement, the crystalline prose apparently so easy but in actuality so difficult to achieve.

A CLERGYMAN'S DAUGHTER

As he wandered through London's slums in 1931, Orwell/Blair listened so carefully to the street people he met that he virtually memorized much of their conversation. One middle-aged female derelict reminded Blair of *The Odd Women*, George Gissing's savage three-volume novel about the wretched lot of "superfluous" Victorian females (Crick 132 n.60). She clung desperately to memories of her more respectable days, convincing Blair that people like her could never explode into revolt, which, he then thought, could destroy England's dehumanizing class system—and so *A Clergyman's Daughter* was born.

HISTORICAL SETTING

By the early 1930s, the Great Depression was raging worldwide. Britain's controversial return to the gold standard kept interest rates high, an economic effect "like putting on the brake while going up hill" (Arnstein 288), and in May 1926 the troubled mining industry set off the only general strike in British history—no trains, trams, or buses moved, no newspapers appeared, docks and power plants and steel mills shut down.

The strikes produced plenty of political rhetoric but little immediate concrete effect. Then with the American stock market crash in October 1929, the whole artificial international financial structure collapsed. Unemployment soared until almost seven million out of the total British population of forty-five million were living entirely on the dole (Arnstein 294). By the late 1930s, conditions were so bad that Hollywood's romantic escapism lured four million Britons a day into theaters where they could forget their diet of "bread and marg" for a little while.

Orwell threw his lot in with those too poor to buy a movie ticket. At least 15 to 20 percent of all British workers could not afford the diet the British Medical Association recommended to maintain minimum health and ability to work. A third of these were unemployed, a third had inadequate old-age pensions, and a third earned less than a subsistence wage (Briggs 280). Women's lot was particularly dismal. Less than a million married women—one out of ten—held jobs in 1931 (Bentley 328), and unmarried women of the impoverished "lower-upper-middle class," like Dorothy Hare, Orwell's "clergyman's daughter," had virtually no options to avoid genteel starvation except marriage, teaching, or housekeeping for male relatives.

PLOT

The five long chapters of *A Clergyman's Daughter*, each subdivided into short sketch-like scenes, trace eight months in Dorothy's life. As the story begins, she is a browbeaten victim of her social position, doing unpaid parish work and keeping house for her tyrannical father, an Anglican rector who has managed to alienate everyone in every parish assigned to him. Bitterly resentful at not living in a past where a nobly-born clergyman was assured slavish obedience from his congregation, and furious at being tethered to the age of Lenin and the left-wing *Daily Mail*, he has only Dorothy, who represents exactly half of his daily communicants, to bully while he gambles away his meager income.

One midnight, still working though she is exhausted, Dorothy suffers a nervous collapse. She loses her memory, wandering away from the rectory and falling in with migrant hop-pickers in Kent. She then descends to begging in Trafalgar Square, only escaping prostitution because an effete, wealthy relative fears public embarrassment. After her memory returns, she takes a horrid job teaching in a repellent London suburb where the headmistress Miss Creevy, who never read an entire book and was proud of it (*CD* 235), loves to do people "bad turns" so she can get "spiritual orgasms" from them (*CD* 236).

Repulsed by her father and finally rescued by Mr. Warburton, a genial roué from her hometown who offers to marry her, Dorothy rejects Warburton and returns to her father's prison-like rectory in Suffolk (*CD* 214). As Orwell's device for Dorothy's temporary escape, her abrupt collapse and her mysterious amnesia seem awkwardly contrived, although they allow Orwell to contrast the poor with Dorothy's spiritually desolate "lower-upper-middle class" existence. Orwell knew both lives firsthand. In the summer of 1931 he had bloodied his own hands picking hops, a thorny crop used in brewing beer; he had shivered through nights outdoors in Trafalgar Square, and he had taught in a fourth-rate suburban school where parents demanded the mediocrity that doomed their children to wretched lives exactly like their own. For a man, such experiences would be shattering enough, but Orwell broadened the scope of his social criticism by making this victim of social injustice a woman.

CHARACTER DEVELOPMENT

Orwell used many of his own experiences in this novel, but his protagonist seemed unable to learn or profit from hers. At twenty-eight, Dorothy Hare still looks vulnerable and inexperienced, a reflection of her abysmally low self-esteem. Like Flory, she feels her face is her weakest point, though Dorothy wears her disfiguring scars where they cannot be seen. Like Flory's birthmark, Dorothy's incapacitating insecurity results from prenatally-determined factors. Her parents' unpleasant personalities, their tenuous position in the British class system, and their precarious financial situation, all matters beyond Dorothy's control, combine to create the pressures that temporarily snap her mind.

Dorothy's forbidding father, the widowed rector of St. Athelstan's, was the younger son of the younger son of a baronet, the lowest rung in the stratified British peerage. Under Britain's legal code, the Law of England, only eldest sons could inherit family titles and wealth, so the rector took the usual younger-son path of least resistance (and usually least income) and went into the Anglican Church, where he tried to make everyone around him as unhappy as he was.

As the product of "a diabolically unhappy marriage" (*CD* 23), all the more vicious for being hidden because a clergyman could never openly quarrel with his wife, Dorothy grew up loathing the very thought of "*all that* [Orwell's italics]" (*CD* 93), her euphemism for sex. Recollections of "dreadful scenes" she had witnessed as a child brought on Dorothy's fatal frigidity, a condition, according to Orwell, "too common nowadays, among educated women, to occasion any kind of surprise" (*CD* 94).

Because her fear of sex blocks the traditional escape route of marriage, Dorothy forced herself into the time-honored self-sacrificial mode of British spinsters—"odd" women. She bathed in icy water, deprived herself of food, and stabbed her arms raw with pins until one night, overcome with fatigue, she succeeded in blocking out her whole world. She awoke days later in the brutal world of the destitute, a world ignored by the Christian churches supposedly founded to help them.

Orwell's characterizations in *A Clergyman's Daughter*, especially the sadistically domineering Miss Creevy and Dorothy's tyrannical father, owe a great deal to Dickens' minutely observed social satire, just as Dorothy's plight resembles the wretched existence of Gissing's *Odd Women*, which Dorothy read during the Christmas she spent teaching in London. Orwell, however, did not develop his characters as fully as Dickens usually did. Orwell also had a gift for incisive humor never seen in Gissing's thoroughly bitter novels.

Orwell used that humor to good advantage in drawing plump, well-to-do, middle-aged Mr. Warburton, a good-natured rake who had done his best to seduce Dorothy two years earlier. She still visited his home alone, late at night, attracted by his conversation, "Oscar Wilde seven times watered" (*CD* 50), which to Dorothy's sheltered sensibilities seemed audaciously "modern." Even though Warburton's designs on Dorothy were originally less than honorable, he, not her father, rescues her and decently proposes marriage, but she rejects him. Dorothy is fond of Warburton, Orwell comments ironically, because "the pious and the immoral naturally drift together" (*CD* 49).

THEMATIC ISSUES

As social fiction, *A Clergyman's Daughter* attacks Britain's traditional class system for its damage to the individual, and the established Anglican church's neglect of its people's needs. Dorothy's father is obnoxious, but by posing the rector before an empty fireplace grate, warming himself at an imaginary fire (*CD* 19), Orwell reminds readers that Britain's traditional inheritance laws deprived this man, raised on the fringes of the leisure class, of the means to support the lifestyle the social system had led him to expect, the only lifestyle he knew and wanted. It had deprived him, too, of any healthy desire to make his own way effectively in the world by working.

The class system even more cruelly victimized Dorothy, a woman completely dependent on her father's position. Despite her supposedly lofty position, she worked physically as hard as any poor scrubwoman. Since her father, like the dictatorial Stuart monarch Charles I whom he worshiped, aristocratically refused to bother himself about tradesmen's bills, Dorothy helplessly tried to run the household on a miserly eighteen pounds a month. The seemingly peaceful town, she concludes sadly, is so different when an enemy or creditor lurks back of every window (*CD* 41). Orwell saw no hope of escape for Dorothy. She condemns herself because she lacks the desire and courage to break free. She returns to her old rut, pasting up paper Cavalier jackboots for a children's play—the crushing symbols of a class system that keeps her willingly serving a religion in which she no longer can believe.

By the early 1930s, the Anglican church, as an instrument of Britain's class system, offered Dorothy and thousands of individuals like her little but meaningless busy work. Despite spending her time visiting old and sick parishioners (which her father ought to have been doing) when she would have been far happier out in the sunny fields with the cows, Dorothy fails to overcome the "vague, black disbelief so common in the illiterate" (*CD* 57), eventually realizing her beliefs are as far gone as theirs. Mr. Warburton lays out the hopeless future that awaits her, where she will wither up like the scrawny aspidistra, an ugly hard to kill houseplant, that Orwell chose as the symbol for the perpetual minimal existence the British lower-middle class condemned itself to living, but Dorothy can not and will not and does not want to change "the spiritual background of her mind" (*CD* 308). Because Orwell felt the entrenched British class system destroyed the self-respect that individuals would need to carry out a successful change in society, he concluded that any kind of English revolution, whether personal or societal, was doomed, the greatest betrayal, in Orwell's opinion, that the Church of England could inflict upon its followers (Gilman G1).

STYLISTIC AND LITERARY DEVICES

In *A Clergyman's Daughter*, Orwell employed the same brutal realism with which Dickens and Gissing described the poor, their oppressors, and the conditions in which the various English social classes lived. Where Dickens tended toward sentimentality, especially in his treatment of helpless female characters, and Gissing succumbed to mournful gloom, Orwell intensified his black humor throughout *A Clergyman's Daughter*. Outrage early in the novel at the rector who refused to get up to baptize a dying baby (*CD* 29) modulates into the blackest humor when Orwell ferociously describes the rector's reaction to Dorothy's departure: "a frightful, unprecedented thing—a thing never to be forgotten this side of the grave; the Rector was obliged to prepare his own breakfast—yes, actually to mess about with a vulgar black kettle and rashers of Danish bacon—with his own sacerdotal hands. After that, of course, his heart was hardened against Dorothy for ever" (*CD* 205). Orwell unexpectedly puts concrete details side by side with extravagant discrepancies between what is and what, in the rector's warped mind, should be in order to lay bare the moral depravity that Orwell felt the British class system fostered.

In Chapter III of *A Clergyman's Daughter* Orwell made his only stab at a literary avant-garde technique, influenced by the "Nighttown" episode of Joyce's *Ulysses*, a novel Orwell praised highly for its sexual frankness, its "marvelous" descriptions and the use of varying styles "to represent different patterns of thought" (Crick 152). Written in dramatic form, Orwell's chapter does accurately convey the speech patterns of various derelicts, but he failed to integrate Dorothy's experience convincingly with any development in her character.

Orwell's problems with characterizations accompanied his tendency to intrude his own commentary into the narrative, like his mini-dissertation on education in the chapter on Dorothy's teaching "career." Once he completed this novel, he realized that that technique didn't work. He called this novel "a good idea," but he feared he had "made a muck of it," though he thought it was as good as he could do for the time being (quoted in Shelden 1991: 190).

KEEP THE ASPIDISTRA FLYING

Immediately after finishing *A Clergyman's Daughter*, Orwell moved to London to take a job at a shop called Booklovers' Corner in London's Hampstead district, full of "young writers and artists on the make or on the mend" (Crick 159), and again he tried hard to shape his own experiences into a novel. *Keep the Aspidistra Flying* violently satirizes the life of a failed writer—the life Orwell probably thought he was living—and denounces the British capitalism that he blamed for his failure. Shortly before he died, Orwell observed that this novel was among the two or three of his that he was ashamed of. He wrote it, he said, because he was starving and desperately needed the one hundred pounds or so it might make (*CEJL* 4:205).

HISTORICAL SETTING

Between 1931 and 1936 in Orwell's England, "the natural had yielded to the social, and the immemorial landscapes were now obscured by the industrial city, with its dereliction and unemployment" (Berthoud 91). Richest and poorest alike bore the brunt of economic hardship. Tripled postwar taxation broke up estates and prevented the upper class from investing. Unemployment soared, almost twice in Wales and Yorkshire what it was in Greater London (Robbins 291). The dole only increased workers' reluctance to move where jobs were available or to shift from declining industries to expanding ones.

Most British workers simply concluded that "Millions were starving but the Tories did nothing" (Arnstein 298).

The interwar birth of new industries shifted labor needs. Manual-labor jobs phased out in favor of white-collar work in the service and distribution sectors of the economy (Mellers and Hildyard 29), so the comparatively well-employed middle class seems to have profited most. By reducing the size of families and bringing emigrants from Ireland, the Dominions, and the Continent into Britain, the depression augmented interclass animosity and changed the fabric of British politics, although British workers generally proved surprisingly placid when faced with protracted joblessness and a lowered standard of living. Only a small minority of them embraced political extremes like communism or fascism (Arnstein 301).

Orwell's new employers belonged to that small minority. His aunt Nellie Limouzin had found him a job with kindly, poor, and rather unworldly Francis and Mary Myfanwy Westrope, a connection that acquainted him with members of the Independent Labour Party (ILP), "left-wing, egalitarian, a strange English mixture of secularized evangelism and non-Communist Marxism" (Crick 162). Jon Kimche, a fellow employee of the bookshop and later editor of the left-wing periodical *Tribune*, recalled Orwell as "a kind of intellectual anarchist" chiefly fulminating against the inequities of the Roman Catholic Church. Until 1935 Orwell described himself, in fact, as a "Tory anarchist" (quoted in Crick 430 n.13).

PLOT

In *Keep the Aspidistra Flying* Orwell angrily attacks the capitalistic value system which traps his protagonist, the impoverished money-obsessed bookstore clerk Gordon Comstock, in a demonic dilemma: if he prostitutes his literary talent in the newly burgeoning advertising business, he can live comfortably, but if he keeps clear of commercial contamination, he will probably starve to death.

As the novel opens, Gordon works days in a shabby little London bookstore, while he struggles to write in a chilly rented room each night. In a long second-chapter flashback, Orwell recounts Gordon's family history. His father died when he was eighteen, and Gordon's mother and sister Julia made heroic sacrifices to educate Gordon, "the boy," and get him a "good" job. Gordon doesn't want a dull "good" job, he wants to write, but when his mother falls ill, he takes a clerical position, which he holds six years, until she dies.

Though his family thinks he has lost his senses, Gordon then abandons the "money-world" (*KAF* 49) and tries to write, first sponging off his family, principally poor Julia, but he almost starves. He then takes an advertising agency job, where he meets sweet, practical Rosemary. The development of their relationship parallels his attempt to become a serious writer, but lack of money warps Gordon's moral values, too. Though he found it hard "to make love in a cold climate when you have no money" (*KAF* 122), Gordon made an outdoor tryst with Rosemary, only to have his budget blasted by an expensive unplanned hotel meal and their intimacy soured by his own selfishness. When at a crucial moment she protests that he has not brought a condom, he arrogantly insists that Rosemary must "take her chance" on an unwanted pregnancy, dousing the romantic mood completely.

Gordon shows promise in public relations, but he feels he is prostituting his literary talent. He throws up that job, too, and for two years, despite the efforts of Rosemary and his wealthy, liberal friend Ravelston, Gordon gradually sinks into successively more grim stages of destitution while he tries arrogantly and ineffectually to produce a great modern epic poem, which of course he will never accomplish, blaming his poverty for his own shortcomings—lack of inspiration, talent, and ability to concentrate.

At last, fallen nearly as far as he can go and abusing nearly everyone who tries to help him, Gordon hits bottom, blowing the little money he earns on fancy food, pricey wine, and loose women. Then Rosemary, in the most squalid setting possible, redeems him sexually. She saves Gordon from himself by risking her own job to get him another position at the advertising agency where they met. She also becomes pregnant, so Gordon marries her and embraces the suburban respectability he had spurned for so long. Finally Gordon sets out to buy himself and Rosemary their own aspidistra plant, relinquishing his literary aspirations and joining the aspidistra-flaunting lower-middle class. This "happy ending" does not seem to fit the generally frustrated, acrid atmosphere of the novel.

THEMATIC ISSUES

For Orwell, the spiky aspidistra ("snake plant"), a homely but hardy houseplant beloved by the British middle and lower classes as an emblem of respectability, symbolized their physical ugliness, their capacity to survive almost anything, and their fatal insistence on keeping up appearances. An aspidistra in the window, however lowly the dwelling, meant that its inhabitants, like the poor woman tramp he met who kept insisting she really didn't belong on the streets, thought of themselves as only temporarily badly off—and so prevented themselves from revolting against the system that held them down. Accordingly, the theme which *Keep the Aspidistra Flying* embodies may be stated simply: money and the desire for possessing it, the basis of Britain's class structure, are inherently evil, corrupting influences that destroy an individual's creative impulses.

Orwell keynoted this novel, one of his strongest denunciations of capitalism, by changing the famous passage from I Corinthians 13 to celebrate not love, but money: "And now abideth faith, hope, money, these three; but the greatest of these is money" (*KAF* epigraph). Money, meaning the capitalistic system, was the root of all the specific social evils he addressed here—poverty, immorality, destruction of personal freedom, class prejudice, perversion of literary talent, even what he considered as the baited hook of socialism.

Like Dorothy, the clergyman's daughter, Gordon Comstock is the victim of a family decline that took place before his birth. Gordon's self-made "Gran'pa" had crushed the spirit out of his children by driving his sons into professions for which they were unfit, turning them into "semi-genteel failures," "grey, shabby, joyless people" obsessed with financial worries because they frittered all Gran'pa's money away (*KAF* 38–39). Gordon repeated their mistakes by quitting one job after another. Finally, his success as an ad writer frightened him because he feared it would smother his "art," so he threw it up to "write," only to discover that poverty—a bookstore job at two pounds a week—"kills thought" (*KAF* 48) and that failure was "as great a swindle" as success (*KAF* 57).

Poverty, Gordon thought, had restricted his personal freedom so ruthlessly that he yearned to see his whole society obliterated. Several passages in *Keep the Aspidistra Flying* describe the new and horrifying kind of war Orwell foresaw while he was finishing the novel in 1935. Even before the Spanish Civil War, aerial bombing was a recurrent theme in many European novels and poems, but Gordon's reaction reflects Orwell's anger at his society's restriction of an individual's liberty to create, to love, to realize his potential: "Only a little while before the aeroplanes come. Zoom—bang! A few tons of T.N.T. to send our civilization back to hell where it belongs" (*KAF* 282).

Class distinctions also motivated Gordon's desire to see his civilization annihilated. Orwell landed some vehement shots on Gordon's—and his own—snobbish bookstore customers: "hen-witted middle-aged women trying to be literary" (*KAF* 64), and "moneyed young beasts who glide from Eton to Cambridge to the literary reviews" (*KAF* 8) as Orwell had not been able to do. Gordon's well-meaning, wealthy friend Ravelston, modeled on Orwell's Socialist friend Sir Richard Rees, tries to help, but Gordon only sinks further into despair. Gordon's surly conviction that "Life had beaten him, but you can still beat life by turning your face away," resembles Orwell's own determination to atone for his own moral deficiencies as an Imperial policeman by embracing failure.

Ravelston urges Gordon to choose once and for all between capitalism and socialism, but sex with Rosemary in Gordon's flea-infested bed, not politics, made Gordon return to the capitalistic world he loved and hated. Gordon declared early in the novel that at sixteen he had not seen "the hook striking out of the rather stodgy bait" of socialism (*KAF* 43), a sign of a deep-seated desire for "respectability" that try as he might, Gordon could not get out of his system.

CHARACTER DEVELOPMENT

Flory of *Burmese Days* and Dorothy of *A Clergyman's Daughter* are passive victims of social ills they cannot change. For all his whiny self-pity, Gordon Comstock is a better defined, more three-dimensional figure. In making Gordon sacrifice his admittedly minor (and as Orwell describes it, ridiculous) literary talent to the capitalistic culture Gordon and Orwell himself occasionally thought deserved to be blown up, Orwell reveals that Gordon's "secret heart" (*KAF* 236), and perhaps his own, longed for the security of the self-satisfied bourgeoisie.

In *Keep the Aspidistra Flying*, Orwell also created more convincing female characters than he had previously done, focusing on Rosemary and the long-suffering Julia. He based both on people he knew. Rosemary is a composite of several young women he was close to at this time, including Eileen O'Shaughnessy, whom he eventually married, and Julia is a portrait of his sister Avril.

Rosemary is a sensible and outgoing young woman who responds to Gordon's childish tantrums with understanding and compassion. Her common sense and warmth contrast vividly against his selfishness and irritability and ultimately triumph over his self-centeredness (Hammond 110–11). She loves Gordon but initially refuses to sleep with him, which Gordon sullenly blames on his poverty, not on her moral principles. Rosemary sensibly suggests that she pay her own part of the expensive hotel meal Gordon can't afford, but he petulantly refuses, spoiling their outing. Subsequently faced with Gordon's deliberate wallowing in the "deep sluttish underworld" (*KAF* 203), Rosemary offers herself out of "pure magnanimity" (*KAF* 219), a surprising twist that reverses ordinary moral standards. The act leaves Rosemary "dismayed, disappointed, and very cold," but in the spring it resurrects Gordon, like the dying aspidistra in his garret, when Rosemary tells him she is pregnant.

Julia, Gordon's sister, is just as forgiving, though Orwell portrays her more flatly. She is one of those "odd" Englishwomen whose parents sacrificed their futures so "the boy" in the family could attend "wretched, pretentious" schools (*KAF* 41) in order to retrieve the family fortunes. Since World War I destroyed many of the young men they would otherwise have married, a whole generation of Englishwomen found themselves thrown on their own slender resources, working in tea shops like Orwell's sister Avril, unwanted and unappreciated even when their male relatives despise them and bamboozle them out of their pitiful savings. Like the lowly aspidistra, though, Julia not only survives but in her small way prospers, conspiring with Rosemary to get Gordon employed again and happily scraping up money for a "rather dreadful" occasional table as a wedding present.

Ravelston's inherited wealth, on the other hand, makes Gordon uncomfortable and resentful. Ravelston generously prints poems by penniless poets like Gordon in his journal *Antichrist* (Orwell could not seem to resist a jab at Rees' *Adelphi*, which by 1935 was printing Orwell's work fairly often). Ravelston represents the decency Orwell in spite of himself could see in the moneyed class, but Ravelston's haughty lady friend Hermione is Elizabeth from *Burmese Days* grown wealthy, despising the lower classes because they smelled—or as Orwell put it, they had "spiritual halitosis" (*KAF* 92).

STYLISTIC AND LITERARY DEVICES

D. H. Lawrence was evidently still setting off sparks for Orwell, because he incorporated some sensuous Lawrentian nature-description—which Gordon mocks—into Gordon's outing with Rosemary (*KAF* 130). Joyce, too, "before he went off his coconut" (*KAF* 12) inspired Gordon's eternally unfinished *magnum opus,* the epic "London Pleasures" that was supposed to immortalize Gordon's wanderings through London, much like the odyssey Joyce's character Leopold Bloom took through Dublin.

Orwell's own style was maturing in *Keep the Aspidistra Flying.* He was indulging and sharpening his taste for the killing phrase, often tying offensive specimens of humanity to the animals, particularly swine, like the "docile little porker, sitting in the money-sty" (*KAF* 15), Gordon's bitter description of the modern man immortalized in contemporary advertising posters.

Through Gordon Comstock, Orwell also satirized the poetry he had been writing for *Adelphi* in the early 1930s. The one poem which Gordon Comstock managed to finish, though it took him half the book (*KAF* 150), reveals excessive reliance on stock "poetic" diction and phrases. After 1935 Orwell still liked lyric poetry, but he seems to have abandoned the notion of writing it himself.

Despite its obsessive insistence on money as the root of all evil, *Keep the Aspidistra Flying* is an intense novel exhibiting Orwell's growing literary self-confidence. He himself later downplayed the book, calling it "lifeless" because it did not convey a political purpose (*CEJL* 1:7). On the other hand, it had allowed him to get his tendency toward luridly sexual "purple passages" out of his system. As the last of Orwell's apolitical novels, *Keep the Aspidistra Flying* marked the end of his literary apprenticeship.

ALTERNATE CRITICAL PERSPECTIVE: FEMINISM

Since feminism is a social movement striving toward the equality of the sexes, a feminist approach to Orwell's first three novels would examine the social, political, and economic roles of his principal female characters to ascertain the extent to which he seems to advocate or deny gender inequality there. In *Burmese Days, A Clergyman's Daughter*, and *Keep the Aspidistra Flying*, Orwell seems to exhibit a profound ambivalence about the change in attitudes toward gender roles that was taking place in the 1920s and 1930s, a change he, like many men of his generation, did not wholeheartedly welcome.

Around 1914, the constitutional demands of British suffragettes and the demographic shift toward smaller families foreshadowed an erosion in traditional sexual roles. After suffragette leader Christabel Pankhurst called down "God's vengeance on the people who held women in subjection" (quoted in Briggs 262), women made such significant contributions to the British war effort that in 1918 Parliament granted female British householders and wives of householders over thirty the right to vote, then in 1927 extended the "flapper vote" to women on the same basis as men. Women did not immediately rush into the British workforce or into politics, but Victorian certainties about their role in the home had evaporated. Shifting attitudes toward sexuality, marriage, childbearing, and the function of the family resulted in smaller British families and even broken families, a rise in illegitimate births, the conquest of syphilis, and widespread use of contraception, by 1919 available from every village chemist (Briggs 264). Orwell opposed contraception both in his personal affairs and in his fiction.

Dorothy Hare, the clergyman's daughter, had no need of contraception because she was frigid. In her, Orwell tried to portray woman-as-victim without a clear-cut sense of how women's personalities functioned. He made Dorothy, who demonstrated that given the right circumstances she might have developed into a capable, even an inspiring teacher, slink home in failure, suggesting that Dorothy was her own worst enemy, unable to overcome either her lack of willpower or her sexual frigidity.

The anything but frigid female characters in *Burmese Days* and *Keep the Aspidistra Flying* act more forcefully and/or effectively than the insecure failure-embracing male protagonists of these novels, despite their traditional female roles. In *Burmese Days*, Elizabeth and Ma Hla May, each in her own way, help destroy Flory by playing out the female roles the Empire expects of them, Elizabeth's venomous snobbery and Ma Hla May's native-woman-scorned revenge.

Orwell's attitude toward domineering women like Elizabeth and Ma Hla May was clearly negative, because their actions placed them among the social oppressors he found so repugnant. However, he also seemed to relish the comeuppance the ultra-traditional Oriental wife of the dastardly U Po Kyin gives her husband.

In *Keep the Aspidistra Flying*, Rosemary and Julia together haul Gordon back from artistic starvation to respectable aspidistra-ownership, illustrating the power of "good" women to change a man's life—whether he wants them to or not. Orwell treated Rosemary and Julia much more sympathetically than the women in *Burmese Days*. Rosemary and Julia are kept subservient by their society's class structure but are still capable of acting within those roles to "save" their man, no matter what it cost them.

From a feminist perspective, all three of Orwell's first novels show that he recognized an increase in women's power to change men's lives, though he seemed to want them to remain in traditional roles, a reflection of the ambivalence about gender equality that existed in 1930s England.

5

From Mandalay to Wigan Pier: "Shooting an Elephant" and *The Road to Wigan Pier*

"SHOOTING AN ELEPHANT"

On June 6, 1936, three days before he married Eileen O'Shaughnessy, Orwell finished one of his most famous sketches, "Shooting an Elephant" (Shelden 1991: 644; *CEJL* 1:235ff). He had been immersed for a month in a larger project, a "sort of book of essays" (*CEJL* 1:235) eventually titled *The Road to Wigan Pier*, but when John Lehmann, editor of the respected journal *New Writing*, invited him to contribute, Orwell seized the opportunity to describe an incident that had recently come back to him "very vividly" (Shelden 1991: 244). Even though the 1920s Burmese setting of "Shooting an Elephant" seems far removed from the miseries of the largely unemployed English North in the Great Depression of the 1930s, the ideas Orwell addressed in that sketch provide a remarkable introduction to the unorthodox socialist position he presented in *The Road to Wigan Pier*, much to the consternation of his left-wing publisher, Victor Gollancz.

Orwell wrote "Shooting an Elephant" in about two weeks, and it contains some of his finest prose—economical, concrete, powerfully paced. In *Burmese Days, A Clergyman's Daughter*, and *Keep the Aspidistra Flying* respectively, he had tried to fictionalize his disgust at British imperialism, the English class system, and the ruthless capitalism that dominated British culture, but he had not completely satisfied either his readers or, more significantly, himself. Now, however, in only seven pages, Orwell crystallized his views on the three-headed socioeconomic juggernaut of imperialism, class, and capitalism that he believed was inexorably crushing both its victims and their "masters."

As with all tragedies, the story line of "Shooting an Elephant" is brutally simple. A working Burmese elephant in *must*, a periodic hormonal frenzy, had broken its chains and in the absence of its *mahout* (handler) damaged considerable native property in Moulmein, Lower Burma, where Orwell was stationed as the town's sub-divisional police officer. The natives demanded that Orwell, who embodied hated British authority, track down the elephant. Then the beast killed a coolie, unconsciously sealing its own fate because then Orwell had to kill it. It also sealed the fate of Orwell's career as an Imperial policeman. After a decade of reflection, killing the elephant became his indelible metaphor for the swiftly approaching demise of the British Empire.

Like the heat and humidity of the tropics, the natives' hatred enveloped and dehumanized Orwell, the central figure and narrator of "Shooting an Elephant." Orwell liked animals and he pitied this hapless creature, whose live economic value was worth twenty times the price of its tusks, hide, and flesh. Having already decided that imperialism was evil and that he must give up the job he loathed more each day, Orwell also found himself caught blisteringly between his hatred of the Empire he had agreed to serve and his rage against "the evil-spirited little beasts" who were trying to make his job impossible (*CEJL* 1:236). When he reluctantly took the beautiful German elephant gun into his hands, Orwell became a victim of both the Empire and the Burmese, feeling like an absurd marionette controlled by the will of the natives behind him (*CEJL* 1:239). The elephant's protracted death agony killed part of Orwell, too, because as he concluded in shattering self-revelation, he had killed it only to avoid appearing foolish (*CEJL* 1:242).

By the time he wrote "Shooting an Elephant," Orwell's literary style had matured considerably. Using the old Aristotelian deductive movement from an abstract general statement to specific details that powerfully impact all the senses, he conveyed the full horror of the dual murder his position forced him to commit—the destruction of both the innocent animal and his own self-respect—with clear, approachable syntax and diction and stark, powerful images.

Both Orwell and the elephant fell victim to interrelated forces they could not control—imperialism, the British class system, and the capitalism that undergirded European society. At the mercy of his physical condition, the elephant involuntarily set off the events which brought him down, just as Orwell, born into the "upper-lower-middle class," and bending to his father's choice of his career, sentenced himself to a form of suicide doing what he called the Empire's dirty work in Burma (*CEJL* 1:236).

Orwell realized that his duties as an Imperial policeman were stripping away his humanity, making him perform acts, like shooting the elephant, contrary to his innate compassion and his intellectual judgment. Worse, though, was the effect of the dirty work on his self-image, because it forced him to confront ugly elements of his own personality, like his sadistic contemplation of "the greatest joy in the world"—to jam a bayonet into the gut of a Buddhist priest (*CEJL* 1:236). Orwell's recognition that by serving the Empire he was exacerbating his most vicious tendencies led to a shattering and long-lasting disgust with himself, and he concluded he was a coward because he had given in to the system's demands. Killing the elephant permanently demonstrated to Orwell that when a white man becomes tyrannical, he destroys his own freedom (*CEJL* 1:239). That realization was awakened in him by the tortured gasps of a dying Burmese elephant he himself, yielding to pressures he hated, had shot. Then it was only a small step for Orwell to change "white man" to "English capitalist"—the crucial step on his road to Wigan Pier.

In 1934 Orwell already felt so revolted by British society, corrupted by the thirst for money and power, that he told Brenda Salkeld he was tempted "to start calling down curses from Heaven" (*CEJL* 1:140), an image that reflected his boyish fascination with explosive experiments. He decided that the capitalistic Western governments would refuse to oppose Hitler and Mussolini, because he thought capitalism had too much in common with fascism, which he considered its outgrowth. He also felt the British rule in India was every bit as evil as German Fascism (*CEJL* 1:284).

In Orwell's opinion, the only system that could oppose the growing threat of fascism was socialism, but as yet he had not worked out his own meaning of that term nor identified himself with the British socialist movement, which at this time he had encountered principally through his publisher, Victor Gollancz; the Westropes, his employers at Booklovers' Corner; and his friend Sir Richard Rees. Through Rees, Orwell wandered into a Socialist meeting one Saturday in May 1935, where he argued for several hours about what socialism represented and how it should be implemented, questions that occupied him for the rest of his life (Shelden 1991: 219).

After Orwell completed *Keep the Aspidistra Flying* that December, Gollancz offered him the considerable advance of five hundred pounds for a documentary book about the unemployed workers in England's industrial North. This income, about the same amount as his father's pension, confirmed Orwell as a professional writer and allowed him to give up his bookshop job and marry Eileen, to whom he had proposed almost as soon as they met in March of 1935.

In sending Orwell to report on the impoverished North, Gollancz was hoping for a book similar to *Down and Out in Paris and London*, but directed toward poverty-stricken and unemployed workers instead of tramps and dishwashers. Orwell speedily accepted Gollancz's offer, and on January 15, 1935, he headed north to spend about two months, not just visiting but living, in some of the most impoverished conditions England had to offer.

THE ROAD TO WIGAN PIER

HISTORICAL SETTING

Ever since the Industrial Revolution, England's north "Black Country" had been paying a heavy price for the nation's capitalistic progress. Industrialism caused a population shift from rural areas to urban centers like Coventry, Birmingham, Sheffield, and Manchester, and in the mid-1840s the Irish potato famine flooded northern England and southern Scotland with Roman Catholic immigrants. The early marriages and high fertility rate of these groups turned England into an urban society (Rose 277).

An appalling decline in living standards ensued. Wealthier townsfolk fled to the unpolluted suburbs, leaving decaying urban housing crammed to the rafters with immigrants lacking "adequate paving, drainage and water supply, let alone schools, shops or open spaces for recreation" (Rose 277). In 1936, almost a third of Yorkshire's working-class families lived in primary poverty. Nationwide, British unemployment bottomed out in 1932, when nearly three million workers were on the British dole. In northern areas like Yorkshire, unemployment hit 67.8 percent in 1934.

British regional disparities paralleled class differences during the 1930s. The area around London was relatively prosperous, with a much lower infant mortality than in the economically depressed North. Diet was another important social indicator. A 1930s working-class family ate a good deal more bread and flour and 16 percent more potatoes than a middle-class family, like Orwell's parents, who enjoyed more meat, over twice as much fish and fresh milk, more eggs, 56 percent more butter, and only half the quantity of margarine (Briggs 281).

In the 1930s the British upper class was so far removed from the lower that it seemed to inhabit "a different world with lifestyles which were too exotic to provoke envy . . .[but] there appears to have been far less envy within the society than there had been twenty years before and was to be forty years later" (Briggs 280–81), at least in the relatively affluent southeast. In the industrial areas like Lancashire, though, economic stagnation produced the sour, embittered mood that dominated popular memories of the 1930s (Supple 324).

Wigan, a small Lancashire town outside of Manchester, had long been the target of music hall comedians who made its name synonymous with sordid working-class life. When Orwell arrived there on January 30, 1936, slowdowns and closures of the area's cotton mills and coal mines had caused high unemployment, and symptoms of unrest among laid off and marginally employed workers were beginning to appear.

The discontent of the coal miners in the North who had held out longest in the general strike smoldered long after the strike had ended, and they increasingly supported labor movements like the International Labour Party (ILP) and the National Unemployed Workers' Movement (NUWM). Richard Rees and John Middleton Murry of *Adelphi* supplied Orwell with letters of introduction to Northern trade union leaders, and one of them, Frank Meade of Manchester, put him in touch with ILP and the NUWM members in Wigan. Orwell spent about six weeks in February–March of 1936 in the North, and he wrote *The Road to Wigan Pier* between the following April and October.

The capitalistic British Coalition Government (1935–40) assumed that artists and intellectuals calling for industrial regeneration, economic stimulation, and improved public services were "enemies of society" (Mellers and Hildyard 28). By going in person to the North, living intimately with its out-of-work workers and miners, and writing with brilliant accuracy and compassion about their lot, Orwell put himself high on the list of those enemies, but he managed to upset the left as well as the right wing of British politics by doing it his own unconventional way.

STRUCTURE

The Road to Wigan Pier is a collection of essays closely based on Orwell's experience in the North. It contains two major sections, the first comprised of short chapters coolly and realistically presenting the conditions and people Orwell observed, and the second discussing the sociopolitical implications of these facts and his theories about them. Orwell's opponents called the book a "misshapen creature" with a "good" first part and a "bad" second one. Gollancz issued Part I by itself as propaganda for the Left in order to avoid what he considered Orwell's embarrassing personal commentary in the second part. For both the British Left Book Club edition and the first American edition, not published until 1958, Gollancz added a thirteen-page Foreword explaining why Orwell's views and those of Gollancz's Left Book Club did not agree.

Because *The Road to Wigan Pier* is not a novel, it has no plot or story line. The first four chapters of Part I describe specific horrors of un- and underemployment in the North. Chapter I (Orwell used Roman numerals) portrays the awful room above a reeking Wigan tripe shop (Orwell shared it with three out-of-work men and pensioners), his landlords the Brookers, and the moral decay their poverty has forced on them. Chapters II, III, and IV reveal the subhuman working conditions in the mines which undergirded British industry and the hardships of the miners and their families. Chapters V and VI treat the equally miserable living conditions of those who work but cannot earn a living wage—miners' dependents, the destitute, and old-age pensioners. Chapter VII concludes Part I by exploring the environmental devastation industrialism has caused in the North and celebrating the human decency he found among the workers who lived there.

Part II contains Orwell's unorthodox views on how these people might be helped, which he drew from his own life before he came to Wigan. The autobiographical Chapters VIII, IX and X, respectively, trace his conditioning as a member of the "lower-upper-middle class" (*RWP* 121), which he considers morally inferior to the working class he came to know in Wigan; his schooling, which made him a snob but also gave him a hatred for the "hoggishly rich" (*RWP* 137); and his attempts to rid himself of class prejudice by living among social outcasts and coal miners (*RWP* 154–55). In Chapters XI and XII, Orwell dissected the inadequacies of socialism at that time (*RWP* 171ff), concluding that it appealed chiefly to "unsatisfactory or even inhuman types" (*RWP* 182) and that it was chiefly a mechanized "urban creed" (*RWP* 188), which makes life safe and soft and debauches taste (*RWP* 204). In his concluding Chapter XIII, Orwell presents his suggestion about how socialism might be reconciled with its "more intelligent enemies" (*RWP* 217) through dispelling socialist "crankishness" (*RWP* 222) and its "horrible jargon" (*RWP* 223), and facing the issue of class distinctions realistically (*RWP* 224).

The Road to Wigan Pier is not just an uneasy combination of reportage and personal political views. It represents a remarkable new stage in Orwell's development, where he was able to connect reader and writer as compellingly as he had done in "Shooting an Elephant." In his 1940 essay "Inside the Whale," Orwell described the effect of that connection as able to break down, at least briefly, "the solitude in which the human being dwells" (*CEJL* 1:525). In "Shooting an Elephant," he forced his readers to acknowledge their own cowardice and self-disgust by stripping his own actions and motives bare and showing how universal they are, and soon after, he took them with him to Wigan Pier on his painful road to personal redemption.

THEMATIC ISSUES, PART I: WORKING-CLASS TRIALS AND MORAL SUPERIORITY

According to Gollancz, Orwell's two major concerns in Part I of *The Road to Wigan Pier* were to give a firsthand account of the lives of Wigan's workers and to pay tribute to "their courage and patience—patience far too great." Gollancz had wanted Orwell's book to disrupt the apathy of the "unconverted" (*RWP* xi), but in Part I, Orwell went further, doing his best to arouse profound sympathy and praise for the workers and their fortitude. Orwell moved consistently from the horrifying specifics he directly observed to general, if unconventional, conclusions, gradually widening his focus to Britain's national failures in failing to address these problems adequately and in allowing the overall physical and emotional deterioration of British workers and their families. In his conclusion to Part I, Orwell illustrated the theme he drew from his observations, an important modulation of the theme of "Shooting an Elephant": that self-made businessmen, those cherished icons of British capitalism, were actually despotic corpses who had slain their own souls by abusing the economically downtrodden but generally morally superior working-class men and women.

Most of Part I of *The Road to Wigan Pier* shows in excruciating detail what poverty had done to the poor of the North. Orwell's filthy rented room above Mr. and Mrs. Brooker's tripe shop stank every morning "like a ferret's cage" (*RWP* 6). Brooker's unwashed hands that had previously handled unrefrigerated cattle intestines and organs lingered over the boarders' food, as he "chewed his grievances like a cud" (*RWP* 12). Mrs. Brooker, "a soft mound of fat and self-pity" (*RWP* 14), moaned ceaselessly from her couch, hating the two old-age pensioners who lived above simply because they were there. When the chamber pot under the breakfast table was full, Orwell abandoned this "stagnant meaningless decay," having fulfilled his duty as an investigator—to see and smell, hear and touch and taste such places, but for his own good, not to stay too long (*RWP* 17).

In bleak early March, Orwell went down into the mines, which he compared to hell. He was much taller than most miners though not as strong, and he suffered physically to tell their story. One miner, Joe Kennan, later commented, "I said to him, 'It's a so-and-so good thing [the owners] don't know what you're down here for, to write a book about mining, otherwise the whole roof would come down on top of you'" (quoted in Gross 56). In the old-fashioned British pits, miners walked about three miles stooped over in passages with five-foot ceilings and then worked seven and a half hours at the coal face, moving about two tons of coal an hour in dehumanizing toil that, like the subterranean labor of the luxury hotel *plongeurs*, was absolutely necessary to sustain the glittering upper world of the rich. Only because the miners "sweat their guts out," Orwell remarked, could "superior persons . . . remain superior" (*RWP* 34). For Orwell, "superior" carried the unmistakable reek of moral degeneration.

Orwell unforgettably personalized the plight of the North. In later writing, he frequently returned to the most unforgettable image of his trip, a slum girl, aged before her time, that he had seen from his train window. She was battling a plugged sewer pipe, entirely aware that she would never escape her wretched fate. He backed up his dramatic word pictures with a relentless accounting of the miners' wages and expenses. For about two pounds a week, a miner lucky enough to live to age sixty, produced about 8400 tons of coal. Housing was so inadequate that miners and their families would take anything—at best fifty- to sixty-year-old hovels, which were better than the marginally habitable trail- ers in which about ten thousand British families lived. According to Orwell, much-touted government attempts at housing the indigent were performed ruthlessly and soullessly (*RWP* 71), ruining small shopkeepers and dumping human beings into cheap corporate housing without even a reasonably priced pub in sight.

Such poverty deprived its victims of the most basic human needs. Maintain- ing a decent living standard depended on how few children a couple had to support, necessitating birth control. Orwell sympathized with single men, de- prived of family life because they could not afford to marry, and wives who did all the work whether their men were merely ill paid or completely out of work (*RWP* 81). Orwell visited about two hundred poor homes, where the people's "extraordinary generosity and good grace" toward him, a stranger prying into some of the most intimate details of their lives, amazed him (*RWP* 73).

Beneath the grim symptoms of poverty he described in Part I seethes Or- well's indignation with the capitalistic mentality responsible for it. Dominant in the nineteenth century, self-made businessmen persisted into Orwell's time, taking pride, he believed, in being greater boors after they had made money than before (*RWP* 113). Orwell pointed out that Yorkshire or Scottish busi- nessmen enjoyed a popular reputation for "grit," which he felt underlay that bumptiousness, but he also felt it would be a "great mistake" to assume that the genuine working class of the North shared that unpleasant quality. Generally Orwell felt inferior to the Northern workers, most of all the miners; they could easily outwork him, yet treated him with kindness and courtesy that embar- rassed him (*RWP* 114). He also felt contempt for "the parasitic dividend- drawing class" of the South, insisting on "at least a tinge of truth" in the charac- terization of Southern England as "one enormous Brighton inhabited by lounge-lizards" (*RWP* 114).

THEMATIC ISSUES OF PART II: SOCIALISM AND SOCIAL REFORM

Gollancz found Part II of *The Road to Wigan Pier* so "highly provocative" that in his Foreword he said he marked over a hundred passages in which he differed from Orwell. Lacking space to deal with all of these, Gollancz limited himself to "broader aspects": Orwell's unshakable orientation as a member of the "lower-upper-middle-class"; the devil's advocate position Orwell took against socialism; the faults Orwell found with the Soviet Union's supposed triumph of industrialism; and Orwell's failure to present his own definition of socialism (*RWP* xi–xxi). Whether Gollancz and the readers of the Left Book Club liked Orwell's positions or not, however, Part II of *The Road to Wigan Pier* was the testing ground for literary weapons Orwell was honing into his lifelong concern, the necessity of waging all-out war on unjust collective forces in order to live at peace with oneself.

Going to Wigan and seeing mass unemployment at its worst enabled Orwell to develop his own approach to socialism. Orwell scathingly indicted his class-bound "shabby-genteel" upbringing, not just a matter of money but also of tradition, for turning him into "an odious little snob" (*RWP* 137) who considered workers as his dirty, smelly enemies (*RWP* 122–25). By living with tramps, Orwell had lost his own squeamishness over dirt (less than half the houses in England at that time had bathrooms), but he knew that class hatred was by no means disappearing in England, because he acknowledged traces of it in himself. Part of him did not want to root them out; he used Kipling's poem, "The Road to Mandalay," as a metaphor for what he disliked in British society, but he could not help loving and admiring the poem, too (*CEJL* 1:159).

Orwell ambiguously claimed Eton had turned him into "a snob and a revolutionary" (*RWP* 140), and made him dismiss as subhuman the striking workers and rioting war veterans who now understood they would never have the utopia for which they had fought in World War I (*RWP* 141). As Orwell looked back on postwar lawlessness, he also recalled that young Etonians like himself had mocked all accepted institutions, and adopted notions he now found repugnant, like birth control and "half-baked antinomian opinions" (*RWP* 138). This society-wide disillusion, he concluded in 1936, had brought England closer to revolution than ever before or since. It also helped bring on his personal about-face in Burma, where he finally became physically ill at the reek of sweaty British soldiers (*RWP* 143), a symptom of his disgust with the Empire and himself (*RWP* 148).

Orwell described himself as jolted out of his class-bound opinion that the poor were "alien and dangerous" when a "polite and gentle" unemployed worker (*RWP* 152) handed him a cup of tea. That humble gesture showed Orwell that abolishing class distinctions could not be accomplished by theories; it had to be the individual's responsibility, requiring uncomfortable changes in habits and opinions. In Orwell's opinion, deliberate government-mandated efforts at class breaking, such as birth control, were very serious errors which he felt intensified, rather than abolished, class prejudice (*RWP* 162).

Orwell acknowledged that socialism appeared to offer a way out of England's debilitating class problem, but he saw what most of his contemporaries totally missed: that British Socialism was not really a workers' movement but a highly hypocritical middle-class theory, whose adherents might noisily preach socialist doctrine and even join the Communist Party—but then would marry within their own class (*RWP* 135). Orwell exercised some irony on working-class intellectuals who used Socialist connections to climb into the middle class, but he reserved his most scalding comments for the "poisonous jungle" of the British Socialist literary intelligentsia, a group he said was almost impossible for "decent human beings" to join, where "you get on by kissing the bums of verminous little lions" (*RWP* 164).

Socialism in the abstract, Orwell thought, might seem to promise utopia, but in 1936 with unspeakable horrors on the international horizon, he did not believe that a socialist society could stand up to militant fascism. He found British Socialism an unpalatable and impotent bore. He claimed its literature was "dull, tasteless, and bad" (*RWP* 183), and its adherents were "cranks"—a "dreary tribe of high-minded women and sandal-wearers and bearded fruit-juice drinkers" wanting to impose reforms on everyone else (*RWP* 174).

Orwell had an even more serious moral objection to socialism. He felt that people recoiled from it because it threatened the individual. Looking at the "industrialized" Soviet Union which his Socialist compatriots were praising to the skies, Orwell projected a glittering socialist "remote future" based on machine production and industrialization and intercommunication with the whole world (*RWP* 188)—a half-century before the Internet. Citing Karel Capek's *R.U.R.*, a vision of a robotized future, Wells' pessimistic utopian story *The Sleeper Awakes*, and Huxley's *Brave New World*, which Orwell said portrayed "a paradise of little fat men," Orwell flatly denounced the useful, dangerous, and habit-forming machine for its potential to maim all human activity by severing individuals from productive work—which for Orwell meant separating them from life itself (*RWP* 197).

Orwell found organized socialism so full of "humbug," so dull and flabby, he could not firmly define it. He could, however, describe what he thought it should do. Socialism had to oppose fascism, which he believed was aiming at a world of "rabbits ruled by stoats" (*RWP* 216). Orwell compared his ideal of justice and liberty to a diamond that had to be dug out from under a "mountain of dung," but he did not think English Socialism could do the job. "Socialism . . . does not smell any longer of revolution and the overthrow of tyrants; it smells of crankishness, machine-worship and the stupid cult of Russia." That smell had to be cleaned up soon, he thought, or fascism might win (*RWP* 216). In calling for a humanized socialism (a utopian attempt in itself), Orwell rejected philosophical Marxism (*RWP* 222) and equated socialism with ordinary decency, since the interests of all exploited people, he felt, were the same. No wonder that English Socialists who praised the conformity of Stalin's totalitarian Soviet Union found Orwell's view of socialism unorthodox, unsettling, and unacceptable.

CHARACTER DEVELOPMENT—PART I

In Part I of *The Road to Wigan Pier*, Orwell was reporting about real individuals he met, not creating fictional characters, but he also revealed his own growth, making Part I an important autobiographical statement (Shelden 1991: 230–31). First, Orwell recognized that his disenchanting experiences in Burma, like shooting the elephant, prepared him to understand the social ills he now witnessed. He noted that he had gone to Burma as still a boy (*RWP* 85) and that not until he had come back did he realize the immensity of British unemployment problems. He compared the squalor of miners' housing to the plight of Indian coolies in Burma (*RWP* 62), commenting that he had had to write a novel to try to heal the damage his role as an Imperial policeman had caused him, but he still noted his tortuously ambivalent reaction: "Anything outrageously strange generally ends by fascinating me even when I abominate it" (*RWP* 109).

In Part I of *The Road to Wigan Pier*, Orwell also unabashedly showed his "deep nostalgia" for his prewar childhood and his "sentimental attachment" for Britain's bygone military traditions, recalling that British soldiers used to be bigger and stronger than they were in the 1930s (Shelden 1991: 231). The Britain Orwell loved seemed to have perished at the grasping hands of "lounge-lizards" and "parasitic" dividend-drawing capitalists.

In *Burmese Days, A Clergyman's Daughter*, and *Keep the Aspidistra Flying*, Orwell had revealed many aspects of modern Britain he detested, and his negativity contributes to the bad taste these novels often leave. He was brutally direct about what he disliked about Wigan, too, like the inescapable filth and lack of privacy, but in Part I he contrasted his seamy surroundings with his own pleasures, like gardening and French cooking. Wigan also proved to Orwell he had some admirable qualities himself: the physical courage it took to crawl through dark, dangerous mine passages, the determination to produce thirty novels by the time he turned sixty, and even the descriptive ability, reminiscent of D. H. Lawrence, to savor and convey such sights as the "sinister magnificence" of Sheffield at night, with its smoke "rosy with sulphur," its "serrated flames," "fiery serpents of iron," "redlit boys," and "the scream of the iron under the blow" (*RWP* 107).

Writing Part I enhanced Orwell's ability to make his readers share his experiences. He could—and did—leave the Brookers' appalling breakfast table as soon as the chamber pot was full, but he stayed long enough to have shared their boarders' misery. The plight of the miners and their families moves readers precisely because it moved Orwell himself (Shelden 1991: 231). The difference between Eric Blair of *Down and Out in Paris and London* and George Orwell of *The Road to Wigan Pier*, however, is that now, as after he shot the

Burmese elephant, Orwell knew he shared some of the blame, and he intended to make amends.

CHARACTER DEVELOPMENT—PART II

Between the Orwell of Part I of *The Road to Wigan Pier* and the Orwell of Part II lies the bulk of a slaughtered elephant. Orwell of Part I reveals many valuable details about himself and the attitudes he was developing toward the ills of his society, but the Orwell of Part II had definitely decided to involve himself vigorously in politics. Orwell weighed the morality of his Imperial policeman self by looking deeply into his own motivation for killing the elephant. He found himself wanting and faced up to his own pride and cowardice. That realization showed him that any change in society would have to start with an individual, not a group, and that by experiencing oppression himself and writing about it with integrity, he could bring his readers to identify with the homeless and the hopeless, the victims of society's oppression. Orwell then undertook his self-imposed mission with the zeal of a prophet. Once and for all, shooting the helpless elephant clarified what really mattered to Orwell as a man and as a writer: from now on, he intended to turn political writing into an art (Shelden 1991: 235), an art intended to improve people's lives.

STYLISTIC AND LITERARY DEVICES, PART I

In his Nobel Lecture, Aleksandr Solzhenitsyn suggested that propaganda and scientific proof are powerless to help one individual understand another's "far-off sorrows or joys"; only literature, he felt, could recreate "life-like, the experience of other men, so that we can assimilate it as our own" (Solzhenitsyn 565). That was the kind of literature Orwell was beginning to create.

By the early 1930s, Orwell had discovered two writers whom he felt could produce the identification between writer and reader that he felt was indispensable to this sort of writing. One was James Joyce, whose greatest originality, Orwell insisted to Brenda Salkeld, was presenting "life . . . as it is lived . . . attempting to select and represent events and thoughts as they occur in life and not as they occur in fiction" (*CEJL* 1:126). Another was the American Henry Miller, with whom Orwell was carrying on a mutually respectful correspondence while writing *The Road to Wigan Pier*. Orwell admired Miller's frankness, even if it had gotten Miller's books banned, but Orwell praised Miller even more for assuming that all people, regardless of class, were alike and for characterizing them realistically in his fiction.

Under these influences, Orwell managed in Part I of *The Road to Wigan Pier*, as never before in his writing, to create a fellow-feeling between himself and his reader that swept away barriers between individual human beings. Orwell addressed his readers directly as "you," putting them directly into the tripe shop and the mine with ruthlessly concrete detail. Orwell also established his unique voice, educated but with a common touch, moving easily between the worlds of the poor he had experienced directly and the calm, comfortable world of his reader's study. He accomplished this by balancing "inside" and "outside" perspectives; for him, good prose had to act as a windowpane, stunningly clear and assuming a common bond of humanity (Shelden 1991: 232), as in his famous sketch of the woman struggling with the sewer pipe, which he viewed from the window of the train that took him away from Wigan: "She knew well enough what was happening to her—understood as well as I did how dreadful a destiny it was to be kneeling there in the bitter cold, on the slimy stones of a slum backyard, poking a stick up a foul drain-pipe" (*RWP* 18).

Because Orwell was on the other side of the window, just as he admired and respected the miners without being one of them, he could take the side of the poor effectively. The Eton accent he never lost marked him as a part of the class which was holding them down, but he still felt he had to speak for them because they could not speak adequately for themselves. On the other hand, Orwell had no intention of immersing himself in any movement which would destroy his individuality—as was abundantly clear to Victor Gollancz when he saw Part II of *The Road to Wigan Pier*, Orwell might embrace socialistic aims, but he never was a conventional British socialist.

STYLISTIC AND LITERARY DEVICES, PART II

Orwell's self-portraits in Parts I and II strongly differ in focus, emphasis, form, and style, so that *The Road to Wigan Pier* as a whole illustrates the unusual inside-outside perspective he was beginning to master. His inward-looking autobiographical statements in Part I, while supplying important information about the development of his attitudes, are secondary to his outward-looking reportage about the impoverished Northern workers and their living conditions. He memorably individualized these people instead of treating them in groups like miners, pensioners, the unemployed, and so on. Orwell's inwardly-directed analysis dominates Part II, however, with only occasional observations about the poor and unemployed drawn from his experiences in the North.

By emphasizing his own reactions and conclusions in Part II, Orwell announced a watershed in his career. The political orientation he would sustain for the rest of his life was now becoming as clear as the literary form in which he would present it. Even though Orwell continued to think of himself as a novelist, he only wrote one more genuine novel after 1936, *Coming Up for Air*, since

Animal Farm is a fable and most commentators consider *Nineteen Eighty-Four* a literary thing unto itself (Crick 202). *The Road to Wigan Pier*, Part II in particular, turned Orwell away from fictionalizing his ideas and showed him that the essay form best allowed him to voice his moral and political positions directly.

Orwell's clear, trenchant, mature style, with "a distinctive kick and energy" was also surfacing in Part II of *The Road to Wigan Pier*. He rarely qualifies his statements with a "perhaps" or "probably." He uses short, occasionally uncouth Anglo-Saxon terms like "bum" for "buttocks" whenever possible. This "gives the reader a feeling of relief because . . . [he] refuses to pussyfoot. . . . You feel firm ground under your feet" (Hodgart 35).

The personal essay form Orwell used in Part II of *The Road to Wigan Pier* allowed him to address his readers directly, to present his moral stance without compromise, and to couch his message in economical terms often distilled to the quintessence of savage and concrete accuracy. When Orwell summed up Part II, he demonstrated both his integrity and his command of economical expression, insisting that nothing in society could be repaired unless an effective Socialist Party could be brought into existence; that the interests of all exploited people are the same; and that socialism should be compatible with common decency (*RWP* 230).

As Orwell's first attempt at turning political writing into art, *The Road to Wigan Pier* was a revelation even to some of his closest friends. Richard Rees, reading it for the first time, was astonished, noting that Orwell until now had seemed to be groping and perhaps had hit a dead end with *Keep the Aspidistra Flying*. "But in *The Road to Wigan Pier*, besides revealing what he had seen in the mining towns of the north, he began to reveal his true self" (Rees 48–49).

ALTERNATIVE CRITICAL PERSPECTIVES: SOCIALISM/MARXISM

Applying political labels, especially to Orwell, is dangerous. In 1935, before he accepted Gollancz's project on unemployment in the North, Orwell had prejudices against several groups: Roman Catholics, "Scotchmen" (a term The Scots despise), homosexuals, vegetarians, and Socialists, who became some of his favorite targets (Sheldon 1991: 220, 234). Orwell's trip to the North not only opened his eyes to unemployment, it also proved he was a Socialist, even if an undoctrinal one. It also showed him how to focus his distaste for those middle-class Socialists who had never experienced the workers' lives firsthand.

For their part, few English Socialists were impressed with *The Road to Wigan Pier*. Directing his Foreword chiefly to members of the large Left Book Club, Orwell's socialist publisher, Victor Gollancz, described Part II as extremely provocative, and proceeded to attribute Orwell's reservations about English

Socialism to Orwell's "privileged" upbringing. Gollancz saw Orwell as torn between obligations to his class and to the poor, calling him both a frightful snob and a hater of snobbery. Gollancz refused to accept Orwell's denunciation of Soviet industrialism because Gollancz was convinced that modern methods of production could no longer work under capitalism—only under socialism. Convinced that what Orwell called "the misery of Stalin's slaves" was merely German propaganda, Gollancz bitterly resented Orwell's dismissal of Soviet Communism as "half gramophones, half gangsters" (*RWP* xix).

Gollancz was by no means alone among English Socialists in denouncing what he felt was Orwell's vague and idealistic approach in considering socialism elementary common sense—that in the midst of plenty, everyone should enjoy his fair share. In *The Road to Wigan Pier*, Orwell did succeed in providing a balanced picture of working-class life by including a decent, relatively prosperous family to complement the dominant bleakness, moving toward "validating a socialism based essentially on the English laborer's values" (Kubal 107). Middle-class socialists of his own time, however, resented Orwell's vivid association of socialism with crankery when he declared in Part II that "the mere words 'Socialism' and 'Communism' draw towards them with magnetic force every fruit-juice drinker, nudist, sandal-wearer, sex maniac, Quaker, 'Nature Cure' quack, pacifist and feminist in England" (*RWP* 206).

As for working-class Socialists, one mining electrician, Joe Kennan, perhaps miffed because Orwell never sent him a copy of *The Road to Wigan Pier*, recalled in 1970 that "Several of the boys really on the Left very much doubted Orwell's sincerity. Because he was very cynical and he certainly never expressed any thanks for anything that was done for him . . . he never showed any appreciation of hospitality. . . . I thought, well, what a peculiar type" (quoted in Wadhams 59).

Orwell and the more extreme Left had an even stronger mutual antipathy. By 1936, so far as is known, he had read some of Marx's works directly, and he had become secondhandedly acquainted with Marx's theories by meeting Marxists and arguing with them. Fredric Warburg, who published Orwell's later works, recalled that in 1936 Orwell already detested the Communists and fellow travelers whom he knew through the Left Book Club about as much as he disliked most members of the ILP and British Communist sympathizers. The Communists later got their licks in at Orwell by making extraordinary efforts to discredit Orwell's *Homage to Catalonia*.

The Road to Wigan Pier, published while Orwell was in the trenches in Spain, appeared in an astonishing first edition of 43,690 copies. It also aroused enormous long-lasting controversy, and its initial reviews were mixed. Walter Greenwood, writing for the London *Tribune*, fairly summed up liberal reaction to Orwell's socialistic vision: "[He] has you with him one moment and provoked beyond endurance the next." Harold Laski damned Part II for Orwell's supposed ignorance of socialist theory (quoted in Crick 229), and the Communist *Daily Worker* attacked Orwell personally, dismissing the whole book as the work of "a disillusioned little middle-class boy" who, if he could hear what the Left Book circles would say about *The Road to Wigan Pier*, would resolve "never to write again on any subject that he does not understand" (quoted in Crick 229). The trouble was probably that Orwell, nearly alone in his generation, already understood Marxism and its aims too well.

6

Spilling Spanish Beans:
Homage to Catalonia

Orwell's life changed dramatically during the spring and early summer of 1936. On July 18, while he was working on *The Road to Wigan Pier*, Spanish workers rose up against Fascist General Franco's revolt against the elected Spanish leftist government, and, as Orwell later wrote, "probably every anti-Fascist in Europe felt a thrill of hope" (*HC* 189) for a decisive blow against the rising tide of fascism. He decided to finish *The Road to Wigan Pier* as soon as possible so that he could go to Spain and report the workers' struggle—and perhaps fight on their side against the Fascists (Shelden 1991: 246).

HISTORICAL PERSPECTIVE

Orwell realized that the fighting in Spain was not a localized civil war but an ominous and highly complex ideological struggle involving most of Europe. "Fascism" refers narrowly to the Italian political-economic system begun by Mussolini in 1922. The term also refers to Nazism and Franco's military-led political party in Spain (Nationalism).

Fascism derives from the French ruling classes' hatred for democratic ideals. Fascism inflames national pride and prejudices, claiming to champion law and order against mob rule and often exploiting anti-Semitism. Mussolini seized power by pretending to save Italy from anarchy and Communism. He used his party militia, the Black Shirts, to become Italy's dictator, taking his party's name from the Roman *fasces*, bundled sticks and axe symbolizing the power of the people that balanced the power of the aristocratic Roman Senate.

Adolf Hitler's rise to power in Germany paralleled Mussolini's. In *Mein Kampf* (1923), Hitler appealed to the German masses through nationalism, anti-Semitism, the concept of an Aryan "Master Race" led by a supreme infallible leader (Hitler himself), and the promise of a pan-German empire after annihilation of its enemies, the Jews and the Communists. Though Nazism incorporated certain anticapitalist features, most of Germany's powerful capitalists supported Hitler against the German Social Democrats and Communists.

Nazism and Italian Fascism both stressed youth movements, opposed the Communists and Social Democrats, and completely controlled their nations' economies, using public works projects and relief programs. The real power rested with the leaders and their elites—Mussolini's Black Shirts and Hitler's black-uniformed, lightning-flashed SS (*Schutzstaffel*) and his Gestapo (secret police) who carried out state terrorism. Both dictators also pursued aggressive expansionism, and after Italy forcibly annexed Ethiopia, Hitler collaborated with Mussolini in the first ideological proxy war—the Spanish Civil War.

In this conflict, Hitler and Mussolini opposed the evil and cunning dictator of the Soviet Union, Josef Stalin, who had plotted and assassinated to become General Secretary of the Soviet Communist Party in 1922. Stalin's strongest rival, Leon Trotsky preached the goal of world Marxist revolution, but Stalin solidified his control within the U.S.S.R. through his secret police, originally called the "Cheka," then successively renamed the OGPU, the NKVD, and the KGB, which carried out purges from 1934 to 1938 and cannibalized the Soviet people. From 1935 to 1940, approximately one-quarter of the adult Soviet population, excluding children and the elderly, were sent to Stalin's Gulag prison system. Almost all of them died (Antonov-Ovseyenko 212).

Stalin also attempted to extend Soviet influence into Spain. "Aloof, self-contained, xenophobic," Spain was the European country "least vulnerable to the foreign viruses of totalitarianism" (Johnson 322). The Soviets worked principally through their Comintern, the covert organization which infiltrated other nations' political systems.

The Spanish Civil War is a confusing tangle of political groups. In the 1920s, the Spanish Socialist Party (PSOE), somewhat influenced by British Fabians, had peacefully formed the first Spanish Labor government. Spain quietly became a republic in 1931, so that the term "Republican" identified the Spanish Socialists who opposed Franco's Fascist-backed "Nationalists."

Contention soon broke out within the Socialist Party. The socialist dream of a gradual humane modernization of Spain was wrecked by "entryism," surreptitious intrusions into the Socialist Party and the union cadres by the ultra-

Left, organized by the U.S.S.R. The 1933 peasant uprisings instigated by the Anarchists were savagely put down by the Socialist government, and then the Spanish military, led by Franco, revolted against the government: "the poor were maddened by hunger, the rich were maddened by fear" (quoted in Johnson 323).

The liberal socialist tone of the Spanish republic threatened several powerful interests in Spanish society—the Catholic Church, the upper classes, the military, the monarchists, and the Fascist Falange traditionalists. These groups together formed the backbone of Franco's Nationalists, bent on wiping out the "foreign disease" engendered by what he called "the fronts"—"socialism, communism, and the other formulae which attack civilization to replace it with barbarism" (quoted in Johnson 323).

The militant Spanish Left also included groups with widely differing goals, some of them savage. Dolores Ibarruri, "La Pasionaria," an elected official of the Popular Front, reputedly cut a priest's throat with her teeth (Johnson 325). The Left also included street gangs, the Anarchists, the "Syndicos Libres," and the newly formed revolutionary Marxist party, the POUM (*Partido Obrero de Unificacion Marxista)*, dedicated to Trotskyist aims of world Communism. In May 1936, Spain was almost equally divided between Left and Right, with atrocities being committed by both sides. The Left murdered over a tenth of Spain's Catholic bishops and priests (Johnson 327), and in July, Franco responded with all-out civil war. Like Orwell, Socialists across Europe hailed the workers' struggle against Franco as a chance to defeat fascism and institute their new social order.

In the summer of 1936 thousands of well-intentioned but politically naïve British and American Socialists volunteered for the Republican cause. Soon many discovered that this war was not a battle of good against evil but "a general tragedy" (Johnson 326), though few admitted it. One was Orwell. In his essay, "Spilling the Spanish Beans" (1937), Orwell claimed that the Spanish Civil War had produced "a richer crop of lies" than any event since World War I (*CEJL* 1:269), and he undertook exposing the causes and dimensions of that tragedy. Until *Animal Farm* and *Nineteen Eighty-Four, Homage to Catalonia* (1938) was the book of Orwell's most thoroughly feared and hated not only by Soviet Communists but by any kind of totalitarian thinker. It is also the book that marked the greatest watershed of Orwell's life.

STRUCTURE

Like *The Road to Wigan Pier, Homage to Catalonia* is a collection of Orwell's observations and theories about an historical calamity. The fourteen chapters of *Homage to Catalonia* fall into two sections. Chapters I through VIII (Orwell used Roman numerals) chronicle Orwell's direct experience as a soldier from his arrival on December 30, 1936, until on April 25, 1937. Chapters IX through XIV present his observations of the lethal clash between the POUM and the Soviet-led Spanish Communists from the end of April until he escaped from Spain on June 23, 1937. About midway through this half of the book, Orwell paused to develop his general conclusions about the socialist cause in Spain.

Orwell followed the structural pattern he had established in his earlier documentary works, first presenting specific and meticulously observed details, and then drawing general conclusions from them. In Chapters I through IV, he meticulously observed individuals he encountered and the conditions in which they lived and fought. He presented his generalized ideas about the nature of the conflict in Chapter V, and returned to specific accounts of his experiences at the front in Chapters VI, VII, and VIII.

Most of the second half of *Homage to Catalonia* also contains his personal observations. Chapter IX begins with his recollections of his first leave after 115 days at the front, a visit to Barcelona where his equally committed wife Eileen had been working for POUM leader John McNair since February 15. Chapter X is an eyewitness account of street fighting in Barcelona between the Anarchists, who dragged POUM into the clash on their side, and the Communist-led "Popular Army." As he had done in the first part of *Homage to Catalonia*, Orwell generalized midway through the second half of the book, in Chapter XI, analyzing the causes and results of this conflict and defending POUM against Communist charges that POUM was secretly a subversive arm ("Fifth Column") of Franco's Nationalists. Chapter XII records Orwell's disillusioned return to the front three days after the fighting in Barcelona, his wounding a week after that, and his subsequent hospital stay at Tarragona. In Chapters XIII and XIV, the book's most harrowing passages, Orwell documented the Communist persecution and liquidation of POUM members and his escape from Spain with his wife and John McNair.

THEMATIC ISSUES

In *Homage to Catalonia*, Orwell addressed several important topics: political idealism and disillusion, social equality, the decency of ordinary individuals, and anticommunism. These coalesce in the theme of this book: no matter how decent and honorable an individual's intentions may be as he strives to achieve a better society, he will inevitably be betrayed by groups of amoral opportunists who will not hesitate to stoop to do what his principles forbid.

Orwell's title presents two important aspects of his message about the Spanish Civil War. By "Homage," he honored the ideas of truly egalitarian government and the individuals of decency, integrity, and goodwill who fought to bring those ideals to Spain. Using "Catalonia" rather than "Spain" indicates that though he drew general conclusions about those ideals and how they could be—and were—betrayed, he based his account on his direct observations in the hilly and traditionally rebellious province of Spain stretching southward from the Pyrenees to the Mediterranean, with its capital at Barcelona. Catalonia briefly governed itself from 1932 to 1934 and again from 1936 to 1939, until Franco abolished its autonomy.

Both the Anarchists and the POUM were fighting the Nationalists at the front when the Communists attacked members of these parties on the streets of Barcelona. This betrayal caused the most profound shift in Orwell's thinking about the war in Spain. When he arrived in late December, he had idealistically believed that Spanish workers could abolish the old feudal class system and replace it with a socialistic society where human beings could live equally and decently with one another. After he fought on the Barcelona barricades in April, though, he described the difference in the city as "Mandalay to Maymyo" (*HC* 108), drawing on his Burmese experience, as he had done in *The Road to Wigan Pier* to illustrate his shock and dismay at having those ideals blasted away.

Orwell arrived in Spain intending to report on the war for the *New Statesman* or some other liberal British newspaper sympathetic to the Republican cause (Shelden 1991: 249). He had been inaccurately told that to get into Spain he had to have papers from a British left-wing organization, but he was unable to get them from the British Communist Party, who thought he was "politically unreliable" (*CEJL* 1:327), a view three months later echoed in the *Daily Worker*'s scathing review of *The Road to Wigan Pier*. Orwell then approached the Independent Labour Party (ILP), which speedily gave him credentials to their representative in Barcelona, John McNair. Orwell immediately saw how woefully untrained most of the Republican soldiers were. He himself had had comparatively quite a bit more military training at St. Cyprian's and Eton, so he impulsively decided to join them (*CEJL* 1:318) and fight for "common decency" (*HC* 47). McNair, who had read both *Down and Out in Paris and London* and *Burmese Days* and admired Orwell in spite of his elitist Etonian accent, ascertained that Orwell was not a Stalinist and told him he could join the POUM that very day (Shelden 1991: 251).

His initial experiences in POUM showed Orwell that the conflict in Spain was not a war but a revolution pitting workers against capitalists, so in the first half of *Homage to Catalonia* he insists that to achieve their rightful equality in a society that confirms and supports their human decency, the lower classes had to bring down the unfair existing capitalist order. Not realizing then that the wealthy bourgeois of Barcelona were simply lying low, Orwell thought he saw for the first time the socialist ideal of a town run by its workers, with everyone equal (*HC* 4).

Throughout the first half of *Homage to Catalonia*, Orwell praised the essential decency of most Catalan worker-militiamen, who were terribly poor—many militiamen lacked blankets, firewood, drinking water, and even weapons, let alone training in how to use them. Orwell easily made friends with them, and even though he was often galled to the point of fury with their "mañana" inefficiency and lack of punctuality (*HC* 12), he admired the social equality he saw between officers and men, even the teenaged militia "men," that Orwell considered a "public menace" at the front (*HC* 26–27).

Orwell's original socialist idealism cooled considerably after several weeks in a POUM unit dug in at the stinking, rat-infested Huesca front where shouting matches with the Fascists entrenched a few hundred yards away were the prevailing mode of warfare. He soon realized that the early Republican successes had been achieved through revolutionary fervor directed not against European-style fascism but against Franco's military mutiny, which was attempting to restore feudalistic domination by the aristocracy and the Roman Catholic Church. Hence Orwell saw that the war was actually a triangular struggle with the leftist government battling both Franco and the trade unions, the unions fighting the government and Franco, and Franco striking against both the unions and the government (*HC* 54).

An even worse disaster, the betrayal of the workers' revolutionary cause, became increasingly clear to Orwell. He realized that during October–November 1936, the early spirit of equality he admired so much had been subverted swiftly and deliberately when the U.S.S.R. began to arm Spain's Socialist government. The Soviets then shifted their support from the moderate Spanish Socialists to the Spanish Communists, in return demanding that the Spanish Communists give up their revolutionary ideal. Eventually the U.S.S.R. supplied the Republicans about one thousand pilots and two thousand other specialists, organized international brigades, and shipped in enormous amounts of equipment, some of which was left on the battlefield. All of it carried the Soviet ultimatum: "Prevent the revolution or you get no weapons" (*HC* 53). The Soviets refused to tolerate a Spanish workers' revolution because Soviet Comintern policy put the defense of the U.S.S.R. first. Sustaining the Soviet Union's military alliances, especially with capitalist-imperialist France, which did not want a revolutionary socialist Spain on its doorstep, meant that during the winter of 1936–37, under the direction of the U.S.S.R., the Spanish Communist Party insisted on reducing the war to an ordinary nonrevolutionary conflict (*HC* 70) and did its underhanded best to sabotage the workers' revolution.

Orwell also soon realized that the revolutionary aspect of the struggle in Spain was being covered up in Britain. The pro-Fascist press, of course, spread rumors of Red atrocities, like the 512 Nationalists hurled into the gorge at Ronda, an incident used by Ernest Hemingway in *For Whom the Bell Tolls*, but even the anti-Fascist papers obscured the revolutionary nature of the workers' actions. While glibly preaching humanitarian slogans, Communists, Socialists, and Fascists—the whole world, Orwell thought— hypocritically tried to scuttle the revolution (*HC* 51).

Actually, in the first flush of revolutionary ardor, not even Orwell had seen through the Communist propaganda. For a while he had backed the Communist point of view because he thought it was more practical than the seemingly futile anti-Soviet POUM position, which rejected Stalinism and demanded a revolution leading to total control by the workers. Because Orwell was irked with the inaction he endured in the POUM trenches near Huesca, he never actually joined POUM, but later he declared he regretted not doing so, since he had seen that while the Communist position might have looked good on paper, it failed to work in practice. Then on April 25, as he wrote at the close of the first half of *Homage to Catalonia*, the real trouble in Spain began (*HC* 106).

Orwell found appalling changes in Barcelona that April. The winter's heady atmosphere of freedom and equality had vanished; enlistments were down, soldiers again saluted their superior officers, food shortages were mounting, civilians just wanted the war to be over, and the old distinctions of rich and poor and upper and lower classes were openly evident (*HC* 110–11). Worse, from Orwell's point of view, the Communist Party was mounting a systematic propaganda campaign for the "Popular Army" they backed instead of supporting the militia groups, whom the Communists blamed for their lack of military success against the Nationalists. A little earlier that month, Orwell had asked for a transfer to the Communist International Brigade then fighting on the Madrid front, but during his leave in Barcelona he experienced the Communist-inspired political hatred of groups who wanted a genuine revolution, particularly the Anarchists and the POUM.

When the "unbearable, sickening and disillusioning" street warfare broke out in Barcelona (*HC* 130), Orwell did everything he could expect of himself. After learning that the government was about to outlaw POUM (*HC* 137), he went sixty hours without sleep on no bread and one sardine, rallying POUM supporters to attack, but soon they were beaten back by well-fed government assault guards armed with American-made rifles supplied by the U.S.S.R.—weapons, like the guards themselves, never intended to be used against Franco at the front (*HC* 144). The street fighting gave the pro-Soviet Republican government in Valencia an excuse to bring Catalonia under their control and to suppress the POUM. Sickened by their betrayal of the POUM's revolutionary aim, Orwell returned to the front shorn of his idealism and convinced of the futility of the Socialist cause.

Orwell's near-fatal throat wound—a Nationalist bullet missed his carotid artery by about a millimeter (*HC* 194)— proved his salvation. After a remarkably short hospital stay, he returned to get a medical discharge in the "nightmare atmosphere" (*HC* 198) of Barcelona, where the Communists were now torturing and executing POUM members. The secret police had confiscated all of the diaries he had sent to Eileen for safekeeping and Orwell was under threat of arrest, so he adopted his old tramping incognito, sleeping five nights on the streets, once on the broken masonry of a ruined church (*HC* 212–13). During the day, he and Eileen put principle before their personal safety and visited their POUM friend, Georges Kopp, in a horrifying Spanish prison. For Orwell the horror of seeing his friend in jail and tortured and not being able to help him far outweighed the personal risk he himself was taking (*HC* 217–18).

Since coming to terms with himself after Burma, Orwell had consistently put decency and integrity foremost in his own life. Now, forced to leave Spain due to the Communist betrayal of socialist ideals, Orwell by no means abandoned his principles. When he and Eileen crossed the border into France, they both realized they would have rather gone back to Spain—back to certain prison and possible death. As he insisted in *Homage to Catalonia,* however, the moral obligation to expose Communist lies, oppression, and betrayal carried Orwell back to the beautiful England of his childhood, which he found oblivious to the dual threats of fascism and communism, sunk, he grimly warned, in a deep, deep sleep that would last only until "we are jerked out of it by the roar of bombs" (*HC* 232).

CHARACTER DEVELOPMENT

By opening *Homage to Catalonia* with a touching portrait of a young Italian militiaman who like Orwell had volunteered to defend the Spanish workers' rights, Orwell paid tribute to the decency of ordinary men. Orwell felt an immediate and profound bond with this soldier's "crystal spirit," as if his soul and Orwell's "had momentarily succeeded in bridging the gulf of language and tradition and meeting in utter intimacy" (*HC* 4). Through this nameless individual, Orwell glimpsed the essence of what he was fighting for, human decency, which he believed could flourish only in an atmosphere of economic and political equality achieved, if necessary, by revolutionary means.

Orwell, the political activist who fights for that human decency, is the central figure of *Homage to Catalonia,* but Orwell the narrator had considerable difficulty getting the story written by Orwell the activist into print. Though the Spanish police confiscated the diaries he had kept in Spain, Orwell almost immediately after his escape sent a proposal for a book on his experiences to his publisher Victor Gollancz, but the difficulties he had been having for some time with Gollancz's firm got in his way. The previous February, Orwell had already complained to his agent Leonard Moore about Norman Collins, Gollancz's twenty-nine-year-old deputy chairman, whom Orwell called "that squirt," claiming Collins had ruined the manuscript of *The Road to Wigan Pier*, and Orwell feared it might happen again (Shelden 1991: 225). Worse for Orwell, on Collins' word and without speaking to Orwell at all, Gollancz rejected Orwell's proposal on July 5, writing to Orwell that Collins felt the book would "harm the fight against fascism" (Shelden 1991: 279). Orwell concluded a Leftist conspiracy was obstructing exposure of the truth about the situation in Spain, and he redoubled his efforts to expose the hypocrisy at the heart of organized socialism. When he wrote *Homage to Catalonia,* he did so by presenting contrasting self-portraits before and after he realized the true nature of communism.

As the narrator, Orwell displayed his earlier self in the first part of *Homage to Catalonia* as dedicated, impulsive, initially frightened but hiding his apprehension, disgusted with the boredom and discomfort of the front, and boyishly enthused with patrols and bomb-tossing. He longed, he said, for what all soldiers in trench warfare long for— more cigarettes, a week's leave, a battle—creature comforts, or else the relief of decisive and effective action. "Not bad fun in a way," he commented about leading his first attack on a Fascist redoubt. It proved a modest success, though by volunteering to go back and look for a supposedly missing solder Orwell risked his life for nothing (*HC* 96, 99–100). Bob Edwards, who commanded the ILP contingent where Orwell fought near Monte Oscuro in January, described him as "absolutely fearless" in the face of the enemy, although "he had an absolute phobia against rats" (*HC* 78). These animals, some as large as cats, infested the trenches and the prisons where the Communists held POUM members prisoner.

Orwell's admiration for the decency of ordinary people dominates the first half of *Homage to Catalonia.* Writing in a blaze of moral indignation only weeks after he left Spain, Orwell presented a different self in the second half of *Homage to Catalonia.* After the abortive fighting on the barricades in Barcelona to defend POUM members from the Communists, Orwell was angry, disgusted, above all disillusioned with the vicious abandonment of principles and lack of integrity in those who claimed to represent the workers' interests, like a Soviet secret police operative he saw in a Barcelona hotel—the first time, he said, he'd seen a person whose profession was telling lies, unless one counted journalists (*HC* 140).

The crux of the outrage which changed Orwell from idealistic volunteer to embittered veteran was his conception of a writer's duty to the truth. To be able to live with himself after what he had come to consider the immoral actions forced on him in Burma, Orwell had suffered along with the underprivileged because he felt it was the only way he could write about their suffering with integrity. Having adopted this stern personal standard, he was inevitably disappointed with his fellow journalists. Not only the Communist press but almost all journalists swallowed the Communist line. The British *News Chronicle* treated the May fighting in Barcelona as a "trotskyist revolt" by POUM, and the *New Republic* reported that POUM troops were playing football with the Fascists (Gross 71). Such distortions and downright fabrications made Orwell all the more determined to bring the unpopular truth to light.

The same decency that prompted Orwell to battle hypocritical journalism led him to express his outrage at the fate of POUM members imprisoned and tortured by the Communists. Orwell came out of Spain, he said, with "evil memories"—and more belief in human decency than he had ever had before (*HC* 230). Those memories and that belief affected nearly everything else he wrote.

Since his return from Burma, Orwell had considered society not as faceless groups but as collections of individuals, each entitled to personal hopes, abilities, fears, and dreams. The complex struggle in Spain not only changed Orwell as an individual and as a chronicler of the individual's struggle against domination by an amoral group, it helped him define the difference between people he admired and those he detested. What mattered for him was a human being's essential decency. No matter where he encountered a human "crystal spirit," Orwell admired it—and celebrated it in his writing.

Two men Orwell met in Spain had that quality. One was Russian-born engineer Georges Kopp, a POUM General Staff member who took Orwell and his first unit to the Aragon front near Alcubierre and became a friend of Eileen's in Barcelona, even driving her to visit Orwell at the front in mid-March. Later, when the Communists jailed Kopp in Barcelona, Orwell risked his own life to obtain a letter that might release Kopp, to no avail (*HC* 219–220). For Orwell, friendship came first, then shared danger, then reputation: "He was my personal friend, I had served under him for months, I had been under fire with him, and I knew his history. He was a man who had sacrificed everything—family, nationality, livelihood—simply to come to Spain and fight against Fascism" (*HC* 209). Orwell might have been more loyal to Kopp than Kopp was to him. Kopp probably had falsified his background and, more shocking, Kopp remained in love with Eileen all his life, though whether they had an affair is debatable (Shelden 1991: 272). Despite concerted efforts by English friends to free Kopp, the Spanish Communists tortured him and held him, once in a rat-filled coal bin, until 1938, releasing him shortly before Franco captured Barcelona. Kopp then went to England, where he stayed for some time with Eileen's brother Dr. Laurence O'Shaughnessy and his wife Gwen. Whatever Kopp's relation to Eileen was, Kopp was fortunate to have such a friend as Orwell (Shelden 1991: 274).

Orwell's compatriot Bob Smillie was a grandson of the miners' notorious labor leader Robert Smillie. Orwell met Bob in February 1937 when Orwell joined the POUM's semi-independent British subgroup, and they became fast friends; typically, Smillie was just behind Orwell when their patrol assaulted a Fascist position near Huesca. When Orwell heard that Smillie had died in a Valencia government prison June 12, 1937, he knew exactly where to lay the blame: "this brave and gifted boy" left Glasgow University to fight fascism "with faultless courage and willingness, and all they could find to do with him was to fling him into jail and let him die [probably of appendicitis] like a neglected animal" (*HC* 217). For Orwell, Smillie's fate personalized the utter senselessness of the entire war in Spain. He mourned his friend's death as unforgivable: "To be killed in battle—yes, that is what one expects; but to be flung into jail, not even for any imaginary offense, but simply owing to dull blind spite, and then left to die in solitude—that is a different matter" (*HC* 218).

Kopp and Smillie and the nameless Italian militiaman whose portrait Orwell chose to open *Homage to Catalonia* shared a quality very dear to Orwell, the willingness to "commit murder and throw away [one's] life for a friend" (*HC* 3). In any age, in any crisis, few human beings possess such devotion, and perhaps even fewer today admire or even respect it, but Orwell did. Both before and after he knew the truth about international Communism, he was ready to lay his life down for friendship, and to kill, if he had to, to defend it.

In *Homage to Catalonia*, the human qualities and actions which Orwell found despicable are just as clear. He did not seem to hate the Fascists he had come to fight; instead he rather sympathetically showed them as individuals in trenches just as filthy and miserable as those he and his comrades lived in. Orwell did his share and more of accurate bomb-throwing, but he was no heartless killer. He felt "a vague sorrow" when he heard the screams of a man badly wounded in the explosion of a bomb Orwell had thrown (Crick 217). He could also see the wry humor in war's ironies. Much later, he recalled crawling near the Fascist trenches on a reconaissance and catching an enemy soldier in his sights. The man was holding up his trousers as he ran, and Orwell could not bring himself to pull the trigger. He had come to Spain to shoot Fascists, he later wrote, "but a man who is holding up his trousers isn't a 'Fascist,' he is visibly a fellow creature" (*CEJL* 2:254).

While he praised individual heroism in *Homage to Catalonia*, Orwell did not use the book as a vehicle for personal revenge, though he had encountered a fair share of unscrupulous people in Spain and at home, both among the Communists and among the European journalists covering the war. He preferred to expose the evil that groups of people can create when they feed off one another's insincerity, hypocrisy, deceit, betrayal, and hatred, all fostered and rewarded by corrupt leaders and their deluded followers.

Through *Homage to Catalonia*, Orwell made his own war on two groups he felt had committed the most serious outrages against human decency that he had as yet seen. By brutally suppressing POUM, he believed the Communists had revealed their true nature, even though most of the world refused to see it, and by failing to protest the Communist terrorism, the pro-Communist Left had caused him "a disillusionment that amounted to nausea" (Gross 65).

Left-wing Communist sympathizers revolted Orwell even more than the Communists did. Orwell had studied Marxist theory, which taught that truth was conditioned by class and that objective truth was a bourgeois virtue that should be superseded by proletarian truth, as the Soviets did in rewriting history. The Communists also believed that objective truth should be superseded at any cost by the psychological need for the emotional supports of Party life. To accomplish this, Stalin murdered his former defender, the writer Maxim Gorky; he burned (though not publicly) the literary output of a generation of Russian writers (Johnson 306); and he sent over six hundred writers to the kind of prison camp called *dokhodilovka*, "the place where one reaches the edge," where starved and demented prisoners "gnawed on whatever they could find underfoot, in refuse heaps or in piles of corpses that awaited burial" (Goldberg 17). Orwell recognized that this was the kind of system the Stalinist Comintern hoped to establish in Spain.

Arthur Koestler, who like Orwell was one of the first and few European authors to denounce communism (Koestler spent time in a Spanish jail for doing so), offered a typical example of how a writer toed the Party mark by telling blatant lies for propaganda purposes. According to Koestler, the Communists ascribed to the Fascists the very propaganda technique the Communists themselves customarily used to demonize their opponents (Koestler 334). By unmasking the Communist outrages in Spain, Orwell challenged nearly the whole European literary establishment, which in the 1930s was largely comprised of pro-Communist Leftists. They blindly considered Stalin a lesser evil than Hitler, even after the sham Moscow Trials stage-managed by Stalin himself, who invented the formula "arrest—smear—torture—obtain a confession—try—condemn—execute (=send to a death camp)" in a matter of days, sometimes even hours (Antonov-Ovseyenko 130). In 1934 alone, 300,000 Communists were purged (Antonov-Ovseyenko 144), individuals delivered to courtrooms from the Lubyanka as "disemboweled, physically and mentally exhausted defendants and witnesses, drugged by poisons and terrified by the impending retribution" (Antonov-Ovseyenko 143). The Spanish War opened

Orwell's eyes, so that he, nearly alone, saw the truth of international communism—and he told the world.

STYLISTIC AND LITERARY DEVICES

In each half of *Homage to Catalonia*, Orwell separated his chapters on the militia and on politics, putting one chapter of political analysis in the middle of chapters describing his militia experiences. In the militia chapters, he took pains to use data only from his own observations and those of witnesses he considered reliable, so he could contradict propaganda about the actions in Spain by presenting the stark facts in as undeceived a fashion as he could manage.

In his 1952 Introduction to the first U.S. edition of *Homage to Catalonia*, critic Lionel Trilling attributed Orwell's "ideal of fairness and responsibility" to the considerable residue of middle-class virtues in his mind —love of personal privacy, of order, of manners, fair play, courage, all adding up to survival as a decent human being. For that reason, Trilling saw Orwell less as a twentieth-century socialist than as a spiritual contemporary of early nineteenth-century English essayists William Hazlitt and William Cobbett.

Trilling's comparison is appropriate, though surprising in light of Orwell's own description of himself as a "democratic Socialist." Hazlitt (1778–1830), a literary man and a passionate democrat who like Orwell combined intense subjectivity with strict adherence to his subject, was a literary and dramatic critic respected equally for his perceptive readings of Elizabethan drama and for giving credit where it was due regardless of political persuasion. Orwell resembled Hazlitt in intellect, temper, and unequivocal devotion to the truth. Orwell's criticism of the leftist intelligentsia's inability to recognize the truth about communist hypocrisy (and their own) affirmed the same middle-class virtues: "Orwell had the simple courage to point out that the pacifists preached their doctrine under . . . the protection of the British navy" (*HC* xvii).

William Cobbett (1763?-1835) was a lifelong British social reformer. He championed American Federalists and became a radical working-class leader and apostle of agrarianism in England, and he successfully agitated for the parliamentary Reform Bill of 1832. Trilling observed that Orwell's radicalism, like Cobbett's, referred to the past and to the soil, an orientation that gave Orwell's political radicalism a conservative slant and saved it from "the ravages of ideology": "Like Cobbett, [Orwell] does not dream of a new kind of man, he is content with the old kind, and what moves him is the desire that this old kind of man should have freedom, bacon, and proper work" (*HC* xiii).

Furthermore, both Hazlitt and Cobbett, like Orwell, were far-ranging readers who cultivated lucid literary styles. Stylistically, Orwell's writing resembles Hazlitt's—a natural style that could crescendo to vehement eloquence and glowing imagery, as Orwell's often could do when inspired by outrage against injustice. Hazlitt, who had an agile mind like Orwell's, liked to use paradoxes for effect, a technique Orwell often used, like his unforgettable closing scene of *Homage to Catalonia*, safe, sweet, slumbering England oblivious to the coming bombs. Within the strictures of early nineteenth-century century taste, Hazlitt and Cobbett both employed rich masculine diction, as Orwell did in the earthier idiom of his time, and like Cobbett who wrote a first-rate grammar and rhetoric handbook, Orwell was in love with the English language and defended it passionately against the journalists and literati who in his opinion prostituted it for political purposes. In his retrospective essay, "Why I Write" (1946), Orwell declared that his experiences in Spain "turned the scale": "Every line of serious work that I have written since 1936 has been written, directly or indirectly, *against* totalitarianism and *for* democratic Socialism, as I understand it [Orwell's italics]" (*CEJL* 4:5).

ALTERNATIVE CRITICAL PERSPECTIVE: MARXISM/COMMUNISM

Fiercely determined to expose the Communists' actions in Spain, during the last week in June at Banyuls, Orwell worked on his article, "Spilling the Spanish Beans," and as soon as he arrived in Wallingford in early July he started *Homage to Catalonia*. "Spilling the Spanish Beans" appeared as a two-part article in *The New English Weekly* for 29 July and 2 September. *The New Statesman* asked him to review Franz Borkenau's *The Spanish Cockpit*, but editor Kingsley Martin found Orwell's implication that Martin's "Spanish correspondents are all wrong" was "uncompromising" and rejected the review (Crick 228). Orwell then wrote an equally uncompromising tandem review of *The Spanish Cockpit* and John Sommerfield's *Volunteer in Spain* that was published in *Time and Tide*, July 31, 1937.

Martin's rejection enraged Orwell. He called it "expediency" that demonstrated tolerance of "necessary murder," and showed "the mentality of a whore ... a willingness to string along at any price" (quoted in Crick 438 n.53). The Communists and their sympathizers were already attacking *The Road to Wigan Pier* when Orwell returned from Spain, and "For the next few years, public controversy and Orwell walked hand in hand" (Crick 229).

Orwell completed *Homage to Catalonia* in January of 1938. Although he compared the job of sorting out interparty polemics to "diving into a cesspool" (Shelden 1991: 283), on the whole this is his most optimistic book, testifying to his belief in the possibility of a truly equitable society, one completely free of totalitarianism.

British publisher Fredric Warburg courageously brought out *Homage to Catalonia* in April 1938. Critic Desmond Flower praised Orwell's objectivity and stately, unhurried, unexaggerated clarity (quoted in Shelden 1991: 293), but it sold only about seven hundred copies in its first four months, nine hundred in Orwell's lifetime. Orwell attributed the book's failure to lack of advertising (Shelden 1991: 293–94), but the prevailing pro-Communist atmosphere and venomous assaults from left-wing and Communist writers were probably more responsible for its lamentable sales record.

In the highly political 1930s as never before, writers experienced serious pressures to write for political purposes, under the widely held assumption that art could only be justified as a tool for the reshaping of society (Zwerdling 3). Orwell was well acquainted with Karl Marx's theories (Zwerdling 20; Rees 147), one of which taught that culture and ideology were ultimately determined by the economic conditions of the society that created them. According to Marx, "It is not the consciousness of men that determines their being, but, on the contrary, their social being that determines their consciousness" (quoted in Zwerdling 6), so that the arts do not shape their society, they are its products or commodities.

Under Lenin and Stalin, Marx's concept of the arts' role in society developed into a recognized element of official Soviet ideology, and the manipulation and control of art became the task of the Communist state. Lenin insisted, "Literature must become *part* [italics in original] of the common cause of the proletariat, 'cog and wheel' of a single, great Social-Democratic mechanism" (quoted in Zwerdling 6). Stalin, who called writers "engineers of human souls" (quoted in Zwerdling 7), brutally implemented the centralized control of literature. The mechanical imagery both Lenin and Stalin used reflects the assumption that literature is a controllable product, like the output of any other kind of factory (Zwerdling 7). Furthermore, Communists believe literature must move in one direction only, the Party line (Tertz 43). In the 1930s, the Communist Party spread their concept of literature based on ideology, not observation, through the Western world through convincing writers like W. H. Auden "to go to the front [in the Spanish Civil War and] write some pieces saying hurrah for the Republic." Auden produced an obscure, ironic poem "Spain 1933" (Zwerdling 8).

Communists consistently attack several of Orwell's premises in *Homage to Catalonia*. First, Orwell insisted that the " 'mystique' of Socialism . . . is the idea of equality" (*HC* 112), a utopian notion that Marxists denounce while insisting on the inevitability of class war and revolution. In fact, Orwell recorded the Communists' swift destruction of the spirit of equality in 1937 (*HC* 55). Second, on the basis of his firsthand observation of the Communists' suppression of POUM, Orwell believed that socialism had to be defined, created, and defended, not allowed to evolve itself naturally as the Communists insist, which would lead to a new set of socialist oppressions like the imprisonment and torture of Smillie and Kopp. Third, Orwell recorded Soviet-inspired insensitivity to local conditions which made the Communist Party in Spain a tool of the Soviet Union, a concept contrary to the Spanish workers' hope for equality. Fourth, Orwell attacked the Communist notion that abolishing private property necessarily ends hierarchy and privilege when, for instance, he showed the well-fed and well-equipped Popular Army forces battling the POUM in Barcelona. Above all, Orwell unmasked the merciless "historicist" Communist principle that the end justifies the means. He denounced as a sheer contradiction of reason the Communist view Auden pronounced that the triumph of socialism justifies even "necessary murder" to achieve it as a sheer contradiction of reason. "Doing evil," Orwell wrote to novelist Naomi Mitchison in June 1938, "that good may come . . . in my opinion implies that causes do not have effects" (quoted in Shelden 1991: 209).

According to Communist theory, if a writer's political criticism is "internal," rather than "external," he is helping the enemy. Just as the Communists had falsely claimed that the POUM was Franco's "Fifth Column," so they attacked Orwell as bourgeois, subjective, and pro-Fascist, although in *Homage to Catalonia*, Orwell frankly cautioned his readers about his biases and his possible mistakes (*HC* 160). Communists see Orwell's denunciation of communism's "end justifies the means" mentality and its emphasis on "necessary murder" as breaking faith with the requirements of socialist revolution. They reject Orwell's insistence on objective truth as hopelessly bourgeois, since communist theory demands that the reshaping of history into proletarian truth is a prerequisite to establishing the workers' ideal state. Orwell's intense respect for the individual also contradicted accepted communist dogma, which requires that the happiness of the individual be sacrificed to the happiness of the state, and that the emotional support of the Party must be maintained at any cost to individual privacy and self-respect, concepts Orwell himself fiercely defended.

By declaring that the Communist Party was "now the chief antirevolutionary party" (*CEJL* 1:281), *Homage to Catalonia* exposed communism's real aim as totalitarian domination, not the socialist goal of worldwide revolution to bring about an equitable society where all property would be held in common. Orwell's experience in Spain made his socialism a living faith, but paradoxically, it also planted the seeds of his strongest doubts, because when he first came to Spain, he had seen an ideally classless society—and then he had seen it slain by the Communists, the very group claiming to be its most devoted proponents (Zwerdling 78).

In Orwell's lifetime, the Communists and their sympathizers dismissed *Homage to Catalonia* as his oversimplification and distortion of the events he saw in Spain. V. S. Pritchett called Orwell's appetite for the unvarnished truth "perverse" (Gross 80), and Victor Gollancz argued that "Orwell was always 'a trifle dishonest'" because he never gave "full play to those doubts, hesitations and searchings about the truth which are the lot of us all but which so many try to stifle" (quoted in Wadhams 71). Sam Lesser, a British Communist journalist, claimed flatly, "Orwell did a great disservice to Spain" (quoted in Wadhams 97). In 1945, Orwell told his agent that *Homage to Catalonia* was "about the best I have written" (*CEJL* 3:392). History has shown who told the truth.

7

Orwell's War: *Coming Up for Air* and *The Lion and the Unicorn*

After the dismal reception of *Homage to Catalonia*, Orwell experienced considerable discouragement and depression. His "manifest despair and disgust" arose "as physically and concretely as a smell, from *Coming Up for Air,* his most depressing book," written in 1938 (Gross 80). Orwell knew the Nazi bombs were coming, but nothing seemed able to wake Britain from its false sense of security. From mid-1937 to September 1939, either ignored or vilified by the British intelligentsia, Orwell, unhappy and frustrated, waited for the storm clouds to break over Europe. As he had learned in the Spanish trenches, waiting was one of the hardest trials of a soldier's life, but he tried to keep himself busy with his writing.

COMING UP FOR AIR

HISTORICAL SETTING

In Spain, Franco, supported by the Nazis and Fascist Italy, smothered the hope of socialist revolution that had so briefly flared in Catalonia. The war ended after the Nationalists captured Barcelona in January 1939 and Madrid that March 27. Spain became a dictatorship which reverted to monarchy upon Franco's death.

By this time, alliances for World War II were coalescing, and potential naval enemies threatened Britain in three theaters of war: the home waters, the

Mediterranean, and the Pacific-Indian Ocean. Germany and Japan had signed their own Anti-Comintern Pact in 1936, opposing the Soviet Union. In November 1938, Mussolini announced a fascist racial policy similar to the Nazi Nuremberg Laws, and on May 22, 1939, he signed the "Pact of Steel," a full alliance with Hitler.

Besides making Germany a world power, Hitler intended to "cleanse" the Fatherland of Jews whom he considered "an inundation of diseased bacilli which at the moment have their breeding ground in Russia" (quoted in Johnson 342–43). Upon becoming Chancellor of Germany in 1933, he immediately set up forced-labor concentration camps for Jews, political opponents, and Communists. Within a year he had begun massive rearmament. France and Britain, led by British Prime Minister Neville Chamberlain, whom Orwell called "a stupid old man doing his best [with] public opinion behind him" (*LU* 32), tried to appease Hitler, but when Hitler launched his *Blitzkrieg* at Poland in August 1939 just after concluding a mutual nonaggression pact with the Soviet Union, the world war that Orwell had been predicting for several years erupted.

In the tense prewar atmosphere while he was completing the final draft of *Homage to Catalonia*, the idea for a new novel struck Orwell. On December 6, 1937, he told his agent that this book would not be about politics, but about a man taking a surreptitious vacation as a temporary escape from public and private responsibilities (Shelden 1991: 292). Eileen commented, "The book seethes in his head and he is very anxious to get on with it" (quoted in Shelden 1991: 292), but probably both the growing threat of war and his own increasing physical ailments contributed to its generally gloomy mood. He had already decided to call it "Coming Up for Air" (Shelden 1991: 290) and by the next June, he had sketched out its general plan, but his work was interrupted by a serious bout of chest illness. Orwell wrote the first draft of *Coming Up for Air* in Morocco between September 1938 and a bad case of dysentery in December. He finished the manuscript in March 1939 and hurried to his dying father's bedside at Southwold, where Orwell himself became seriously ill again.

PLOT

Orwell took the epigraph for *Coming Up for Air* from a popular song: "He's dead, but he won't lie down." As the novel opens, Orwell's protagonist George Bowling is gasping in spiritual death throes like a gigantic beached carp, a fat, forty-five-year-old, bourgeois insurance salesman riddled with self-disgust. He loathes his oppressive middle-class situation—his smothering wife Hilda, his monstrously selfish children, his stifling little house in the suburbs, and his dull pedestrian job. He also detests the phoniness of his prewar culture and looks back fondly to his youth in a small English village. In the four chapters of Part One (Orwell's designation), the day after he gets his new false teeth, George suddenly comes into some unexpected money, and he contemplates a few days' escape from being a "good husband" to Hilda, a "good father" to the obnoxious children, and a "good citizen" of Ellesmere Road, "a prison . . . a line of semi-detached torture-chambers" (*CA* 12).

Part I of *Coming Up for Air* develops Bowling's slavery to middle-class values and expectations. As he strolls up London's crowded, noisy Strand which stinks of automobile exhaust, Bowling realizes "the mental swindle" of being bought with his own money; his external and internal punishment for being fat, which prevents "really deep emotions" (*CA* 15, 20); and the increasing threat of the coming war, contrasting all this misery with his idealized boyhood memories of the lovely Thames Valley countryside.

The ten chapters of Part II begin with a flashback to Bowling's early. youth in pre-World War I Lower Binfield, a market town where his father had a small seed business and his plump mother happily cooked and "it was summer all the year round" (*CA* 42). His idyllic memories alternate with his present unpleasant circumstances. The First World War killed off marvelous sweets like Caraway Comfits and Penny Monsters, just as inescapable poverty turned George's babysitter, sweet Katie, into a "wrinkled-up hag" (*CA* 46). George affectionately recalls his father, his Uncle Ezekiel, his mother, and a home where everything went "like clockwork" (*CA* 57). He also recounts happy fishing trips his older brother Joe reluctantly took him on, when George experienced the first big triumph of his life by landing a carp about seven inches long (*CA* 71). Fishing became one of Bowling's passions, and he deliberately reserved a pool of carp he alone had discovered as a prize to savor in his later life, but after they were married Hilda refused to let him fish. As a boy, he also blissfully read old penny dreadfuls and stirring adventure stories (*CA* 103–04). At about sixteen George had a fling with pretty Elsie Waters, the first person who taught him to care about a woman (*CA* 120), not just sexually but emotionally.

Too soon, George's idyllic world shattered. George's father's seed business was wrecked by a bigger competitor, brother Joe became an "ugly ruffian" (*CA* 116) who ran away from the family, and George was drafted into the Great War, a teenage recruit with "no free will and no notion of trying to resist" (*CA* 131). After he was invalided home, Bowling educated himself with a binge of indiscriminate novel-reading, concluding that society was just a "balls-up" (*CA* 140). By 1930, he had married Hilda, settled down, and by 1938, with British industry gearing up for war, George has become "a poor old fatty" with nothing to look forward to but slaving his life out to support his family (*CA* 166).

In the three chapters of Part III, Bowling tries to understand what his society is doing to him. Pondering how to spend his unexpected windfall, he accompanies Hilda to a meeting of the Left Book Club, but he is repelled by the Communist speaker's hatred for his political opponents, the Fascists. When George seeks comfort by celebrating the past with an old friend, a retired schoolmaster, George suddenly sees old Porteous is just a ghost, and the glorious literature and values he celebrates no longer can comfort George—or anyone else. Needing the solace of nature, George then motors out into the countryside on a beautiful spring day and suddenly, happily decides he will plunge back into Lower Binfield, where everything will be good and peaceful, and he can land huge fish in his secret pool. He gets off work, tells Hilda a "watertight" story (*CA* 202), and steps on the gas.

Brutal disillusion greets him. In Part IV, George discovers a dismayingly transformed Lower Binfield. He visits the tackily modernized hotel, the tarted-up marketplace, the cemetery where no one else recalls his parents are buried, and finally the river, which has now become a tawdry, crowded resort spot. After he glimpses poor age-raddled Elsie, now married to a shopkeeper, George flees to his secret carp pool, only to discover it has been turned into the Upper Binfield Model Yacht Club, a blow just as devastating to George as the stray RAF practice bomb that climactically demolishes Binfield's High Street, flooding it with escaped pigs. "If you care about anything," George somberly comments, "say goodbye to it now" (*CA* 269). When he ruefully returns to his dreary home and drearier Hilda, who is crowing over having uncovered his little deception, George's mood shifts yet again. He grimly re-shoulders his eternal row with Hilda and the "mental squalor" of his "awful future" (*CA* 277), Orwell's metaphor for the death of the sleepy rural England he loved. George Bowling is dead, too, and he has only just realized it.

CHARACTER DEVELOPMENT

Like George, all Orwell's characters in this novel, from the least important "extras" to the supporting cast of George Bowling's parents and brother Joe, his babysitter Katie, his girlfriend Elsie, and his wife Hilda, die spiritually long before their bodies give up the ghost. Orwell always detested "crankery," his blanket term for the ineffectual, hypocritical, and phony materialistic faddishness that swept Britain after World War I and destroyed the decent humanity of people like George Bowling's family and friends. "The awful gang of food-cranks and spook-hunters and simple-lifers with £1000 a year" that turned George's sacred carp pool into a garbage dump is Orwell's metaphor for hare-brained English social groups who rushed off into madcap obsessions that ruined the environment and demolished the solid values that had made England great, all the while deliberately ignoring the question that burned at Bowling's—and Orwell's—heart in 1939: "What's ahead of us?" (*CA* 266).

Not much lay ahead for either Katie or Elsie. Grinding poverty brutally coarsened Katie, whose first baby was possibly fathered by a brother. Katie changed from a tiny but conscientious girl draggling along in hand-me-downs to a fiftyish-looking wrinkled crone—at twenty-seven (*CA* 46). Elsie, once tall, pretty, golden-haired, and gentle, with natural refinement and submissive femininity, became listless Mrs. Cookson with a greyish bulldog face and a lower-class accent (*CA* 122, 244–45). Whatever youthful appeal these women had had was drained away by their poverty and their low status in British society.

Orwell's characterization of Bowling's wife Hilda harks back to his unhappy years in Burma. George usually refers to her as "old Hilda," indicating her human qualities are long gone, too. When George first met her she resembled a hare (Orwell particularly loathed rats, and hares are their cousins), and now at thirty-seven she is thin and shriveled, harassed by the fear of poverty, and given to relishing petty disasters like rising gas bills and outgrown children's shoes (*CA* 7–8). Hilda is a malignant reprise of Elizabeth of *Burmese Days*, reincarnated sourly single in England to inflict her own unhappiness on the unlucky man she married. As the daughter of an "upper-lower-middle-class" retired Anglo-Indian family living in genteel poverty, Hilda would have married anyone to escape parents as mentally and physically active "as a couple of shellfish" and their little "cyst-like world" (*CA* 155, 157). Hilda smothers all her family's joy in life in the name of household economy, which becomes her active pursuit, not a passive condition. She justifies dabbling in the "food-crank business," spiritualism, and the Left Book Club (*CA* 163–65) by claiming to save money, driving Bowling to overeating and drinking, adultery, and contemplation of wife-murder (*CA* 158).

Orwell was well aware he had allowed his own personality to intrude constantly into George Bowling. He considered it a novelistic "vice," actually claiming he was not a "real" novelist anyway (Hammond 149–50), but the "Orwell" component of George Bowling enhances the character, not detracts from it. As "fat" is the opposite of the cadaverously thin that Orwell was during most of his adult life, and as marital misery is the opposite of the generally amiable companionship Orwell shared with Eileen, bourgeois (but hating it) George Bowling superficially seems the opposite of democratic socialist and recent ILP member (though nostalgic for Edwardian England) George Orwell—but the one is really a mirror image of the other.

As Orwell's most revealing character in *Coming Up for Air*, Bowling received Orwell's own happy memories of boyhood fishing expeditions, delicious magical hours with older boys who finally let him come along with them, the sun warm above and the smell of wild peppermint "like Mother Wheeler's sweetshop" (*CA* 70).

Early in the novel, Orwell described Bowling as "fat but thin inside" (*CA* 23). George Woodcock, Orwell's contemporary and friend, observed, "the thin man inside him . . . starts looking at fat George Bowling's life and doubting its value" (Woodcock 180). To the objections raised about the literary effect of Orwell's mingling his own ideas into Bowling's, Woodcock noted that Bowling "wins his way into our minds as a kind of probable improbability" having a "consistency of its own . . . speaking in Orwell's most vividly colloquial and imagistic prose, [with] . . . a love for the surface of the earth" (Woodcock 182). Even so, Bowling concludes he has no way out: "The great dark fish will never swim again in the pool of his mind" (Woodcock 186), evidence of Orwell's despair at knowing what was coming—and knowing that almost no one believed him.

THEMATIC ISSUES: IMPERIALISM, CLASS, POVERTY, PERSONAL FREEDOM, LANGUAGE, POLITICS

The contrasts among secure past, in-denial present, and threatening future provide the dominant thematic concern of *Coming Up for Air*. This novel insists that the traditional English values of security, peace, and decency are being dismantled by the English themselves, especially by "cranks" and unscrupulous economic profiteers and everyone else who allows them to get by with it. The bombing that ironically closes *Coming Up for Air* is not an attack from outside, by Fascists, but a military blunder which disappoints the local RAF commander who ordered it because it killed only three people (*CA* 265).

All of Orwell's previous thematic concerns resurface in *Coming Up for Air*: imperialism, class, poverty, personal freedom, language, and politics. Hilda's wretched parents represent the fatal effect of the Empire on its faithful servants, who inevitably become its "decayed throw-out" class (*CA* 158). Retired to their claustrophobic English resort town on a bare subsistence income, the Vincents and George Bowling share vague mutual get-rich-quick aspirations—Bowling hoping to "better" himself by marrying into a family that boasted an ancestral admiral, and Hilda's father looking to touch his new son-in-law for occasional fivers as Hilda's brother already had no scruples about doing (*CA* 158–59).

Bowling's family knew a different kind of poverty. In Bowling's youth, farmhands slaved terrible hours for fourteen shillings a week, ending up as "worn-out cripples with a five-shilling old-age pension and an occasional half-crown from the parish. And . . . 'respectable poverty' was even worse" (*CA* 124). "Worse" for Orwell meant that clinging to appearances often resulted in giving up personal decency and personal freedom: "Small business sliding down the hill, solid tradesmen turning gradually into broken-down bankrupts . . . girls ruined for life by an illegitimate baby" (*CA* 125). World War I, engineered by capitalist international interests, smashed this world and left individuals no free will and no capacity to resist (*CA* 131).

For Orwell, what redeemed all the misery in pre-World War I England was the sense of security and continuity that radiated from the British sense of objective good and evil and permeated their lives (*CA* 125). In Orwell's and Bowling's pre-World War II present, the traditional English respect for the objective concepts of "good" and "evil" had begun to shift into subjectivity, favoring the agenda of one group or another and perverting language to amoral purposes.

When he started *Coming Up for Air*, Orwell claimed it would not be about politics, but he could not keep his political views out of it. One of the novel's most vivid passages is a meeting of the Left Book Club in Bowling's suburb West Bletchly, one of Hilda's "crankish" infatuations because it lets her vaguely feel she is improving her mind without having to pay for it (*CA* 166). It took only one meeting to cure George of leftist illusions. As the nondescript speaker lashed himself and his audience into a fascist-hating, slogan-spouting frenzy, Bowling realized the speaker was just as dangerously amoral as the Fascists were, dishing out "propaganda at you by the hour . . . Hate, hate, hate. Let's all get together and have a good hate . . . [his] vision was . . . smashing people's faces in with a spanner. Fascist faces, of course" (*CA* 175).

After he finished *Coming Up for Air*, Orwell still claimed it was "more or less unpolitical," as much as it could be at that time, describing it generally as pacifist. He communicated his political views, however, through his distaste for "nowadays," the "*ersatz*," (he always used the German term for "phony") frenetic, superheated late-1930s atmosphere which makes this his most political novel prior to *Animal Farm* and *Nineteen Eighty-Four*. After Orwell's difficulties with Gollancz over *Homage to Catalonia*, Orwell suspected some of Gollancz's Communist friends were probably clamoring for the publisher to drop Orwell (Shelden 1991: 309), so he flung down a gauntlet to them in his highly unflattering description of the Left Book Club.

George Bowling's disillusion with all political systems parallels Orwell's own disgust with them—first the laissez-faire capitalism that ruined Bowling's father; the imperialist jingoism that led to World War I and turned ordinary people, Bowling said, into "Bolshies," and finally the vicious communist rabble-rousing. At last Bowling realized that he was doomed, because no air was left for him, like an old carp in a garbage-fouled pool, to come up for any more (*CA* 257). Like Orwell himself, George Bowling also realized that because human beings who desire power are corruptible, every political system, left or right, can be perverted into totalitarianism. Orwell chillingly anticipated *Nineteen Eighty-Four* in Bowling's vision of "The world we're going down into, the . . . hate-world, slogan world. The coloured shirts. The barbed wire . . . The secret cells . . . a million people all cheering for the Leader . . .[but] they hate him so that they want to puke. It's all going to happen" (*CA* 160).

Gloomy as Orwell's view of British life had become, however, *Coming Up for Air* ends on a curiously positive note. Bowling bent to fate and resumed his eternal row with Hilda, but he did return to soldier on rather than reaching for a gun as Flory had. In a minority critical opinion, Orwell's friend Richard Rees claimed Orwell wrote this book in a "blithe and sometimes even optimistic" mood (Gross 88), emotions Orwell invariably exhibited when he had chosen his side, the fight was on, and the enemy was in his sights. Three months after Gollancz published *Coming Up for Air*, Hitler's Panzers rolled into Poland and the biggest fight of Orwell's lifetime was on.

STYLISTIC AND LITERARY DEVICES

Coming Up for Air was Orwell's last conventional novel and the only one in which he used a first person narrator, his major technical experiment here. First person narration allows immediacy and involvement, but an author using it risks excessive subjectivity or even sentimentality. Orwell was evidently trying to refine the inside-outside "window-pane" technique he had admired in Joyce's *Ulysses*, but whether George Bowling is a completely convincing protagonist seems debatable.

Today, critics agree that Bowling is a more complex character than had been acknowledged earlier, "a curious amalgam of attitudes—some of them Orwell's own and others invented" (Hammond 149). By drawing heavily on his own memories and invoking "a complex pattern of impressions and sensations" for the character he gave his own first name, Orwell advanced technically by fusing his materials together "through a *literary* [italics in original] process to achieve an artistically satisfying whole." Orwell also used a technique he had observed in Dickens' *Great Expectations* and *The Pickwick Papers*, having his hero born a decade earlier than his own birth date, distancing the childhood chapters back further into the peaceful nineteenth-century Orwell nostalgically admired (Hammond 150–54) and lyrically described in *Coming Up for Air*, perhaps a symptom of homesickness he felt while writing in Morocco.

On the other hand, Orwell now felt that an author should never yield to the temptation of intruding his personality upon his characters (*CEJL* 4:115). Biographer Michael Shelden agrees, finding Orwell's attempt "to *be* [italics in original]" George Bowling's voice the novel's "one serious defect" and declaring the book succeeds best when Orwell uses his own recognizable voice, not imitating "Fatty" Bowling's. Orwell's attempt to identify with Bowling was another of his experiments with the "window-pane" perspective, but it does not seem to work satisfactorily (Shelden 1991: 311).

Despite his technical experiments in *Coming Up for Air*, Orwell was perfecting his crystalline style as a means of satirizing British suburban life. Orwell was consciously trying to achieve the deceptively simple narrative style he admired in W. Somerset Maugham's work, the power of telling a story "straightforwardly and without frills" (*CEJL* 2:24). In 1940, Orwell claimed that Maugham was the modern novelist who had influenced him most.

Bowling's return to Lower Binfield resembles a similar scene in Maugham's 1930 novel *Cakes and Ale*. Both central characters are disgusted with modernization and dismayed at the loss of their familiar childhood haunts. Orwell, however, was also outraged at the destruction of the values that had shaped his ancestors' lives—"honesty, decency, contentment, concern for the land" by social and technological forces beyond his control (Hammond 155). Bowling's digressions about the evils of modernization reflect Orwell's own savage opinions about British society on the eve of World War II.

ALTERNATIVE CRITICAL PERSPECTIVE: FEMINIST CRITICISM

Feminist critics would pounce with delight on Orwell's portraits of women in *Coming Up for Air*. The most typical feminist reading would analyze these female characters as victims of their male-dominated society, but more aggressive feminist commentators would probably tear Orwell Orpheus-like limb from limb for his supposedly insensitive portrayals of the female characters and their trials.

George's "old Hilda" could be seen as a victim of male economic domination. Her father, by taking up the "white man's burden" and serving the far-flung Empire, doomed her to that class of predatory Englishwomen deprived of careers by their station in life and forced to seize a man—any man— as their only escape from poverty. Hilda's vicious obsession with money, which drives Bowling to engineer his own escape, could be seen as a conditioned response, like Scarlett O'Hara's, to being forced to abandon a comparatively luxurious colonial lifestyle for a greatly reduced income and lowered social status at home. Hilda was never going to go hungry again, but she might starve herself and her family to death doing it.

Feminists would accuse Bowling of heartlessly misusing his adolescent love, the unfortunate Elsie Waters (*CA* 119), since he carelessly discarded her when he went away to war, and more despicably, never considered what twenty-four years could do to both women and men. Elsie's middle-aged appearance depresses him: "a fat hog! . . . This great round-shouldered hag" (*CA* 241, 243). With arrogant male egotism, he refuses to consider that he himself is no longer the lithe young grocery-boy he had been: "No man ever goes to pieces quite so completely as that' " (*CA* 243).

Bowling did reflect on the sad fate of his babysitter Katie, whose sad fate represents the life of lower-class women in the Edwardian England he idealized. Katie came from "a filthy little rat-hole . . . behind the brewery," had a possibly incestuous illegitimate baby at fifteen, and married an itinerant tinker. At twenty-seven, Katie was "a wrinkled old hag of a woman, with her hair coming down and a smoky face" who looked at least fifty years old (*CA* 45–46), tragically aware, like the girl Orwell had seen battling a blocked sewer pipe near Wigan, that her sad lot would never improve. On the other hand, Bowling's mother cooked her Yorkshire puddings and made her jam and died without realizing that "everything they'd believed in was just so much junk" (*CA* 127). Depicting Bowling's mother as incapable of understanding the realities of her situation would, in a feminist view, have been one of Orwell's unkindest male cuts of all.

Each of these female characters could be read by feminists as either a victim or a caricature. As a whole, *Coming Up for Air* might be seen either as Orwell's compassion for a downtrodden segment of society or as a satire on women's foolishness in bringing unhappiness upon themselves. *Coming Up for Air* is full of paradoxes, but Orwell's attitude toward women here seems particularly ambivalent.

THE LION AND THE UNICORN

Immediately before the outbreak of World War II, Orwell was serving in the Home Guard, reviewing a wide variety of books, and writing film and theater criticism for *Time and Tide,* but in the fall of 1940 he produced his best-selling book to that date. *The Lion and the Unicorn* is a 126-page social tract intended to boost British morale. In it, Orwell pays affectionate tribute to traditional English common sense and ferociously indicts Britain's traditional aristocratic rulers (Shelden 1991: 336).

STRUCTURE

Since *The Lion and the Unicorn* is not a novel, it has no fictional story line or plot. It is both a social tract and an extended polemical essay advancing a controversial position. Orwell discusses a wide range of aspects of the English character and attempts to define the possibilities he sees at this dire time for social reform. Significantly, he took his title from the two heraldic beasts that support England's coat of arms. The title *The Lion and the Unicorn* celebrates the quintessentially English sense of tradition, extending from the chivalric heraldry of the Middle Ages to the twentieth century—and probably beyond. The lion, a real animal, represents strength and courage, while the imaginary unicorn represents purity and creativity, forces when in balance symbolically uphold the nation.

The Lion and the Unicorn contains three long essays dealing successively with Britain's past, which Orwell cherished; its perilous wartime present; and its future, which he dreaded unless enormous political and economic shifts could be effected. In Part I, "England, Your England," Orwell offers his definition of English civilization and his reasons for its present peril. Part II, "Shopkeepers at War," presents Orwell's view that capitalism was destroying everything good in Britain. In Part III, "The English Revolution," Orwell draws a blueprint for the only new social order that he felt was capable of saving the country he loved.

As a polemical essay, *The Lion and the Unicorn* of course does not have "character development" in the sense a novel does. In the first section of the book, "England, Your England," however, Orwell carefully defines the overall English character with a survey of the qualities and traits which comprise it. He affectionately concludes that these are first, a distaste for abstract thought, then a desire for personal privacy, gentleness, hatred of militarism, a liking for anacronisms, respect for the rule of law, quiet patriotism, and emotional unity. He also identifies two significant twentieth-century trends, the decay of the English ruling class and the rise of the middle class due to the creation of new technicians and artisans (Hammond 196–97).

In the second section of *The Lion and the Unicorn*, "Shopkeepers at War," Orwell makes a case against capitalism, which he believes cannot work, and for his own kind of socialist society, one now considerably more developed than the one he advocated in *The Road to Wigan Pier*. Orwell advocates a social revolution by ordinary Britishers against "inefficiency, class privilege and the rule of the old" (*LU* 75). The British will overcome Hitler, Orwell maintains, because they are fighting for a better life after the war.

Orwell's third section of *The Lion and the Unicorn*, "The English Revolution," continues his case for a popular socialist movement through a clear definition of the aims of the war which will help bring about that better life. A government able to accomplish these aims will be radically changed, he believes, but it should still carry the characterizing marks that make it English (Hammond 201).

THEMATIC ISSUES: PATRIOTISM AND POLITICAL REVOLUTION

The theme of *The Lion and the Unicorn* might be stated: By celebrating and maintaining their traditional values as individuals, the British people can overcome their outside enemies and destructive internal collective forces, to build themselves a better society through a peaceful social revolution.

By playing on the patriotic expression "England, My England" from W. E. Henley's popular poem "For England's Sake," Orwell was insisting on personal, individual responsibility. "Your England" was the nation of all Englishmen and women, not just the privileged classes. Orwell loved the Edwardian England of his youth, secure in its traditional values—patriotism, civility, courage, respect for individual privacy, unquestioned courage, hatred of war and militarism. He praised the "gentle manners" of the English, their love of flowers, their addiction to hobbies, their ability to draw together in times of supreme crisis, their loathing for the "swaggering officer type," and their incorruptible respect for "the law" (*LU* 11, 14, 20, 22), all characteristics that Orwell drew from his own experience and incorporated into his writing.

England, Orwell felt, was now endangered because its ruling class was rotting; the "idle rich" had turned the land he loved into "the most class-ridden country under the sun . . . a land of snobbery and privilege, ruled largely by the old and silly" (*LU* 33). Its intelligentsia, too, had cut itself off from its roots in the common folk and let itself be "sabotaged" by the Left and its "constipated view of life" (*LU* 49, 45). And yet (and Orwell's "and yet"'s are always highly revealing), the English press, though "deeply dishonest," could not be bribed, while the higher military commanders, drawn from the aristocracy and unable to admit the world and warfare were changing, were still morally sound, ready—like Orwell himself—to be killed defending England (*LU* 43).

If English shopkeepers like George Bowling's father had to risk their lives in war, Orwell felt the war should wipe out the class system and capitalism once and for all (*LU* 55, 59). He was certain that socialism, which he defined here as common ownership of the means of production, could solve problems of production and consumption and bring about a world-state of free and equal human beings, with approximate equality of incomes, political democracy, and abolition of all hereditary privilege, especially in education (*LU* 61–62). For Orwell, this ideal directly opposed the goals of "fascist Germany," a term he invariably used instead of "Nazi Germany" to stress Hitler's authoritarian version of capitalism (Wadhams 123). Orwell believed that the fascist German anti-Semitism and "master race" obsession assumed the inequality of human beings and that fanatical German efficiency presupposed the use of only those socialistic features which enhanced wartime productivity (*LU* 63). Dunkirk, Orwell unequivocally stated, had proved the "utter rottenness" of private capitalism; and he believed the dowager in the Rolls-Royce was more dangerous to British morale than Hitler's whole Luftwaffe was (*LU* 68, 83).

Orwell's solution, "The English Revolution," hinged on the triumph of socialism. He felt it had not worked so far in England because the British Labour

Party concerned itself too much with the prosperity of British capitalism (*LU* 88–89). Now that the war had shown the individual that he was not altogether an individual (*LU* 96), socialism could work in Britain, because patriotism was stronger than class hatred (*LU* 98). On the other hand, Orwell insisted that the "old fashioned proletarian revolution" was now impossible for Britain. He offered instead a six-point recipe for implementing a socialism that he was convinced could work: nationalization of industries, limitation of personal incomes, a democratic educational system, dominion status for India, inclusion of "coloured [*sic*] people" in an Imperial General Council, and formal alliance with victims of fascist power (*LU* 99). Some of Orwell's proposals, like nationalization of industries, became realities shortly after World War II; others, like his notions that the state should impose fifteen–acre limits on ownership of land (*LU* 102) and should suppress Britain's ten thousand private schools, have never been attempted, but his intention, at least, was admirable: to establish a social system capable of respecting the limits of its power. This system, Orwell felt, should be the common man's reward for fighting and winning the common man's war.

Orwell intended that English Socialism should embody the "unmistakable marks" of English civilization, drawing its brain power from a new class of skilled workers, maintaining its tradition of compromise and belief in a law above the state, and disestablishing the Anglican Church but retaining a "vague reverence" for the Christian moral code (*LU* 111–12). In preaching these revolutionary ideals, Orwell rejected not only England's prewar social structure but also Marxism as "a German theory interpreted by Germans" (*LU* 111). Orwell believed that no one "will do our fighting for us" (*LU* 117) (he wrote prior to the Japanese attack on Pearl Harbor), and that going down fighting was far less deadly than some "compromise peace" (*LU* 124). As though he was leading his squad over the top of the trenches at Huesca, Orwell called for England to "go forward or go backward," and out of his faith in traditional English values, he declared "we shall go forward" (*LU* 127).

STYLISTIC AND LITERARY DEVICES

Orwell's direct, easy, conversational style in *The Lion and the Unicorn* is entirely appropriate to his aim of bolstering the patriotic morale of ordinary Englishmen and women during the Battle of Britain. In the opening sentence of "England, Your England," "As I write, highly civilized human beings are flying overhead, trying to kill me" (*LU* 9), Orwell skillfully accomplished several complex purposes in one clear sentence. "I" personalizes the experience of impersonal modern warfare, and Orwell's dramatic use of the present tense, "are flying" and "are trying to kill me," placed himself at equal risk with all the ordinary Londoners being pounded by Hitler's bombers. The bitter irony of "highly civilized" strikes back at the enemy at the same time as it points up the eternal human will-to-war. "As I write," shows that Orwell was fighting the Nazis with his command of language, his weapon of choice to defend himself and his world. Taken as a whole, Orwell's opening sentence speaks volumes about the man, his attitudes, and his values.

The fiery final paragraph of *The Lion and the Unicorn* also demonstrates Orwell's reliance on familiar concrete images to convey a powerful class-system-shattering abstraction:

England has got to be true to herself. . . . The heirs of Nelson and of Cromwell are not in the House of Lords. . . . [They are ordinary people and] at present they are still kept under by a generation of ghosts. . . . By revolution we become more ourselves, not less. (*LU* 126)

By singling out commoners Horatio Nelson and Oliver Cromwell as examples of ordinary Britishers who rose to greatness, Orwell stresses the importance of the individual in opposing outworn and destructive aristocratic systems, "ghosts of a ruling class poisoned by its own decay." *The Lion and the Unicorn* closes on a ringing call for social revolution, "like the spirit of Thomas Jefferson or Tom Paine speaking in a modern voice" (Shelden 1991: 338).

HISTORICAL SETTING

Orwell's *The Lion and the Unicorn* helped bring about an enormous change in British spirits during 1940–41. Quiescent and apathetic during the Chamberlain years, the British now awoke to what Dorothy L. Sayers called an "English war," the kind of heroic, outnumbered combat that had always roused the nation to greatness. In what was arguably his greatest single mistake in judgment, Hitler failed to realize the profound hostility he had aroused in British hearts (Johnson 366). Even while the last British soldiers were being evacuated from Dunkirk, Hitler hoped to make a "reasonable peace" with the British so that he could begin his "great and real task: the confrontation with Bolshevism" (quoted in Johnson 367). Britain opted instead for Churchill and heroism.

Orwell was no stranger to dicey causes, and like Churchill, he marshalled words and sent them into battle. Orwell's words exposed the defeatist and demoralizing elements in British society. First, he worked out his own position regarding the war in three important essays, investigating the directions other writers, like Dickens, Joyce, and Henry Miller, had taken. Orwell concluded that "Good novels are not written by orthodoxy-sniffers, nor by people who are conscience-stricken about their own unorthodoxy. Good novels are written by people who are *not frightened*" [italics in original] (*CEJL* 1:519). During the summer of 1939 he also proved he was not frightened of his critics, even though his mail was censored and police came to confiscate some of his books. He wrote three major and controversial essays, his large-scale study "Charles Dickens"; "Inside the Whale," a penetrating analysis of contemporary writers, including Henry Miller, whose work was then widely considered scandalous; and a pioneering essay on popular culture, "Boys' Weeklies." These essays were published in March 1940 under the title *Inside the Whale*.

In April 1940, Orwell looked back on the eight books he had published over the last eight years and decided to slow up, since he was "incubating an enormous novel, the family saga sort of thing," but at the same time he had to keep busy reviewing to keep food on his table, and he never progressed beyond twenty pages of notes for the huge project he referred to as "The Quick and the Dead" (Crick 262). Had Orwell lived, this work might have become either the first volume of a trilogy capped by *Nineteen Eighty-Four* or "a socialist Forsyte Saga" (Crick 262–63), but he abandoned it to serve his country for three years as a sergeant in the Home Guard. His publisher Fredric Warburg, who had fought as an officer at Passchendaele, served under Orwell as a corporal. Warburg recalled that Orwell was enormously enthusiastic but not terribly competent and nearly blew up his own squad by mistake: "There was practically nothing about the Home Guard that didn't suit Orwell's temperament, until it began to be efficient" (Wadhams 123).

The Lion and the Unicorn was the first volume in Secker and Warburg's Searchlight Series jointly edited by Orwell and Tosco Fyvel, intended "to serve as an arsenal for the manufacture of mental and spiritual weapons needed for the crusade against Nazism" (quoted in Shelden 1991: 336). The book sold over twelve thousand copies and enhanced Orwell's reputation as an effective proponent of democratic socialism (Shelden 1991: 339). More important to Orwell's literary development, it helped him define his own position; the same traditional English qualities, dominated by intensely sincere patriotism, he praised in *The Lion and the Unicorn* were those most deeply embedded in Orwell's own mind and heart.

ALTERNATIVE CRITICAL PERSPECTIVE: PSYCHOLOGY/PSYCHOANALYTICAL THEORY

As established by Freud in the first half of the twentieth century, psychoanalysis holds that human behavior stems from hidden and unconscious motives, thus providing a popular approach to literature. Some psychological/psychoanalytical critics use analysis of an author's unconscious motives to understand and interpret his or her creative process and its artistic products, treating a piece of literature rather like the information that a patient would supply during the therapeutic process.

A psychoanalytical approach to *The Lion and the Unicorn* would take into account both the surface and the hidden motives Orwell had for his position that an English social revolution was necessary. On the surface, Orwell knew that the lives of the working class who would largely have to bear the burden in the coming war were miserable and that some hope of better things ahead for them would be necessary if England was to prevail. In his own unhappy, sick, and frustrated state, Orwell himself needed reassurance that the old values he believed in were worth fighting for.

Psychological/psychoanalytical critics would also feel that the traumatic experiences Orwell underwent at various stages of his early life would have left scars visible in the vehement position he took in *The Lion and the Unicorn*. The psychological wounds inflicted on him at St. Cyprian's and at Eton, where he was made to feel inferior to his wealthier schoolmates, also would have conditioned him against the aristocratic ruling class he denounces in *The Lion and the Unicorn* as outworn and ineffectual. The blows to his ego and his self-respect that he suffered during his tramping days when he had to accept grudging charity from hypocritical representatives of various church groups would have been reflected in the denunciation of the Anglican Church (and others) he makes in *The Lion and the Unicorn*. The Leftist literary establishment, for the most part made up of elitist Oxford and Cambridge men during the 1930s, had greeted many of Orwell's essays and most of his fiction as well as *The Road to Wigan Pier* and *Homage to Catalonia*, the work of his that he then felt was his best, with ridicule and scorn. The psychological scars left by these attacks might have increased Orwell's determination to mount counterassaults in *The Lion and the Unicorn* on "the more soft-boiled [anti-war] intellectuals of the Left" who declared that if England fought the Nazis the English would "go Nazi" themselves (*LU* 111). When in *The Lion and the Unicorn* Orwell celebrated the historical deeds of Horatio Nelson and Oliver Cromwell, commoners who saved England from tyranny, Orwell could have been writing from the deeply felt hurts he believed that members of England's hereditary ruling class had inflicted on him, and he might well have relished the possibility that England's privileged few were committing suicide through their own willful selfishness. The passionate devotion to his country and the equally fervent belief in its working people's resilience that Orwell poured into *The Lion and the Unicorn* seem to have had roots that reached deep into his very soul.

8

All Animals Are Equal,
but . . . : *Animal Farm*

Animal Farm has become Orwell's best-known and best-liked work. When he looked for a publisher for it in February 1944, though, he almost immediately encountered difficulties. The buildup for D-Day was underway, the "Second Front" that Stalin had been demanding from the Allies since 1941. Most British intellectuals wholeheartedly supported the Soviet Union, whose Red Army was diverting Hitler's attention from the Western Front. Gollancz and other British publishers rejected *Animal Farm* because they felt it played into the Nazis' hands by criticizing the Soviets, who, Gollancz told Orwell, had just saved the Allies' necks at Stalingrad (Shelden 1991: 360). Some publishers also shunned *Animal Farm* because of Orwell's contractual obligations to Gollancz. In 1949, Orwell discovered that the Soviets had tried directly to block the publication of *Animal Farm* through a mole (secret agent) in the British Ministry of Information.

After a V-1 rocket destroyed his flat in 1944, Orwell managed to dig the "blitzed" manuscript out of the rubble and took it to T. S. Eliot at Faber and Faber. Eliot missed the book's point completely. Eliot told Orwell that the book didn't need more communism, it needed more pigs with public spirit. The American Dial Press turned it down because they thought it was an animal story for children. By this time Orwell was so desperate he considered publishing *Animal Farm* himself. He eventually submitted it to Fredric Warburg, who had published *Homage to Catalonia* and *The Lion and the Unicorn*. Warburg was delayed by the wartime paper shortage, so *Animal Farm* did not appear in

England until August 17, 1945, after Hitler had been defeated and Stalin's usefulness as a British ally had diminished.

Once published, *Animal Farm* was immediately and astonishingly successful. The British edition sold over 25,000 copies in its first five years, ten times the sales of any of Orwell's previous books. When the American edition appeared in 1946, the start of the Cold War, it sold 590,000 copies in four years and became a popular selection of the U.S. Book-of-the-Month Club. Edmund Wilson praised *Animal Farm* as "absolutely first-rate," declared Orwell a major author, and insisted readers should pick up his earlier, neglected works (quoted in Shelden 1991: 364).

The American success of *Animal Farm* depended largely on its being read simply as anticommunism, but Orwell insisted that his aim had been much broader, not just Soviet Communism but the general corruption of socialist ideals caused by the lust for power. Since the 1930s, fascism and communism were widely considered polar opposites (Zwerdling 47), but Orwell was one of few observers to see that these systems were actually more similar than different, especially in achieving their goals through propaganda. He also fleshed out their fearsome common denominator of authoritarian autocracy in four-footed form as the ruling swine of *Animal Farm*. Eventually, due largely to George Orwell, the world came to know such systems as totalitarianism.

Animal Farm has enormous literary merit. It is totally different from any of Orwell's previous works, the only one in which he did not insert himself as a narrator or a principal character or a commentator on the action. On the surface, the story of barnyard beasts who revolt against their cruel master in order to run their own society is so simply told that it can be enjoyably read by youngsters, who respond enthusiastically to Orwell's obvious affection for animals, but it can also be read as a clever and powerful political satire of Stalinism and as a sophisticated allegory warning against the dangerous abuses of political power and the necessity of placing limits upon it. Orwell's fluent, easygoing, highly approachable style is enriched by sly, generally good-natured humor influenced by his wife Eileen, who listened and commented delightedly each night as Orwell read his day's work to her. The humor here is mostly good-natured, which makes the scenes in which the ruling pigs reveal their ruthlessness and treachery even more shocking. Overall, Orwell claimed that *Animal Farm* was the first book in which he tried, knowing exactly what he was doing, to fuse political and artistic purpose into one literary entity (*CEJL* 1:7).

PLOT

Animal Farm also "is the only book which shows what Orwell could do when he had made up his mind about a subject all the way through" (Gross 126). He said that the central idea for this book came to him immediately after he escaped from the Communists in Spain (Shelden 1991: 364, 368): How could the genuine revolution he had fought for there have let itself fall to a foreign dictator? A little later, he saw a boy near Wallingford whipping a huge cart-horse and reflected that if only such animals realized their strength, humans could never dominate them, comparing animals to Britain's exploited workers (*CEJL* 3:110). He also realized how damaging the Soviet myth had become to western socialism. All these ideas became his masterful fable of farm animals who eject their cruel human owner only to be betrayed by their power-hungry leaders, the pigs.

Orwell's plot is simple. After drunken Farmer Jones, owner of Manor Farm, had been exploiting his farm animals for years, an old boar named Major tells them his dream of expelling Jones and ruling themselves, inspiring them with the catchy hymn "Beasts of England" sung to the tune of "My Darling Clementine." Soon after, Major dies, and two younger boars, Snowball and Napoleon, who have taught themselves to read and write, formulate the creed of Animalism and secretly teach it to the others. One day Jones forgets to feed them and the animals spontaneously revolt, expelling Jones and his wife and Moses the raven. The animals begin to build their new life.

The intelligent pigs take responsibility for organizing the others, but they also take over decision-making. One of their first decisions, to take the cows' milk for themselves, is the first sign of their corruption which will inevitably lead to the ruin of everything else. Their most devoted listeners are the draft horses Boxer and Clover who have slow wits but the great strength needed to build the new society.

At first the animals' revolutionary enterprise prospers and they are happier than they had ever been before, but soon Napoleon begins to quarrel with Snowball, who has ideas about the animals' self-government quite different from Napoleon's. Napoleon exerts his will to power through his subordinate pigs, especially his propaganda-maker Squealer. They help him convince the other animals to work harder and harder on less and less food, and their lives become much more miserable than they had been under Farmer Jones.

From his exile at the Willingdon pub, Mr. Jones plots with Farmer Pilkington and Farmer Frederick, who fear that the animals' rebellion may spread to their own farms, to recapture Manor Farm. On October 12, subsequently called the Battle of the Cowshed, Snowball skillfully leads the animals against the human invasion, losing only one sheep, taking a wound himself, and receiving the medal of "Animal Hero, First Class," with Boxer, whose great strength convinces the humans to retreat.

During the following winter, Napoleon begins to consolidate his own power, using the windmill Snowball wants to build as a pretext for ejecting his rival. Napoleon orders a purge of animals who have opposed him, commanding his loyal dogs to slay several and forcing Snowball into exile. This allows Napoleon to become an absolute dictator, reshaping Animalism and history through his subordinate swine and controlling the remaining animals through the young dogs he has trained to be loyal only to him. When Farmer Frederick successfully tricks Napoleon, the animals have to fight the Battle of the Windmill against the humans, a costly victory which exhausts and depresses them. Life at Animal Farm becomes virtually indistinguishable from life at Manor Farm.

Shortly before he is supposed to retire, Boxer collapses from overwork. Napoleon has him carted off to slaughter, using the price of the poor old horse to buy whiskey for himself and his swinish comrades. Finally the remaining weak and underfed animals sadly watch Napoleon and his followers partying noisily on their hind legs with the humans they now strongly resemble—the incarnation of Napoleon's motto:

ALL ANIMALS ARE EQUAL
BUT SOME ANIMALS ARE MORE EQUAL THAN OTHERS. (*AF* 133)

The animals' sad fate is a tragedy they brought on themselves. Their first mistake was abandoning their right to decide who would have the cows' milk and the apples. They made this mistake because most of them could not read or write or profit from the bitter lesson of history that, as Lord Acton famously put it, power tends to corrupt, and absolute power corrupts absolutely. A few, like Benjamin the donkey, knew better but chose not to act, and so all the good animals were vulnerable to the wicked pigs, who used their facility with language to bring about an evil totalitarian system of government for their own selfish purposes.

HISTORICAL-BIOGRAPHICAL CONTEXT

As the Second World War stretched into a long and deadly struggle, Orwell's perspective began to darken, while his physical condition deteriorated sharply. He was, in fact, facing a death sentence, because he had tuberculosis ("TB" or "consumption"), which is prevalent in overcrowded slums and is aggravated by stress.

Orwell's tendency to overwork also escalated during the war. In December 1940, the *Partisan Review*, a left-wing American journal sympathetic to Trotskyism, asked him to contribute "London Letters" exploring aspects of British politics and attitudes that American readers couldn't learn from news reports (*CEJL* 2:49). In his "London Letters," Orwell could refer to any personality and be as gossipy and outspoken as he liked (Shelden 224), probably adding to the animosity he aroused among the British intelligentsia.

Meanwhile the war was changing profoundly. Hitler suspended his plan to invade Britain and instead on June 22, 1941, fatally launched a surprise attack on Stalin, his former treaty partner. Not only did the Nazi invasion of the U.S.S.R. help destroy the Nazi war machine, but it also carried Soviet totalitarianism straight to the heart of Europe (Johnson 376). It also brought British intellectuals, who had criticized Stalin's alliance with Hitler, back into the ranks of Stalin's admirers and sympathizers.

Hitler tried to "cleanse" the U.S.S.R. by issuing the "Commissar Order" of June 6, 1941, calling for ruthless measures against Bolsheviks and Jews, executing about 500,000 Russian Jews and an equal number of Russians. This proved Stalin's salvation. Being betrayed by Hitler had undone Stalin badly, but it did not stop him from carrying out a war on his own people so terrifying that prisoners in the Soviet Gulag concentration camps volunteered for front line duty as preferable to their captivity. Stalin turned the Nazi invasion into the Soviet Union's "Great Patriotic War," calling for relentless guerrilla warfare and a scorched earth policy, even allowing religious observances again and cynically invoking the same saints and warriors of Imperial Russia that Communists customarily reviled. The Russian people responded with unparalleled heroism and sacrifice. The Red Army's costly victory at Stalingrad sparked a mighty Soviet drive that by 1944 stretched deep into Poland and Hungary and forced the Axis armies out of the Balkans.

George Orwell was one of the few British writers who realized that the so-called "Great Patriotic War" was only the latest of a terrible series of sufferings Stalin had brought on the people of the Soviet Union. Orwell commented in a 1946 *Polemic* article that he never could have been disappointed by Stalin and his government, because he had never expected anything good from them, an opinion he said he had held since the 1920s, when he had carefully studied Marx's works, which he fundamentally admired. Orwell's own bitter experience with Soviet-backed Communism in Spain had taught him that Soviet Communism had unacceptable aims and methods of implementing them. In Spain, Orwell had also become suspicious about internal Soviet policies. Orwell's views on Soviet Communism "progressed from doubt to certainty, from vague distrust to positive rejection" (Zwerdling 50).

In the late 1920s and early 1930s, many Western socialists ecstatically praised the supposed Soviet utopia, or at least those wonders Stalin allowed them to see, but by the mid-1930s evidence of Soviet state-organized terrorism was beginning to surface. In reviewing Eugene Lyons' scathing 1938 exposé of Stalinism, *Assignment in Utopia*, Orwell wondered, "Is it Socialism, or is it a peculiarly vicious form of state-capitalism [*sic*]?" His satiric answer foreshadowed the satiric technique of *Animal Farm*. He translated Stalin's persecution of Trotsky and the Moscow show trials into a wickedly funny hypothetical English context, tossing Churchill into exile in Portugal and attributing "dastardly acts of sabotage" to him, like causing an outbreak of hoof-and-mouth disease in the Royal racing stables (*CEJL* 1:333). In 1940, Orwell openly declared that since 1928, Soviet policy had simply been an instrument to keep the ruling clique in power. Furthermore, he felt that the Soviet Union and Nazi Germany were rapidly evolving towards the same system—"a form of oligarchical [*sic*] collectivism" (*CEJL* 2:25, 26).

What Orwell realized and most Western leftists ignored was that Stalin was stoking a monumental lust for power. Stalin was not Russian; his father was a Georgian shoemaker and his pious mother was Armenian. Stalin was arrested as a Bolshevik revolutionary and exiled for life to Siberia in 1913, but after the 1917 October Revolution he became People's Commissar for Nationalities in Lenin's cabinet. He lay low just before the revolution and during the 1918–20 Civil War when the Bolsheviks solidified their control of the country, but in 1922 he was elected General Secretary (chief executive) of the U.S.S.R.'s ruling Communist Party.

When Lenin died in 1924 Stalin began to eliminate his rivals, principally Leon Trotsky, at that time the strongest proponent of international communism. Under Lenin, Trotsky had functioned effectively, organizing the victorious Red Army in the 1918–20 Civil War. Trotsky also led the leftist opposition to Stalin, so by 1927, Stalin had Trotsky expelled from the Soviet Communist Party. Stalin then engineered the murder of popular Leningrad Communist leader Sergei Mironovich Kirov and blamed it on Trotsky, exiling him from the Soviet Union. Continually protesting his innocence and hurling counter-charges at Stalin, Trotsky lived abroad until he was killed in 1940 by a mysterious axe-murderer who had wormed himself into Trotsky's confidence.

The murder of Kirov gruesomely illustrates Stalin's methods, which Orwell paralleled in Napoleon's bloodthirsty reprisals against his enemies. Just before the Seventeenth Communist Party Congress in 1934, some Soviet leaders secretly discussed replacing Stalin with Kirov, whose sincerity, enthusiastic perception, and energy had won Party members' hearts (Antonov-Ovseyenko 79). This sealed Kirov's fate. While Stalin effusively maintained his public affection for Kirov, he directed the secret police to eliminate him, and by the end of 1937, all of Kirov's former supporters and Stalin's former corulers, Kamenev and Zinoviev, had been "tried" and executed. In four years, Stalin removed his main rival and many other prominent Party leaders, began the annihilation of the Leninist Old Guard, and intimidated the entire Soviet population, all the while publicly praising Kirov to the skies. The Soviet people knew what had happened, but the scope of Stalin's terrorism ensured that they dared not rebel

(Antonov-Ovseyenko 103), just as most of Orwell's animals knuckled under to Napoleon after he had some sheep and hens killed as "examples."

STYLISTIC AND LITERARY DEVICES

Eileen may have contributed significantly to the gently humorous tone of much of *Animal Farm*, a tone unprecedented and unequaled in Orwell's fiction. In his more vehement passages, however, Orwell unleashed his talent for ferocious Swiftian satire, the variety of irony which pokes fun at a societal evil in order to correct it. Irony depends on the perception of incongruity, the difference between what is and what ought to be, and Orwell, with Eileen's encouragement, lodged some memorable direct hits on his swinish targets, showing Napoleon hoggishly slurping his refreshments from Farmer Jones' Crown Derby soup tureen and Snowball idealistically attempting to establish the cows' Clean-Tail League.

Orwell's satire was reinforced by his choice of an ancient literary form, the animal fable, a short allegorical tale that points to a moral truth. Starting with Aesop in fifth-century B.C. Greece and flourishing in such modern works as Kipling's *Jungle Books* and *Just So Stories,* the animal fable is a special kind of allegory that satirically portrays the follies of mankind. Allegory, the favorite teaching device of the largely illiterate Middle Ages, is a narrative form of extended metaphor, an implicit one-to-one comparison between concrete objects, characters, and actions and abstract meanings outside the narrative itself. The allegory sets up a dual interest, the concrete surface story and the author's abstract message (theme), which is independent of the surface story's action and embodies moral, religious, social, or political significance.

The farm animals' successful revolt and their leaders' subsequent betrayal of them forms Orwell's simple surface story, told with remarkable economy, exquisite wit, and enormous insight into the evil machinations of the Soviets, who were held in high esteem by the British intelligentsia during the 1930s and World War II, as well as illuminating the features and motives of totalitarianism.

CHARACTER DEVELOPMENT

Orwell said that he had sweated hard to achieve *Animal Farm* (Warburg 58). In this book, he unabashedly revealed his love for animals and meticulously portrayed their personalities. This was a culmination of a lifelong tendency to use animals and imagery about them in his works. In his posthumous autobiographical essay "Such, Such Were the Joys," he indicated that most of his good memories up to about the age of twenty were related in some way to animals

(*CEJL* 4:86). He also used a great deal of animal imagery in his novels, describing many characters, especially the unpleasant ones, as beasts. Conversely, he was able to endow animals with convincingly human emotions. The animal characters of *Animal Farm* are not just cartoon figures but completely credible individuals (Hammond 163).

Animal Farm also continues the character structure Orwell had been portraying from the start—a group of underprivileged and abused protagonists and a group of their own kind who betray and prey upon them. Both groups are trapped by the implacable lust for power, which encourages exploiters to misuse the exploited and debases the masters far more than the honest beings they dominate. Orwell's revolutionary animal society corresponds perfectly to the socio-political structure of the Soviet Union.

Manor Farm: the Soviet Union, the "workers' paradise"

Mr. Jones: Tsar Nicholas II, whom the Communists drove from the throne and killed

Major: Karl Marx, whose theories sparked the Communist revolution

Boxer: the Soviet workers, largely illiterate and thus easily manipulated

Napoleon, the only Berkshire boar on the farm: Stalin, a scheming Georgian who dominated the Russian Communists

Snowball: Trotsky, who insisted on "snowballing" the worldwide Socialist revolution and who was accused of vast anti-Stalin plots

Squealer: *Pravda* ("Truth"), the official Communist newspaper, preaching the Party line

Minimus: Mayakovsky, a poet who prostituted his art for Party purposes

The Pigs: the Bolsheviks who launched the October Revolution

The Dogs: the Soviet secret police (successively the Cheka, OGPU, NKVD, KGB)

Moses the crow: the Russian Orthodox Church, promising its followers paradise while allying itself with the Communists to stay alive

Mollie, the pretty mare: the Tsarist White Russians who drained Russia for their own luxury

Farmer Pilkington: capitalistic Churchill/Britain, which the Russians distrust

Farmer Frederick: militaristic Hitler/Germany, which the Russians fear and hate

Benjamin the donkey: cynical Jewish philosophers

The farm house: the Kremlin, where plots are hatched to corrupt Marxist aims

The Rebellion: the Bolshevik Revolution

The Battle of the Cowshed: the anti-Communist invasion of Russia in 1918–19

The windmill: Stalin's Five-Year Plans, designed to industrialize the Soviet Union

The Battle of the Windmill: the German invasion of 1941

"Beasts of England": the rousing Communist anthem "l'Internationale"

Orwell's friend Hugh Kingsmill noted that Orwell "only wrote sympatheti-cally about human beings when he regarded them as animals" (Bright-Holmes 374). His most sympathetically-drawn animal protagonists in *Animal Farm* were Boxer, the powerful draft horse, and Clover, a stout motherly mare. Though Boxer was not very bright, he was widely respected for his good na-ture, his dependability, and his willingness to work harder and harder (*AF* 26), qualities which the ruling pigs constantly abused. Smitten by the simple social-istic ideals of "Beasts of England"—freedom from cruel human masters, enough barley, hay, oats, and sweet water for all—Boxer takes on the heaviest labor of building the new society, aware that he should learn to read but putting it off until too late. Under his personal mottoes, "I will work harder" and "Na-poleon is always right," he hauls stone until his mighty lungs collapse, going blindly to his death because he cannot read the letters spelling out the butcher's name on the van that carries him away.

Orwell completely avoided sentimentality, the usual pitfall of animal sto-ries, by depicting Boxer's own shortcomings unsparingly. Boxer is a round character with the capacity to surprise, not just a stupid hard-working slave. He feels remorseful when he thinks he killed a stable boy in the Battle of the Cow-shed, and he puzzles over Napoleon's reshaping of history to defame Snowball, who, Boxer knows, had led the animals bravely against Farmer Jones in the same confrontation. Boxer's great failing is the lack of sufficient intelligence and education to sift truth from Napoleon's propaganda. His female counter-part Clover, who can read a little, distrusts the pigs' distortion of Animalism, but she lacks the strength, imagination, and daring to act on her suspicions. She saves herself from liquidation by keeping quiet, but she dooms herself to slavery.

Clover remains silent, Benjamin the donkey philosophically grieves for his friend Boxer, Mollie the pretty carriage mare defects to Mr. Pilkington for a few ribbons and lumps of sugar, and the sheep are too stupid to do anything but bleat out the slogans the pigs teach them. Moses the black raven, absent during the early period of the animals' revolt, suddenly returns, preaching a Sugar Candy Mountain afterlife for all animals who believe in Napoleon's creed and meekly accept Napoleon's selfish leadership. The few who dare to rebel, like the black Minorca pullets, are savaged by the new generation of hounds Napoleon separates from their parents and raises to be loyal to himself alone.

Orwell treated Boxer and Clover with relatively gentle humor, but he poured out his most scathing satire on Napoleon and his hoggish hangers-on. Significantly, Napoleon is the only Berkshire boar on Manor Farm. The Berk-shire, a dish-faced long-bodied black hog with white face and feet, is named for the English county where the breed was developed, a prime swine-raising area also home to Windsor, the British Royal Residence, so the Berkshire is known throughout Britain as the Royal Swine—a clear indication of Napoleon's aims. Conspicuous by his absence from the Battle of the Cowshed, the fierce-looking Napoleon is not a military strategist but a corrupt politician, distorting language in order to manipulate all the other animals through his clever literate fellow pigs. Napoleon shapes the younger pigs' selfish personalities and makes them his closest associates, putting one, Squealer, in charge of circulating Napoleon's plans and pronouncements through the animal ranks and "explaining" them to poor puzzled Boxer. At the outset, if Boxer had only realized the difference between what Napoleon was saying and what really was so, he could easily have kicked the Berkshire bully to Sugar Candy Mountain.

Napoleon also shrewdly sniffed out real or imagined plots against himself and his regime. When Boxer defends Snowball's heroic conduct at the Battle of the Cowshed and a few daring pigs protest Napoleon's abolition of the animals' Sunday Meetings, Napoleon enacts a swift, terrible vengeance. At his shrill squeal, his loyal dogs fall upon four of the pigs while others assault Boxer, who easily pins one hound down with his enormous hoof. Then, looking to Napoleon for guidance, he lets the dog go. First the four unfortunate pigs, then the three rebellious hens, a greedy grain-stealing goose, and several empty-headed sheep confess to crimes they might or might not have committed—all allegedly under Snowball's long-distance direction. The dogs slay them on the spot, "And so the tale of confessions and executions went on, until there was a pile of corpses lying before Napoleon's feet and the air was heavy with the smell of blood, which had been unknown there since the expulsion of Jones" (*AF* 93). In this fearsome passage, Orwell interrupts the gentle tone of his narrative to shift into bitter realism.

Snowball, who had masterminded the Battle of the Cowshed and fought bravely, bears the brunt of Napoleon's envious wrath. Snowball was more lively than Napoleon and he had a greater facility with language, but he did not seem to have the same strength of personality. He tirelessly tries to organize the animals into Committees which Napoleon rejects in favor of training the young, especially the submissive dogs, according to his own principles. Some of Snowball's initiatives, like the Re-education of Wild Comrades, fail because they contradict the nature of the animals they were supposed to "improve," but some of his other ideas, particularly his literacy campaign, succeed dramatically. Snowball also reduces the original Seven Animal Commandments to one principle: "Four legs good, two legs bad," which the silly sheep bleat mindlessly all day long.

Squealer the propagandizing pig and Benjamin the elderly donkey represent the two extremes of the animals' involvement with the revolution.

Squealer opportunistically uses his glib tongue and gift for writing to revise the theory and history of Animalism according to Napoleon's wishes. Benjamin, on the other hand, keeps his distance from the revolution, working slowly and obstinately but not risking anything by openly taking a position. Benjamin's invariable comment is, "Donkeys live a long time"; he has seen everything and survived by keeping his furry nose clean. He does try to save his friend Boxer from the butcher's wagon, but his efforts prove too little and too late.

Orwell made the humans in his story just as reprehensible as the swine who exploited their fellow beasts. The drunkards Farmer Jones and his wife bring their difficulties on themselves. Neighboring Farmer Pilkington of Foxwood connives with Napoleon against wily Mr. Frederick of Pinchfield Farm, who sadistically misuses his animals and even cheats the cunning Napoleon. Pilkington hypocritically praises Napoleon while they drink up the profits of Animal Farm, insisting that Pilkington and his friends have their own lower classes to exploit, just as Napoleon has his lower animals (*AF* 136). Humans and pigs share a lust to dominate the less fortunate that makes the two groups virtually indistinguishable. Malcolm Muggeridge suggested to Orwell that at the end of the novel, a herd of British fellow travelers (Communist sympathizers), like "the infamous 'Red Dean' of Canterbury and writer Kingsley Martin should come on the scene on all fours." Orwell laughed, but he didn't use the suggestion (Wolfe 226–28).

THEMATIC ISSUES

The simple-appearing story of *Animal Farm* conveys a complicated theme: no revolution promising equality and democracy can achieve its lofty aims because all revolutions tend to produce ruling elites which become corrupt through their thirst for power. Once firmly entrenched through terrorism and the perversion of language, they ruthlessly destroy their opposition.

The question Orwell explored through most of his life was stamped into his very being by the Communists' suppression of POUM in Spain: How are the wicked able to exploit the honest and the idealistic? His answer was: They do it through terror and the perversion of language.

Animal Farm superbly explores the terror tactics of totalitarianism, which depend heavily upon the perversion of language by unscrupulous leadership. Orwell was familiar with Soviet tactics from books like Andre Gide's *Retour de l'U.R.S.S. [Return to the Soviet Union]* (1936) and Eugene Lyons' *Assignment in Utopia*, both written by people who had visited the U.S.S.R. thinking they would find a workers' paradise and discovered instead "a terror-ridden state" (Zwerdling 50). An even stronger influence on Orwell, however, was his own experiences— being hunted by the Communists on the streets of Barcelona and having his friends imprisoned and tortured there, and then returning to an England whose intellectuals refused to believe that such things were taking place.

Orwell also had direct personal experience of how language could be used to shape human responses. After years of observation, experience, hard work, and self-discipline, after scores of book reviews and essays where he had to crystallize his opinions before sitting down to the typewriter, Orwell had developed his characteristically clean, lucid, economical prose style into a finely-honed instrument perfectly suited to the satiric allegory form he chose for *Animal Farm*. Because he had worked so hard to develop his own writing as a vehicle for social, economic, and political change, Orwell profoundly respected the shaping power that language can exert over human society. *Animal Farm* arose from his desire to expose the truth about the perversion of language by totalitarianism in general and by the Soviet Union in particular.

Language is a two-way street: some write or speak while others read or listen, and for effective communication, speakers and listeners then have to change roles. In *Animal Farm*, the wicked pigs, who like most revolutionaries have a facility with language, do almost all of the speaking and writing, while the honest workers Boxer and Clover read and say very little, and they do not write at all. The wily old boar Major, allegorically representing Karl Marx, shares his dream of an improved society with the beast-citizens of drunken Mr. Jones' Manor Farm, which stands for Russia drained by its extravagant tsars. Major inspires his fellow animals with the rousing hymn "Beasts of England," adding the emotional power of a communally-sung anthem to his appealing message, but the fearsome Napoleon/Stalin abolishes "Beasts of England" (the Communist hymn "L'Internationale"), replacing it with a feeble made-for-the-occasion ditty composed by his tame poet Minimus/Mayakovsky. Under Stalin a whole generation of writers grew up mindlessly glorifying the Great Leader. Those writers who refused, like Pasternak, Akhmatova, and Mandelstam, were silenced or deported or executed (Shentalinsky 103).

Not only did Napoleon/Stalin smother genuine artists and reward the mediocre, he also molded language to his evil purposes through Squealer/*Pravda*, which rewrote Major/Marx's socialist commandments in support of Napoleon's totalitarian aims. Faced with the repression of truth in art and in their news media, Orwell's animals failed to see through the lies for a variety of reasons, all fatal to their freedom. The silly sheep, like Soviet Communists and their sympathizers throughout the world, believed everything the regime told them. Boxer and Clover were as easily rendered helpless as the Soviet workers were because the horses/workers lacked the ability to read well enough to recognize the regime's lies, the intelligence to interpret their observations accurately, the time to learn to read perceptively, and the judgment to recognize evil when it took advantage of their trusting good nature. Benjamin, like some cynical European philosophers, had the intellectual equipment to sift right from wrong, but he closed his eyes to the regime's excesses until too late—whereupon he disappeared from the last pages of *Animal Farm*, perhaps also loaded into one of the vehicles camouflaged as butchers' vans that the Soviet secret police always used for their late-night arrests.

Soviet-style distortions of truth through the perversion of language ran as rampant in the Communist Party as on Animal Farm. After his exile, Snowball/Trotsky was unmercifully vilified despite his heroic service to the 1917 revolution and international communism. The pigs like Squealer, representing the Soviet press and intelligentsia, used their considerable mental talents to blind the less gifted others, while Napoleon/Stalin, by directing the education of the young himself, perverted the fidelity of the new generation of dogs into a fearsome secret police instrument of his ferocious amoral will, savaging everyone like Kirov who stood in his way.

For Orwell, the Soviet technique of constantly rewriting history to make it conform to their present aims was one of the most sinister new manifestations of the Soviets' will to power. He had already noted in *Homage to Catalonia* that no unbiased account of the Barcelona uprising would ever be possible because future historians would have nothing to work with but "accusations and party propaganda" (*HC* 160). By 1942, in his essay "Looking Back on the Spanish War," Orwell had generalized his experience in Barcelona into the fear that "the very concept of objective truth is fading out of the world" (*CEJL* 2:258). When he projected that fear in the cautionary fable *Animal Farm,* he clearly demonstrated the danger of rewriting history. If the animals had remembered that they had had the strength to carry out their heroic rebellion, they could have easily overthrown Napoleon, so the dictator systematically revamped actual events in order to erase that threat forever, even secretly rewriting the Seven Commandments on the barn door, reshaping history by perverting language.

After the 1950s, the reasons for the success of *Animal Farm*, especially in the United States, changed radically. The initial admiration for the novel as a political satire, a one-to-one condemnation of Stalinism, gradually developed into an understanding of the tendency toward totalitarianism inherent in any and every political system, and then into profound respect for the moral and even spiritual positions Orwell presented in the novel.

While Orwell's primary goal in *Animal Farm* was to show that the Soviets had dramatically and sadistically failed to carry out the idealistic promises of socialism, he also intended the novel to unveil the inherent dangers of all totalitarian systems. By doing so, he gave this work a profound moral dimension which some early reviewers, even sympathetic commentators, like Cyril Connolly, missed (Connolly, 1945: 216). Through his highly sympathetic treatment of most of the animals, Orwell again put himself squarely on the side of the oppressed, where he always stood, no matter whether they were beasts, or children, or the poor, and vehemently against the oppressors, whether they were farmers, teachers, British colonial officials, or party bosses (Woodcock 194–95).

The moral reading of *Animal Farm* developed from Orwell's stinging portrayal of the potential for corruption in political leadership. The animal fable, in which each beast represents one aspect of human nature that the author wants to analyze, was tailor-made for Orwell to analyze the various moral decisions made within a political system. Critical views on the moral dimension of *Animal Farm*, however, varied greatly. T. S. Eliot, who seemed never to understand Orwell or his works, complained that *Animal Farm* failed to excite sympathy with what Orwell wanted, a decent, equitable society, but critic Alex Zwerdling accurately recognized that in *Animal Farm* Orwell not only tried to achieve a realistic view of revolution, he was presenting his moral position. Zwerdling noted that in Orwell's important essay on Dickens, Orwell distinguished between the moralist, who insists that social institutions cannot be changed without "a change of heart," and the revolutionary who wants to turn institutions upside down. According to Zwerdling, at the moment "when a given revolution has more to preserve than to transform . . . it is ripe for the moralist's exposé" (Zwerdling 93).

Although Orwell never espoused any conventional religious belief, his deep concern with spirituality in its broadest sense also animates *Animal Farm*. He often drew analogies between pre-World War II British Socialism and the Roman Catholic Church: both emphasized official dogma and insisted on a priestly caste that dominates its followers by interposing itself between the ordinary persons and truth (Zwerdling 45). In *Animal Farm*, Napoleon and his pig-followers make a pseudo-religion out of "the truth" that they claim has been revealed to them alone. They pass it on to the other beasts, insisting that Snowball knows "the truth" and is rebelling against it for his own selfish reasons. Moreover, the Roman Catholic Church did not abolish its *Index* of prohibited books until 1961 and continues its system of censorship, and the Soviet Union, until its dissolution in 1991, practiced a comprehensive system of supervision of manuscripts prior to state publication—the only kind allowed.

Still more broadly, Steven Greenblatt in 1965 advanced a psychological interpretation of *Animal Farm* as an expression of Orwell's loss of faith in democratic socialism, concluding that the novel's major concern was not the Russian Revolution but "the essential horror of the human condition" (Greenblatt 59). In *Animal Farm*, Orwell condemned the West as roundly as he did the Soviets, because the pigs do not become monsters, they come to resemble rival human beings, Mr. Pilkington who represents British Capitalism and Mr. Frederick who personifies National Socialism (Nazism). Orwell thus shows communism as no better or worse than capitalism or fascism, since all three, like the promise of sweet eternal life on Sugar Candy Mountain which Moses the crow preaches, are merely illusions leaders use to satisfy their greed and lust for power and divert the minds of the suffering masses. "The horror of both *Animal Farm* and the later *1984* is precisely the cold, orderly, predictable process by which decency, happiness, and hope are systematically and ruthlessly crushed" (Greenblatt 66).

In the horrifying passage of *Animal Farm* where the animals "confess" to trumped-up crimes and are summarily liquidated by Napoleon's dogs, Lee sees "the very essence of this strange psycho-political phenomenon of our times, the ritualistic, honestly believed but obviously spurious confession" (Lee 127) that however dismaying is still subsidiary to the denial of objective reality shown when Napoleon deliberately falsifies history.

Orwell himself claimed in "Why I Write" (1946) that *Animal Farm* was the first book in which he consciously tried to fuse his political and artistic purposes into a coherent whole. Most readers believe that he succeeded on at least one other level—allegorical, moral, or spiritual—as well as the concrete level of his little animal tale, but leftist commentators predictably find Orwell's views unpalatable. Stephen Sedley, writing (ironically) in the year 1984, claimed that *Animal Farm* was unsound both ideologically and as a literary work. Sedley believed that "it is or ought to be the experience of every socialist that it is not shared assumptions but shared experience that makes good literature a humanising [*sic*] and encouraging force" (Sedley 155). In comparing Orwell to Swift, Sedley accuses Orwell of lacking humor and he mistakenly sees Orwell's premise as a claim that in politics people are no better than animals. Sedley further insists that *Animal Farm* offers little that is creative or original. He instead trumpets out the customary leftist accusation that in denouncing the Soviet Union, Orwell was preaching "a virulent and often unreasoning anti-communism" (Sedley 162). In his preface to the Ukrainian edition of *Animal Farm*, rather than preaching, Orwell refused to comment on *Animal Farm*, preferring the novel to speak for itself—as indeed it does so brilliantly.

ALTERNATE CRITICAL PERSPECTIVE: ECONOMIC DETERMINISM

Economic determinism was one of the major political concepts of the nineteenth century. According in Karl Marx, the primary influence on human life was economic, the drive to possess or control goods. Therefore, human society was always a clash between the capitalist class (the "haves") and the working class (the "have nots"). Literature that derives from this theory always shows individuals caught up in the class struggle, so the struggle of the beasts in *Animal Farm* to eject Farmer Jones and create their own society is a classic class conflict.

Economic determinist literature, sometimes called "proletarian literature," also emphasizes characters from the lower class—the poor and oppressed laborers who have to spend their lives in endless drudgery and misery. The animals' wretched condition under Jones—their poor and inadequate food, their hard work, the threat of whips, the lack of adequate education and decent retirement—involved complaints that determinists justifiably lodge against the exploiters of the working class.

The passages of *Animal Farm* which describe poor Boxer's hitching himself to mercilessly heavy loads of stone for the windmill, endlessly plodding back and forth until his lungs give out, are classic economic deterministic descriptions of the burdens of the workers—the crucial difference between Orwell's novel and a Marxist proletarian novel being that Boxer, deluded by Napoleon's propaganda, is not the victim of cruel capitalists; deluded by propaganda, he takes the lethal burdens upon himself.

In the initial period of their revolution, the good beasts of *Animal Farm* are successful. Determinists would point to this as proof that the original ideal of revolution was beneficial and indeed necessary. In addition, determinists would see the "outside" forces of capitalistic Farmer Pilkington (representing Britain) and sadistic Farmer Frederick (representing Nazi Germany) as "ganging up" on the animals. In the determinist view, such outside capitalistic forces would be largely responsible for derailing Major's revolutionary dream.

Determinists might also interpret *Animal Farm* in light of the exploitation of the Third World by industrialized nations with the connivance of Third World leaders themselves. Such a reading would treat corrupt Third World leaders as "Napoleons," who through their charisma and talent with words are able to rise to positions of power, and then drain off the resources of their countries into Swiss bank accounts, while their impoverished citizens gaze longingly through the windows of luxurious palaces at their rulers banqueting in opulence—and starve.

9

In Front of Our Noses:
Nineteen Eighty-Four

In the last few years of his life, Orwell drove himself furiously. As a rule, the more he fictionalized his experiences, the longer it took him to turn them into books, so his more successful fiction needed a long time to gestate. In 1943, he had outlined a work tentatively titled "The Last Man in Europe." Wracked with tuberculosis, he completed it in November 1948, and it became *Nineteen Eighty-Four*, his last and most powerful novel.

Under grueling physical and emotional conditions, Orwell wrote most of *Nineteen Eighty-Four* at Barnhill, a drafty old house he bought on the remote Hebridean island of Jura, though he spent the brutal winter of 1946–47 in London. He was looking for a wife, but woman after woman turned him down. Because his lung condition was deteriorating so badly, his friend David Astor obtained the new U.S. drug streptomycin for him, but the side effects proved too violent for Orwell's weakened state.

Orwell's literary success came too late, and he knew it. In January 1949, he and Warburg decided on a title for his new book, reversing the last two digits of the year he had finished it. He at last found a wife, Sonia Brownell, to take care of his literary estate, though he had plans for five more books he wanted to write. When he died on January 21, 1950, Orwell "had lived and written his own biography" (Wolfe 175), and *Nineteen Eighty-Four* remains its towering final chapter.

HISTORICAL SETTING

While Orwell battled ill health and personal rejection by various women to write *Nineteen Eighty-Four*, Britain was fighting the harsh legacy of World War II. Everything about Britain's postwar situation seemed gloomy. The new Labour government imposed a harsh austerity program based on moral principles, but their agenda soon proved disheartening to the British public. Social changes carried an enormous price tag, which meant heavy taxes and a grinding rationing program of most necessities of daily British life—fuel, furniture, clothing—until 1948. Food was not completely de-rationed until 1954. The Labour government nationalized the nation's railway system, the steel, electrical, and mining industries, civil aviation, the Bank of England, and the entire medical system, but soon British voters found the costs outweighed the promises made by Labour's welfare state.

At the same time, the Soviet Union was increasingly threatening the Western democracies. Winston Churchill, almost alone, had been warning the world about Soviet totalitarianism, which he called "a new kind of barbarism" since 1918 (Johnson 74), but for a long time Western governments refused to listen.

The Yalta Conference in March 1945 brought exactly what Churchill feared and Stalin most wanted to hear: the ailing Roosevelt agreed to remove all American forces from Europe in two years and allowed Stalin to swallow up Poland. Serious consequences ensued. In the now famous "Iron Curtain" speech at Fulton, Missouri, two years later, Churchill bluntly defined the new Cold War, and the same year, the United States, not Labour-led Britain, supported Greece and Turkey against Soviet pressures. In 1948, a Communist coup toppled the government of Czechoslovakia and the Soviets blockaded Berlin. On October 1, 1949, after Communists proclaimed the People's Republic of China which Britain recognized as well as the Nationalist Chinese Taiwan government, the United States spearheaded the formation of the North Atlantic Treaty Organization (NATO). Having begun, like World War II, over Poland, the Cold War ripened over Korea and eventually embraced the whole world: "Stalin had polarized the earth" (Johnson 452).

Stalin's power base was a Soviet Union gripped by a savage totalitarianism whose like the world had never seen. Since Stalin feared a possible revolt by the Russian masses, stability at home was his greatest priority, and he maintained it by waging a secret war against his own people (Tolstoy 278ff and Shapiro and Reddaway 172).

Following the Khrushchev-era "thaw" around 1956, Soviet demographers estimated that the Germans were responsible for only a third, or at most half, of the thirty million Soviet deaths in World War II. Most of those deaths were civilian casualties attributable to Stalin's policies, which he tried to cover up by ruthlessly minimizing the number of foreigners allowed inside the Soviet Union. Anyone who had had even accidental contact with non-Soviet ideas—journalists, engineers, scientists, serving officers like Nobel Prize winner Aleksandr Solzhenitsyn, and several million returned prisoners of war, including two million handed over by the British and Americans, were either massacred on arrival or consigned to the Gulag (Stalin's prison system) where an estimated seven million perished in 1940 alone (Tolstoy 283). Stalin's compulsory internal deportations of large sections of the population suspected of German sympathies— Crimean Tartars, Caucasian peoples, and Volga Germans—also resulted in widespread epidemics and starvation.

In spite of these horrifying facts, readily available to the West in the late 1940s through fugitives from the U.S.S.R., from Western visitors like Orwell's friend Malcolm Muggeridge, and even from published Soviet sources, Western support for Stalin "often took the form of neo-religious adulation . . . What was glaringly obvious to Arthur Koestler and George Orwell might have been equally so to [Soviet sympathizers] Louis Aragon . . . or Lillian Hellman" (Tolstoy 436 n.32)—but it was not.

The Western adoration of Stalinism took some strange forms. Some women intellectuals even confused Stalinism with feminism, feeling that sexual freedom was worth its weight in starvation, forced labor, and the extermination of the intelligentsia. "All kinds of personal and social inadequacies drove a troubled generation into projecting its neuroses on to a perfected proletarian Utopia" (Lyons 324). Orwell, who himself was lonely, rejected, exhausted, and incurably ill, relentlessly exposed the individual and collective neuroses by extrapolating totalitarianism into the awful "perfected proletarian Utopia" of *Nineteen Eighty-Four*.

PLOT

The pattern or design of *Nineteen Eighty-Four* is Winston Smith's harrowing descent to the obliteration of his personality. Orwell divided the novel into three approximately equal parts. As he had done in earlier works, midway through *Nineteen Eighty-Four* he incorporated his own sociopolitical theories in a long abstract narrative. He also added an Appendix, "The Principles of Newspeak." "Newspeak" was his term for the minimized and perverted form of English that the ruling regime of *Nineteen Eighty-Four* used to control its population.

Part I of *Nineteen Eighty-Four* records the growing antagonism of Orwell's protagonist Winston Smith to the regime that pressures him to distort the truth. It begins with Smith, hurrying home on a windy cold day in April, just as the clocks ominously strike thirteen. As Smith goes about his daily grind, constantly reminded that "Big Brother is Watching You!" (*NEF* 5), Orwell depicts the sleazy, regimented, repressive world of 1984. This world is separated into three geographical nations: Oceania (created when the United States absorbed Britain), Eurasia, and Eastasia, perpetually fighting with one another for social control. Nuclear warfare has been outlawed, but Oceania keeps its people hysterically fearful of foreign attack. The ruling elite is led by the absolute dictator Big Brother, whose ruggedly handsome features and heavy black mustache resemble Stalin's at the time of the Spanish Civil War. Big Brother controls Oceania through terror. His ruling elite is the Inner Party like the Soviet Politburo about two percent of the population. The Outer Party is about thirteen percent. Everyone else belongs to the Proles, the oppressed masses who labor like poor doomed Boxer at the mercy of the Party. The Party drugs them into insensibility with meaningless work, films, football, beer, gambling, and State-produced pornography (*NEF* 29, 61–62). Ninety-eight percent of Oceania thus staggers along in a wretched existence resembling England's postwar misery.

Big Brother's regime hypocritically calls its instruments of repression by marvelous-sounding names. The Ministry of Plenty assures that citizens scrape by on a bare subsistence diet of horrid food that recalls Orwell's detested boarding-school diet based on margarine and lard, with anything appetizing, like chocolate, severely rationed. The Ministry of Peace conducts constant meaningless subatomic warfare against Eurasia and Eastasia with fearsome new weapons like rockets, keeping the population in a state of perpetual war fever. The Ministry of Love enforces Big Brother's will by terrorism and brute force, and the Ministry of Truth relentlessly bombards the regimented citizens with patriotic propaganda, constantly spying on them with the latest technological devices—and their own Party-indoctrinated children.

In Oceania, language has become the perverted servant of the state. With their electronic gadgetry, the Thought Police observe all sounds, all movements, even heartbeats. They hunt down and destroy all books printed before the mid-1960s, carrying out what Orwell considered the most reprehensible abuse of all, "Newspeak," a reduction of the supple multifaceted English language into terms so general they become sinister, absurd opposites of their original meanings, like the names of Big Brother's various Ministries. Winston Smith works at the Ministry of Truth. He slavishly produces trashy literature and revamps Big Brother's speeches to accommodate the regime's self-serving revisions of history (*NEF* 35). Even though he has only a few sketchy recollections of his childhood, Smith fears he is the last man in Oceania to possess a memory—hence Orwell's working title, "The Last Man in Europe," which implies that removing the memory of the past deprives individuals of their very selves.

Winston Smith, a thirty-nine-year-old member of the Outer Party, suffers from an unhealing varicose ulcer on his leg that, like Flory's birthmark, sets him apart from the rest of Oceania's population. Smith has become uneasy about his work and his life, and he has begun keeping a diary. A diary is strictly forbidden, both because it demonstrates and records individuality and because he is writing it in "Oldspeak," the infinitely flexible English language which Big Brother justifiably fears as a demonstration of individual freedom. Smith covers the first page with the revolutionary forbidden statement, "Down with Big Brother!" (*NEF* 19).

Part II traces Smith's sexual involvement with Julia, an attractive young member of the Anti-Sex League. With some difficulty Julia manages to seduce Smith. The progress of their relationship parallels Smith's growing fascination with a mysterious book by Emanuel Goldstein, a declared and exiled enemy of the State. Smith carries on a clandestine affair with Julia in a room he rents above Mr. Charrington's dark little antique shop. Smith finds its "beautiful rubbish" (*NEF* 84) from the past irresistible, like the useless but lovely lump of glass that he buys for four dollars despite knowing that the Party could use it as evidence of his disloyalty. After Smith has been seeing Julia for some time, a man named O'Brien contacts them, offering them membership in a secret Anti-Big Brother group called "The Brotherhood."

Through O'Brien, Smith receives a copy of Goldstein's forbidden book, *The Theory and Practice of Oligarchical Collectivism*, an exposition of the ideas Orwell used to construct *Nineteen Eighty-Four*. One evening shortly afterwards, Smith begins reading the book to Julia in Charrington's little upper room. They both fall asleep, only to awaken hours later betrayed by Charrington to the Thought Police who crash into the room in their iron-shod boots, brutally arrest Julia and Smith, and almost casually smash the beautiful glass paperweight to smithereens on the hearthstone.

Part III is devoted to O'Brien's lengthy interrogation and torture of Smith deep in the bowels of the Ministry of Love, where the Thought Police deliver Smith and Julia. O'Brien is really a high-ranking member of the Thought Police who knew about—and just possibly engineered—their affair from the start. He alternately tortures Smith and debates with him, trying to make him succumb to loving Big Brother. Neither indoctrination nor various forms of torture break Smith, until O'Brien has him taken to "Room 101," the place that contains what each individual fears most—in Smith's (and Orwell's) case, rats. Faced with a ghastly mask through which an enormous sewer rat will attack his eyes, Smith surrenders to O'Brien. He begs O'Brien to torture Julia instead, giving up the last shred of his self-respect, so that he can now believe he loves Big Brother. Smith is then released and given a better job at the Ministry of Truth. Considerably later, he meets Julia and discovers they betrayed each other. Orwell closes *Nineteen Eighty-Four* with a devastating glimpse of Smith swilling Victory Gin in the Chestnut Café, completely brainwashed into loving submission to Big Brother.

CHARACTER DEVELOPMENT

Orwell had read about Soviet totalitarianism in the 1930s and 1940s, and he fictionalized it through the chief characters of *Nineteen Eighty-Four*. He also shaped the inner view of Smith's tragedy out of his own experiences with political terrorism—being hunted by Communists on the streets of Barcelona and later feeling enormously guilty at living with the knowledge that while his comrades Bob Smillie and Georges Kopp suffered imprisonment and torture, he, Orwell, had been able to escape. As Orwell seemed to be, Winston Smith is also trapped by the contradictions of his personality. His gift for language, the creative ability humanity has always associated with divinity, forces him to rebel—and condemns him, too, just as Orwell was condemned by left-wing intellectuals because he insisted on paying homage to Catalonia and exposing the truth about Soviet-backed international communism.

Complex motivations underlie the story pattern of *Nineteen Eighty-Four*. Oceania's monolithic foundation rests on state-mandated terror, orchestrated by the ruling elite and carried out not only by its various agencies but by almost all of the citizens themselves. Each of Orwell's three major characters, however, responds to Big Brother's state terrorism differently, representing Orwell's attitudes toward three segments of modern society: women, rulers, and thinking individuals.

In 1933, apropos of James Joyce's *Ulysses*, Orwell set down the aims he considered paramount in writing a novel. The author's simplest job, Orwell felt, was to "display or create character"; second, to incorporate "a kind of pattern or design"; and finally, toughest of all, to produce "*good writing*" (Orwell's italics)—if the novelist was up to doing so (*CEJL* 1:126).

To display and create character in *Nineteen Eighty-Four*, Orwell again used the dual perspective he admired in *Ulysses*, where Joyce conveyed the opinions of a common man from within while still portraying that man from an outside, intellectualized point of view. Orwell's inside-outside perspective allowed him to unveil one of the most sinister horrors of totalitarianism, its ability to brainwash its victims into believing that they deserve their own punishment and love their tormentors. He illustrated this grim principle in his three major characters of *Nineteen Eighty-Four*—his protagonist Winston Smith, Smith's lover Julia, and Smith's antagonist O'Brien, the quintessentially corrupt bureaucrat.

Winston Smith's name is a supremely appropriate example of battling totalitarianism with words. "Winston Smith" ironically links the first name of totalitarianism's greatest modern opponent, the inspired orator Winston Churchill, with one of the commonest British names. "Smith" denotes a craftsman or "maker," which in the English Renaissance tradition connects a writer's creative talent with divine creativity. Orwell placed Winston Smith, whose one talent is his facility with words, at the focal point of the brutal light Orwell wanted to shed on totalitarianism, mercilessly portraying him from both within and without. To view Smith from the outside, Orwell drew on the intellectualized knowledge and analysis of the victim's role in a totalitarian society he had gleaned from his reading, but to portray Smith from the inside, he drew upon his own experiences as a tramp in London, a dishwasher in Paris, and a common soldier in Spain.

Smith himself is a bundle of conflicting motivations. His fear of being denounced as a rebel coexists with his frequent subconscious slips, like leaving his diary where it might have been observed by the old woman who wants him to fix her drain (*NEF* 21). As soon as he begins to defy the system, he experiences revealing dreams, symptoms of self-analysis and the subconscious realization of his need to be acknowledged as an individual. As he gradually realizes how shabbily he had treated his mother when he was a child, he also dreams about idyllic nature scenes, a stream with big fish waiting to be caught and an entrancing birdsong later echoed by the Prole woman doing her washing.

Throughout *Nineteen Eighty-Four*, Winston Smith tries to use language to maintain the reality of a world outside himself. Keeping his surreptitious diary, a form of speaking out against the regime, is his first forbidden step toward asserting his individuality. Next, after he and Julia become lovers, Smith reaches out to others by trying to piece together the nursery rhyme "Oranges and Lemons" (Orwell never used its title in *Nineteen Eighty-Four*), about the individual bell-voices of London churches. The rhyme echoes a humanizing tradition of England's forbidden past, since the Church of England customarily baptized and named each church bell as symbolizing a note in the voice of God. Smith learns another scrap of the rhyme from Julia, one more from Charrington, the owner of the flat where he and Julia make forbidden love, and the end of the rhyme from O'Brien, who initially pretended to be Smith's sympathizer and mentor in the fictitious rebel "Brotherhood." Finally Smith's own words betray him when, threatened by the ultimate torture that lurks in Room 101, he saves himself by hurling his last shred of integrity, his moral obligation to Julia, into the abyss.

Orwell also admired Joyce's frankness about sexuality and tried to emulate it in *Nineteen Eighty-Four*, principally through Julia, whose rebelliousness chiefly involves matters below the beltline. As the expression of ultimate intimacy and genuine love capable of inspiring idealistic individualism, human sexuality also threatens Oceania's ruling elite. Big Brother tries to stamp sex out by converting it into a mechanical child-producing function devoid of emotion. The regime wants to remove any vestige of rebellious traditional values in which a whole system of thought like Big Brother's could be swept aside by one consciously heroic individual human gesture, like Julia's flamboyant disrobing in Smith's dream (*NEF* 29).

Orwell gave Winston Smith a lover whose sexuality, like Eve's, helped destroy her mate's chances for happiness. In ancient Rome, the name "Julia," Orwell's choice for Smith's last-name-less lover, signified any and every daughter of the Julian clan, so Orwell's Julia was the Anywoman of postwar England, superficially brassy, selfish, weak, sensual, and opportunistic, a rebel only in matters sexual. Like another Julia, the exploited sister of the protagonist of *Keep the Aspidistra Flying*, Julia of *Nineteen Eighty-Four* deprives and abases herself to feed the appetites of a selfish man, though for Julia of *Nineteen Eighty-Four*, as for those "neurotic" intellectual women who yearned for the "liberation" Bolshevism seemed to offer, everything comes back to her own sexuality. Breaking the rules as best she can and still staying alive is all the creed Julia knows, so she is incapable of understanding either Smith's passion for objective truth or his desperate desire to stop the Party from annihilating the past (*NEF* 109, 128).

In Julia, Orwell captured all the mysterious ambivalence he seems to have felt about women. When Smith begins his one-man revolt, he suddenly notices that dark-haired young Julia, a red-sashed member of the Junior Anti-Sex League, is making advances toward him. Described in terms disturbingly explicit for their time, Smith's sexual relationship with Julia proves not liberating but lethal to his personality, just what the Party intends.

Conditioned by his own less than satisfactory relationships with women, Orwell portrayed Julia as motivated by her pursuit of forbidden pleasures, sexual desire compounded with thrill-seeking, lying, and opportunism. A member of a younger generation than Smith's, she has become cunning and practical, less susceptible to propaganda than older citizens are, and she feels that rebellion is possible only through secret disobedience or isolated acts of violence (*NEF* 127), so her lovemaking is politically, not emotionally, driven, though it catalytically inspires changes in Smith.

As a result of his relations with Julia, Smith suddenly recalls a suppressed memory of his mother, who had nothing to give him but love: she disappeared after he demanded his dying little sister's food. The pity and remorse he feels is reinforced when the singing of a poverty-stricken Prole woman doing her laundry awakens his sympathy. Smith's compassion derives from Orwell's own sensitivity toward the poor, like the prematurely aged girl struggling with a sewer drain near Wigan, an image that haunts several of his works. Julia's softening effect on Smith thus allowed Orwell to portray the downtrodden women of *Nineteen Eighty-Four* sympathetically.

Like Julia, and like real-life icons of totalitarian societies—Hitler, Lenin, Stalin—Winston Smith's antagonist has only one name. O'Brien is a first-name-less, hence universal, dehumanized and dehumanizing symbol of despotism. Smith is initially attracted by O'Brien's urbane manner, his impressive physique, his courteous manners, and his knowing glance, but Smith misreads them all as evidence that O'Brien has the individual integrity to defy the regime. O'Brien entices Smith into revealing his anti-Big Brother sentiments, then as Smith's torturer, diabolically manipulates language and through Smith's greatest fear, the hungry sewer rats, breaks Smith, body and soul, forever.

O'Brien, Big Brother's instrument of terrorism, thrives on power and exerts a malignant charisma to acquire, maintain, and extend it. Like Goethe's Mephistopheles, O'Brien consistently tells the truth in the service of evil, and Smith believes him, because he mistakes O'Brien's perversion of truth for the goodness he wants to believe exists. Smith also wants to believe in the rebel Brotherhood that O'Brien has adroitly created through hint and innuendo. When Julia and Smith, seeking the nonexistent Brotherhood, approach O'Brien, he immediately tells them that no help, only the means of suicide, will ever come from the Brotherhood. This is the literal truth, because the Brotherhood does not exist, but O'Brien is also deceiving them by playing on their idealistic readiness for individual sacrifice. Later, when Smith meets O'Brien in the dungeons of the Ministry of Love, O'Brien continues to tell the truth by revealing the state's monstrous vision of a boot stamping on a human face—forever (*NEF* 220).

O'Brien cunningly sets about destroying Smith's recollections of a free and peaceful world and warps Smith's sense of responsibility. He fosters Smith's growing sense of guilt and helps Smith destroy himself by causing Smith to love him, his torturer (*NEF* 207). In Orwell's day, this was a frequent and well-documented phenomenon in studies of Stalinism, where Party members, who after the peasants were Stalin's chief victims, "managers and specialists, writers and scholars, who [in the 1930s] alone might have prevented or stopped their country's descent into utter lawlessness . . . submitted or cooperated . . .The most astonishing aspect of the process [was] their tendency to worship the man in charge of their torment" (Joravsky xvii).

THEMATIC ISSUES

In *Nineteen Eighty-Four*, Orwell returned to topics he had treated in other works—imperialism, class, poverty, morality, freedom, and language—in the context of a drab future dystopia, a hopelessly wrong society, where the greatest heresy is the expression of common sense. As its working title, "The Last Man in Europe," suggests, *Nineteen Eighty-Four* opposes the free world within one human being's consciousness to the vast totalitarian realm outside it, which inexorably seeks to crush individuality, free choice, and common sense—all incorporated in humanity's defining ability, the capacity to shape thoughts into words.

All of Orwell's major topics coalesce in the great message he had been working toward all his creative life and now achieved in *Nineteen Eighty-Four*: that one man, even if doomed, must fight with everything he has against unjust collective forces like capitalism and totalitarianism that use the perversion of language to dehumanize and destroy him.

Orwell's literary career had been sparked by his disgust with British imperialism, the "white man's burden" of domination over the brown, black, red, and yellow races, and he had originally hoped that British Socialism could solve the socioeconomic conditions of class, industrialism, and capitalism which condemned so many human beings to poverty. In the bitter aftermath of World War II, however, Orwell realized that socialism was causing more problems inside Britain than it could possibly solve, and that internationally, when perverted by Stalinism, it could lead to disaster. In 1949, he still insisted that he supported the British Labour Party and that he never intended *Nineteen Eighty-Four* as an attack on socialism, but he targeted "the perversions to which a centralised [*sic*] economy is liable and which have already been partly realised [*sic*] in Communism and Fascism." Further, he insisted that *Nineteen Eighty-Four* was not a protest against one dictatorial system, like Hitler's or Stalin's, but a warning against totalitarianism in general. "Totalitarianism," Orwell maintained, *if not fought against* [Orwell's italics], could triumph anywhere" (*CEJL* 4:502).

Orwell's desire to air the evil purposes of totalitarianism ran counter to the prevailing atmosphere of the late 1940s, which still demanded admiration of "Uncle Joe" Stalin and his regime as respected wartime allies. The forbidden "Book" Winston Smith read, supposedly authored by exiled Emanuel Goldstein, a Trotsky-like theorist Big Brother denounced as the chief enemy of the state, is really Orwell's own economic-political theory, and it deliberately shows that Big Brother's Oceania, supposedly the realization of idealistic socialistic goals, was actually a despotic dictatorship.

As he had done in several of his other books, Orwell incorporated his theories in a long, demanding passage central to *Nineteen Eighty-Four*. "The Book" teaches Smith that Oceania is far from being the proletarian Party paradise. The Inner Party, a privileged parasitic minority, maintains itself not only by terror but by constant war. War, fueled by the regime's mind-twisting collective demonstrations of Hate, keeps Oceania's industries working while draining the nation's wealth from its citizens. War sustains the Inner Party's exclusive power, provides an emotional basis for the hierarchies of this society, and upholds Party morale by creating a population of paranoid, dependent, "credulous," and "ignorant" fanatics (*NEF* 157–58).

While Big Brother's regime used war, with all its deprivations, its hatred, and its hysteria, to enslave its populace collectively, it devoted just as much energy to stamping out any expression of personal freedom. In order to conquer the Earth, the Party had to dominate history totally and eradicate any expression of independent thought. To implement these actions, the Party's chief instrument was the Ministry of Truth. Orwell modeled his portrait of the Ministry of Truth on Stalin's official body of historical theoreticians, with a healthy dash of his own experiences in the British Ministry of Information. Soviet historians had to follow Party precepts or be deported to the Gulag as enemies of the state. First, the Party's history had to be viewed as the completely admirable chronicle of the all-wise leader's perfect policies carried out by his virtuous people. Next, any notion unacceptable to Big Brother either had to be attributed to the despicable pre-Revolutionary past; or it had to be declared the work of foreign enemies; or to the mistakes of leaders like Goldstein or Snowball who wickedly had worked themselves into public trust and who were speedily ejected when their views clashed with the leader's. Finally, the policies of the all-powerful, all-admirable leader, Big Brother or Napoleon the Royal Berkshire Swine, always dictated the definition of what was acceptable and what was not. Historians had to elaborate and illustrate the leader's views at any given moment, even if these views changed arbitrarily (Joravsky xvii–xviii). In addition, no Soviet historian dared admit that the Russian Communist leaders of the U.S.S.R. had misused their subject nationalities as savagely as any empire in the past had done.

Commenting sidelong in *Nineteen Eighty-Four* that the best books are those which tell their readers what those readers already know, Orwell pointed out that Goldstein's Book was what Winston Smith would have written if he could have overcome the effects of Big Brother's abuse sufficiently to put his thoughts in order (*NEF* 165). The Book showed Smith, a talented writer, the extent of the Party's perversion of history, but it also forced Smith to realize how fatally his own freedom as a creative individual had been perverted. The Stalinist theory of history on which Orwell modeled Big Brother's repression of objective truth rests on the debatable premise that "Nothing exists except through human consciousness" (*NEF* 218), an early version of the holy mantra of subjectivity—"Perception is reality."

Outraged by the denial of objective truth and the extent to which that denial was being accepted in Britain, Orwell insisted that since freedom and morality were anchored in objective truth, totalitarianism uses the most subversive methods to destroy truth where it is born and lives, in the core of each human soul. In order to break its citizens' spirits and force them into total obedience to the state, servants of totalitarianism like O'Brien broke down each individual's belief in objective truth, making each victim first accept the repression of truth, then welcome it, and finally become its adoring accomplice (*NEF* 221).

Winston Smith's experiences in the depths of the Ministry of Love at first follow the same sequence that every repressive human agency—the Inquisition, the Gestapo, and the KGB are only a few—has used to obliterate its victim's belief in objective truth. Smith first endures physical deprivation— no food, no sleep, no companionship—then physical torture and drugs which intensify the constant nagging questioning by Party intellectuals, while O'Brien promises to save him and to cure him of the mistaken beliefs which have brought him such torment. Even after shock therapy forces Smith to capitulate during the culmination of the first stage of torture, he retains his grip on truth: he knows the evil system will kill him, but he will die defying it. He has not yet betrayed Julia, and he knows "to die hating them—that is freedom" (*NEF* 231).

But Big Brother's regime is more dehumanizing, Orwell says, than Nazi Germany or the Soviet Union because it pursues power for its own sake (*NEF* 217). The Party cannot allow Smith the freedom to hate evil or the serene self-respect that comes from witnessing to the truth, as Goldstein's Book does. It knows anyone can break if the pressure is great enough, and it uses the diabolical Room 101, the thing each individual fears most, to break Smith forever. To save himself from O'Brien's hungry sewer rats, Smith commits the one betrayal he can never forgive himself for making, relinquishing not just Julia, but his own morality, his belief in truth, for which he had made her name his symbol. Winston Smith's tragedy is not death; it is a bigger salary at the Ministry of Truth, more gin to wallow in with other broken souls, the mutual contempt he and Julia now share—in short, a life of loving Big Brother, the worst form of slavery the human race has yet devised.

STYLISTIC AND LITERARY DEVICES

Orwell believed that "good writing" was the novelist's most difficult task. Despite all the serious problems he had to face while writing *Nineteen Eighty-Four,* it contains some of his most powerful writing. He had his own hard-won memories and experiences to draw on. In addition, well before writing *Nineteen Eighty-Four* Orwell had analyzed the strengths and weaknesses of other authors' "dystopias," fictional future societies based on everything wrong in human relationships and power structures. By observing their styles and literary devices, Orwell was able to polish his *Nineteen Eighty-Four*, not only claiming but demonstrating how insidiously language can be distorted for sinister purposes.

Prophecy was a subject Orwell simply could not let alone (Gross 139). Since his youth, Orwell had been fascinated by dystopian novels, which often denounced capitalistic oppression. He compared four of them in his 1940 essay "Prophecies of Fascism." The common ancestor for several modern dystopias was H. G. Wells' *When the Sleeper Wakes* (1899) (Hammond 171). Orwell thought Wells offered a vision of a glittering and sinister materialistic and purposeless world with a frozen class system that depraved its upper class and enslaved its workers, but according to Orwell, Wells failed to show how technology could be used to control a population. Orwell's own answer was through terror and the sinister manipulation of language. These required images of violence, like those Jack London used in *The Iron Heel* (1909). Orwell noted that in writing *The Iron Heel*, reputed in the 1940s to be a prediction of Nazism, London had realized that the struggle between capitalism and socialism would be the most unscrupulous and violent ever seen. London's savage streak evidenced itself in cruel and shocking images (*CEJL* 2:30) That novel may have given Orwell images like Smith's glass paperweight, a relic of fine craftsmanship from an earlier, more civilized age, wantonly smashed by Big Brother's Thought Police. London's title may well have inspired O'Brien's unforgettable image of a boot smashing a human face—forever.

Compared to Wells' book, Orwell found *The Iron Heel* lacking Wells' convincing grasp of scientific possibilities, weaker in characterization, and clumsily written, all qualities that Orwell seems to have tried to improve upon in *Nineteen Eighty-Four* by incorporating modern military weaponry like rockets into Big Brother's arsenal, by delving deeply into the complex motivations of his leading characters, and especially by meticulously honing his trademark crystalline style, which he used in the main narrative of *Nineteen Eighty-Four.*

Orwell felt that Aldous Huxley's *Brave New World* (1930), which also owed a debt to *When the Sleeper Wakes*, turned the future into a Riviera resort, lacking the pseudo-religious dimension which makes *Nineteen Eighty-Four* so morally disturbing. The ruling system of *Brave New World* did not elevate its leadership to near-divinity as the regime of *Nineteen Eighty-Four* did, mesmerizing its population through fanatical state-mandated hate-chanting invocations and its cult of the all-powerful leader's personality. Big Brother's regime insisted that its subjects/victims "love" him, perverting the word that occurs at the heart of almost all human forms of worship. Huxley's dystopia also lacks the technology which enables near-perfect surveillance of the citizenry and the universal obligatory Hate rallies.

Similar distortion of vital words occurs in Evgeny Zamiatin's *We* (1924), which Orwell reviewed while he was writing the early drafts of *Nineteen Eighty-Four*. Orwell felt *We* was intriguing, though not a first-rate novel, but he did observe Zamiatin's use of the word "Guardians" to denote the political police responsible for tracking down and obliterating dissent, and Zamiatin's title "Benefactor," for the great leader unanimously elected each year. These terms carry a bitter irony matched by Orwell's own "Ministry" titles and the obligatory "love" for Big Brother that O'Brien forces on Winston Smith.

Orwell knew that even if language could be corrupted by regimes like Big Brother's, it also was the best means to bring about salutary changes in society. In his reviewing, Orwell had seen many examples of both the bad writing he intended to avoid and the good writing he worked so hard to achieve. Although *Nineteen Eighty-Four* has flaws, notably sketchy characterizations of minor figures and the awkwardly incorporated theoretical material in Goldstein's Book, this novel proves that Orwell could produce some of the most effective literary satire seen in English fiction since Dickens and Swift. Michael Hodgart calls *Nineteen Eighty-Four* a "comic inferno, a descent into an unchanging underworld" comparable to Book III of *Gulliver's Travels*, the voyage to Laputa, an "immensely funny vision of hell" (Gross 14).

Orwell probably would have agreed with Dorothy L. Sayers that Hell is work that has no meaning (Sayers 1956: 46). One of Orwell's primary targets was the entire intellectual establishment of England, who toiled mindlessly away at the Ministry of Information and the BBC, like Big Brother's minions churning out reams of meaningless but politically correct trash, "showing immense energy while they pursue[d] their imbecile and deadly careers" (Hodgart 141).

In Dante's medieval Christian universe, no vengeful deity sent souls to the eternal Inferno; human beings sentenced themselves by choosing to sin. Despite his animosity toward the Roman Catholic Church, Orwell agreed, placing the responsibility for an individual's reward or punishment squarely on himself. Prostituting the gift of language was one of the most heinous sins Orwell, who had spent his entire creative life perfecting his utterly lucid prose style, could imagine, so he scorchingly satirized the condemned souls of the British literary establishment who had chosen their own fate.

In "Politics and the English Language," which Orwell wrote at the same time he was beginning *Nineteen Eighty-Four*, he insisted that illogical thought and misused language corrupt each other, but he optimistically believed that this moral-linguistic decay should and could be cured. He presented six sublimely straightforward rules of language usage that can maintain intellectual integrity and improve the use of language as an instrument not to conceal or prevent thought, but to express it. His "thou shalt nots" of honest and effective language usage prohibit using trite figures of speech, long words instead of short ones, passive verbs instead of active ones, and pretentious jargon instead of plain English, always cutting out unnecessary verbiage and avoiding anything that was "outright barbarous" (*CEJL* 4:133, 139). If writers and speakers followed Orwell's exquisitely clear advice, readers could easily distinguish between truth, the foundation of freedom, and propaganda, the servant of totalitarian oppression. *Nineteen Eighty-Four* remains Orwell's proof that language can easily be corrupted for evil manipulative purposes. When the novel first appeared, a number of booksellers who read it were frightened into insomnia (Bright-Holmes 330) and *The New York Times* reported that ninety percent of the novel's first reviews were "overwhelmingly admiring, with cries of terror rising above the applause" (31 July 1949).

"The Principles of Newspeak," Orwell's Appendix to *Nineteen Eighty-Four*, carries distortion of language to a black-humorous extreme. Newspeak is Oceania's official language, the vehicle for promulgating the worldview and mental habits of the supporters of totalitarian "Ingsoc" (English Socialism) and for making free thought impossible. Newspeak strips all words of their enriching shades of meaning and ambiguities. It makes all parts of speech interchangeable, barbarically regularizes grammar ("good-gooder-goodest"), and fatally diminishes vocabulary by tacking syllables onto simple words ("good-ungood"). Big Brother's regime intends that Newspeak be ugly, skeletal, depraved, and as independent as possible of human consciousness. Over time, as language usage deteriorates and literacy in the Western democracies diminishes, Newspeak is becoming less a darkly absurd exaggeration than an all too frightening possibility.

Whether the lasting impression of *Nineteen Eighty-Four* is optimistic or pessimistic has always been debatable. Certainly its bleak tone reflects Orwell's severe physical deterioration and many of the unhappy circumstances of his life, especially his hatred of injustice that started at St. Cyprian's and mounted throughout his life, but the general tendency to read *Nineteen Eighty-Four* as totally pessimistic has made it Orwell's most misunderstood work (Shelden 1991: 430). Orwell put many of his own memories into this book, and some of them were very positive, even idyllic, like Winston Smith's adored "Golden Country" based on Orwell's beloved rural Thames Valley landscapes and like Smith's antique paperweight, a cherished memento of the peaceful prewar Edwardian era of Orwell's youth.

Like Swift, whose ferocious satire shocked his public into recognizing social abuses like Britain's deliberate starvation of Ireland, Orwell satirized threatening totalitarian trends not to counsel gloomy passivity but to jolt his readers into resistance. The terms "Big Brother," "Newspeak," and the title *Nineteen Eighty-Four* itself have become accepted English nouns, permanent reminders that humanity must eternally battle the dangerous will to power and its servant, the perversion of language which eternally menaces the freedom of the human soul.

ALTERNATIVE CRITICAL PERSPECTIVE: FEMINISM

From the feminist perspective, much traditional literature is "patriarchal," negating or at best downplaying the role of women. Since feminist criticism is often associated with the feminist political movement, a feminist critique of a traditional novel usually attempts to raise consciousness about the importance and unique nature of women in literature. Feminist criticism thus often insists that male writers have ignored women and/or presented inaccurate or prejudiced opinions of them. Feminist criticism also tries to foster a more balanced view of the nature and value of women, generally evaluating literary works according to how these works present their female characters.

Feminist critiques of *Nineteen Eighty-Four* focus on Orwell's treatment of women characters and on the possible changes in his understanding of women and their roles that treatment reflects. Crucial to this approach is the importance of women characters in the novel, which in *Nineteen Eighty-Four* might seem relatively minor. Julia is the means to Orwell's end of presenting Winston Smith's tragedy; any object of Smith's "love," that is, anyone or anything he desired as an expression of his individuality in opposition to Big Brother's rules for behavior, would have served equally well as the instrument of the ultimate price—his self-respect—he pays to "save" himself. Orwell never showed Julia from within and never explored her individuality beyond her desire to get by with what she could for her own pleasure. In Parts I and II, he showed her as an irresistible threat to Smith, because even their stolen moments of sexual union demonstrated only selfish gratification, not genuinely shared experience. Like other women in Orwell's life and novels, Julia seemed to live for the moment, preying on men to please herself alone.

A narrowly feminist reading of *Nineteen Eighty-Four* would condemn Smith and Orwell for their apparent lack of sympathy for Julia as well as for their distaste for the elderly prostitute Smith visited before Julia, for Smith's selfish demands on his poor mother, for his cruelty toward his feeble former wife Katherine, his loathing of the repellent little girl spies, and his general fear and loathing of young, pretty girls. Daphne Patai maintains that Orwell directly belittled women in his conversation and that he portrayed women, especially protective mother-figures, as positive, which was really his form of contempt for them as mere "breeding animals" (Patai 258). She castigates Orwell for alleged inability to see issues from the feminist perspective and for promoting destructive masculinity by accepting the masculine ideology of domination, violence, and aggression as the human norm. Patai's reviewer Arthur Eckstein, however, notes that she completely avoids the context of *Nineteen Eighty-Four*: "Patai would prefer not to think very much about the real world of the Gulag" (Eckstein 53).

A wider view, however, might treat Julia's liberated sexual activity as her only means of rebelling against the Party. Her flinging aside the red sash of the Junior Anti-Sex League is one of those forbidden grand old gestures that Smith so admired in his dreams. In Big Brother's realm, physical release is the last possible exercise of personal freedom. The Party is trying to control its citizens' sexuality expressly because it is the most intimate area of an individual's life and least likely to be subject to outside restriction. Julia's determination to exercise her sexuality might be seen not as neurotic, but as a form of protest against the male-dominated Big Brotherly society which is trying to smother all possible individual activity (Shelden 1991: 432). In this reading, when Smith and Julia meet at the end of the novel, each bitterly full of "contempt and dislike" for the other (*NEF* 241), Julia shares Smith's tragedy. Feminists might see her fate as even worse than Smith's, because as Lord Byron observed, a man's love tends to be separate from his work and life—Smith had his literary work, his memories, his rebellion—but love, in the physical sense she wanted, had been Julia's whole existence.

If Julia is seen as a sympathetic figure, other minor female characters in *Nineteen Eighty-Four* might seem to signal a change in Orwell's attitude toward women. Like several female figures in his other works, the red-armed singing laundress of *Nineteen Eighty-Four* has Orwell's sympathy and compassion. She cannot change her hopeless fate, but she sings anyhow, one reason that Orwell saw hope in the common people. Many values he cherished most among the workers and the poor whose lives he had shared were demonstrated by women and symbolized in the little gifts that are all these women can afford to make—the numberless humble cups of tea he drank with miners' wives at Wigan, and the comforting asexual embraces of street women who, like Winston Smith's mother, had nothing to offer but their love.

The circumstances of Orwell's last months might reinforce the broader feminist reading of *Nineteen Eighty-Four*. Aware that he was mortally ill as he struggled to finish *Nineteen Eighty-Four*, Orwell's attitude toward women seems to have changed for the better, as Smith's epiphany at the end of *Nineteen Eighty-Four* seems to indicate. Full of cheap gin and self-disgust, Smith recalls a day when his mother, unable to give him the toys or even the food he demanded, played tiddlywinks with him. "For a whole afternoon they had been happy together, as in his earlier childhood" (*NEF* 243). In a flash, Winston Smith realized what he had lost: his soul. When he saved himself from O'Brien's rats by flinging away his moral obligation to Julia, Smith, not O'Brien or Big Brother, doomed himself to a living hell because he had surrendered to the injustice that eternally strives to crush the individual human spirit under its iron heel. Smith would have to live knowing that he had rejected peace with himself by betraying the innocence of his soul. By thrusting this bitter epiphany on Winston Smith, Orwell celebrated women's role as a catalyst for human freedom. Orwell's hospital-bed marriage to Sonia Brownell, whom he knew did not love him but who was willing for her own reasons to share her life, however briefly, with him, testified to the belief in the saving grace of women's love that Orwell seems to have worked out in the harrowing pages of *Nineteen Eighty-Four.*

10

Halfway to 2050: It Depends on You

George Orwell's best known essays are "Shooting an Elephant" and "Politics and the English Language." Both showcase his translucent English style, his political views, and his personal integrity. His most widely read books are *Animal Farm* and *Nineteen Eighty-Four*, both often read, despite his firm statement of wider aims, as attacks on Stalinism. Today, halfway between Orwell's death in 1950 and 2050, Big Brother's projected date for the destruction of all previous human history and literature, Stalin and his Soviet Union have all but disappeared. Are Orwell's works still relevant?

Orwell's Appendix to *Nineteen Eighty-Four*, "The Principles of Newspeak" leaps from Everyman to every social system, from the doomed individual to any society that dooms itself by perverting language and its servant technology to conceal, mystify, and deceive. As Orwell suggested allegorically in *Animal Farm*, fictionally in *Nineteen Eighty-Four*, and explicitly in "Politics and the English Language," the subversively easy way means subjectively reducing complex nuances of language to often opposite-meaning minimal units—in the process abandoning the objective truth that keeps us free.

Orwell knew that even democratic government, humanity's best hope yet for balancing the welfare of the individual against the welfare of the group, could be subverted this way. In "The Principles of Newspeak," he showed how the opening passage of the Declaration of Independence could be distilled into one opposite-meaning Newspeak word, *crimethink,* proving how easily a free society which insists on the individual's inalienable rights to life, liberty, and the pursuit of happiness can relinquish them in the name of supposed user-friendliness.

Orwell also knew that technology could be combined with twisted language to destroy privacy, manipulate information, and intimidate citizens. Halfway to 2050, how far have we come? A popular suspicion exists that technology, especially computer technology which often demands uncomfortable shifts in individuals' habits and lifestyles, might be used to bolster the power of any group in authority —bureaucrats, politicians, the police, the military. Distortions of language, especially in educational-business theory, are proliferating. The Total Quality Management (TQM) theory proposes, for example, that "quality is not a state of being (a noun) but something people do (a verb) (Chaffee and Sherr 19).

Orwell saw language abuse as the key to totalitarian control. He likely would have denounced current abuses of language which seem to be metastasizing via computer technology, whose vendors tend to preach fervent but nebulously defined Big Brotherish visions of the future: "Education is too important to exist without controls, without licensing, or without credentials. . . . Means are superfluous; it is results that count" (Twigg and Oblinger 8). Orwell probably would also have deplored as ominous other educational trends: many of the great books of the Western literary heritage are rapidly disappearing from university "core curricula," and some are even homogenized into bland prime-time television miniseries, while students' reading scores plummet despite bold innovative grant-generating educational thrusts.

Orwell saw it all coming. In his bitter autobiographical essay "Such, Such Were the Joys," he leaves no doubt that he believed his early schooling had tried to warp his talents, stifle his spirit, and smother his individuality under a hypocritical facade of phony language. All of Orwell's protagonists share his "primary alienation, the unearned outcast's mark. He saved his individuality, his 'crystal spirit,' by exorcising his original self through all his writing so that he could as George Orwell objectively look on the agonies of Eric Blair" (Woodcock 88).

Orwell's earliest published writing, particularly *Down and Out in Paris and London*, concentrates on the individual, the "one man" who even though doomed, must battle the unfair collective forces in his world, like capitalism, that are trying to dehumanize him. He soon found other targets to denounce—British imperialism in *Burmese Days*, religious hypocrisy in *A Clergyman's Daughter*, the British class system and capitalism again in *Keep the Aspidistra Flying*. After Orwell developed his concept of "democratic socialism" in *The Road to Wigan Pier* and passed through the crucible of the Spanish Civil War, he realized that socialism and its extension communism could be twisted into paths, like their ostensible enemy fascism, to totalitarianism. Orwell announced the truth about communism in *Homage to Catalonia,* which at first seemed futile, and far more successfully in *Animal Farm* and *Nineteen Eighty-Four,* which finally took the world by storm. In both novels he insisted that totalitarianism seized the power it craved by distorting language, the only means by which individuals, acting together, can defeat it.

Halfway to 2050, truth badly needs its defenders. "It is best to be wary of movements with large blazing truths in hand and the firm conviction that petty, pesky, literal truth therefore almost doesn't matter . . . that dishonesty or indifference to truth is justified by one's commitment to a cause" (Leo 16). Orwell always claimed that the message of *Nineteen Eighty-Four* was that only the individual who had the guts to tell the truth could halt totalitarianism: "Don't let it happen. It depends on you" (Woodcock 89). When a chief executive can quibble over the meaning of "is" and an on-line encyclopedia firm adapts historical fact to the country where it is sold (*Wall Street Journal* 15 June 1999), perversion of language to conceal, mystify, and deceive is debilitating Western society, aided and abetted by "the folklore surrounding computers—the images of power, the illusions of well-being, the fantasies and wishful thinking that have grown up around the machine" (Roszak xiii). The term "information" has come to mean "all good things to all people," but "Words that come to mean everything may finally mean nothing . . . their very emptiness may allow them to be filled with a mesmerizing glamour" (Roszak xiv)—precisely Orwell's message in *Nineteen Eighty-Four.*

Just as doomed Winston Smith still saw hope in the Proles, ordinary individuals still can and do point out that some contemporary emperors are stark naked. Each individual, Orwell believed, can exercise clearheaded common sense and reject the perversion of language and the blithe and lethal disregard of historical fact and objective truth—if the individual is willing, as he was, to pay the price.

Unless the eternal forces of totalitarianism that mask themselves as caring apostles of futurism succeed in Big Brothering Orwell's work out of existence in some malignant 2050 where writing allegedly "too hard" for students must be translated into a version of Newspeak, his work will continue to fight for freedom of thought and expression, staving off the horrors of Room 101 in the Ministry of Love, where totalitarianism relentlessly forces individuals to enslave themselves. Orwell was nothing more nor less than a truthteller who wrote his hard-won messages in a plain prose style "of a rhythm and a shapeliness to seduce the angels" (James 74). Because he believed that liberty means telling people what they do not want to hear, he knew that freedom depends on each person's courage to tell the truth, though few are able to do it. He did it nobly.

Selected Bibliography

Numerous books and critical articles on Orwell and his works have appeared yearly since 1977. The following lists offer only a sampling of the more accessible material.

WORKS BY GEORGE ORWELL

Note: Abbreviations used in the text appear in parentheses

COLLECTIONS

(*CEJL*): *The Collected Essays: Journalism and Letters of George Orwell*. Ed. Sonia Orwell and Ian Angus. 4 vols. New York: Harcourt, Brace and World, 1968.

The Complete Works of George Orwell. Ed. Peter Davison. 20 vols. London: Secker, 1998.

The Penguin Complete Longer Non-Fiction of George Orwell. Harmondsworth: Penguin, 1983.

The Penguin Complete Novels of George Orwell. Harmondsworth: Penguin, 1983.

The Penguin Essays of George Orwell. Harmondsworth: Penguin, 1984.

INDIVIDUAL WORKS

(*Down and Out*): *Down and Out in Paris and London*. London: Gollancz, 1933; New York: Harper, 1933.

(*BD*): *Burmese Days*. New York: Harper, 1934; London: Gollancz, 1935.

(*CD*): *A Clergyman's Daughter*. London: Gollancz, 1935; New York: Harper, 1936.

(*KAF*): *Keep the Aspidistra Flying*. London: Gollancz, 1936; New York: Harcourt, 1956.

(*RWP*): *The Road to Wigan Pier*. London: Gollancz, 1937; New York: Harcourt, 1958.

(*HC*): *Homage to Catalonia*. London: Secker and Warburg, 1938; New York: Harcourt, 1952.

(*CA*): *Coming Up for Air*. London: Gollancz, 1939; New York: Harcourt, 1950.

(*LU*): *The Lion and the Unicorn*. London: Secker and Warburg, 1941.

(*AF*): *Animal Farm*. London: Secker and Warburg, 1945; New York: Harcourt, 1946.

(*NEF*): *Nineteen Eighty-Four*. London: Secker and Warburg, 1949; New York: Harcourt, 1949.

BIBLIOGRAPHY

Meyers, Jeffrey, and Valerie Meyers. *George Orwell: An Annotated Bibliography of Criticism*. New York: Garland, 1977.

BIOGRAPHIES

Crick, Bernard. *Orwell: The First Complete Biography*. Boston: Little, Brown and Company, 1980.

Gross, Miriam, ed. *The World of George Orwell*. New York: Simon and Schuster, 1971.

Rees, Richard. *George Orwell: Fugitive from the Camp of Victory*. London: Secker and Warburg, 1961; Carbondale: Southern Illinois University Press, 1962.

Shelden, Michael. *Orwell: The Authorized Biography*. New York: HarperCollins, 1991.

———. "Revealed: George Orwell's Big Brother Dossier," *The Daily Telegraph* 22 June 1998: 12.

Stansky, Peter, and William Abrahams. *The Unknown Orwell*. London: Constable, 1972; New York: Alfred A. Knopf, 1972.

———. *Orwell: The Transformation*. London: Constable, 1979; New York: Alfred A. Knopf, 1980.

Woodcock. George. *The Crystal Spirit: A Study of George Orwell*. Boston: Little, Brown and Company, 1966.

Zwerdling, Alex. *Orwell and the Left*. New Haven, CT: Yale University Press, 1974.

CRITICAL STUDIES OF GEORGE ORWELL'S WORKS

Ash, Timothy Garton. "Orwell in 1998," *The New York Times* 2 October 1998: 10–14.

Carey, John. "Speaking His Mind," *The Sunday Times: Books* 5 July 1998. http://www.Thetimes.co.uk/news/pages/sti/98/07/05.

Greenblatt, Stephen. "George Orwell" in his *Three Modern Satirists: Waugh, Orwell, and Huxley*: New Haven, CT: Yale University Press, 1965.

Hammond, J. R. *George Orwell Companion: A Guide to the Novels, Documentaries and Essays*. London: Macmillan, 1982.

Jacobson, Dan. "The Invention of Orwell," *Times Literary Supplement* 21 August 1998: 3–4.

James, Clive. "The Truthteller," *The New Yorker* 18 January 1999: 72–78.

Krich, John. "Literary Pilgrimages: George Orwell," *The New York Times on the Web*. http:www.nytimes.com/books/98/05/10/specials.

Kubal, David L. *Outside the Whale: George Orwell's Art and Politics*. South Bend, Ind.: University of Notre Dame Press, 1972.

Lee, Robert A. *Orwell's Fiction*. South Bend, Ind.: University of Notre Dame Press, 1969.

Marks, Peter. "Where He Wrote: Periodicals and the Essays of George Orwell," *Twentieth Century Literature* 4 (Winter 1995): 266–84.

Naftali, Timothy. "George Orwell's List," *The New York Times on the Web* 29 July 1998. http://www.nytimes.com/library/books.

Patai, Daphne. *The Orwell Mystique: A Study in Male Ideology*. Amherst: University of Massachusetts Press, 1984.

Richardson, J. M., ed. *Orwell x 8: A Symposium*. Winnipeg, Canada: Ronald P. Frye and Co., 1986.

Wain, John. "A Toast to a Lonely Voice," *Encounter* September 1990: 31–33.

DOWN AND OUT IN PARIS AND LONDON

Astier, Henri. "Spilling the Beans in Paris and London: George Orwell and Jean-François Revel," *Contemporary Review* 264 (June 1994): 289–95.

THE ROAD TO WIGAN PIER

Greenwood, Walter. Review of *The Road to Wigan Pier*, quoted in "George Orwell," *Contemporary Authors* 132 Detroit, MI: Gale Publishing Co., 1991.

Hodgart, Richard. Introduction to *The Road to Wigan Pier*. Rpt. in *George Orwell: A Collection of Critical Essays*. Ed. Raymond Williams. New York: Prentice Hall, 1974.

Laski, Harold. Review of *The Road to Wigan Pier. The Left News* 20 March 1937.

Review of *The Road to Wigan Pier. The Daily Worker* 17 March 1937.

HOMAGE TO CATALONIA

Flower, Desmond. Review of *Homage to Catalonia. Observer* 19 May 1938.

ANIMAL FARM

Connolly, Cyril. Review of *Animal Farm*. *Horizon* 12 (September 1945): 216.

De Hezedus, Adam. Review of *Animal Farm*. *The Commonweal* 44 (12 September 1946): 528–30.

Sadley, Stephen. "An Immodest Proposal: 'Animal Farm'," in *Inside the Myth: Orwell, Views from the Left*. Ed. Christopher Norris. London: Lawrence and Weshart, 1984.

NINETEEN EIGHTY-FOUR

Howe, Irving, ed. 1984 *Revisited: Totalitarianism in Our Century*. New York: Harper and Row. 1983.

"POLITICS AND THE ENGLISH LANGUAGE"

Trail, George Y. "Teaching Argument and the Rhetoric of Orwell's 'Politics and the English Language' " *College English* 57 (September 1995): 570–84.

ADAPTATIONS OF ORWELL'S WORKS

Animal Farm. 1955, film. Produced by the Louis de Rougemont company, written and produced by John Halas and Joy Batchelor.

Animal Farm. 1965, play. Produced by Samuel French and adapted by Nelson Slade Bond.

The Merry War. 1998, film (adapted from *Keep the Aspidistra Flying*). Produced by Robert Bierman and starring Richard E. Grant and Helena Bonham-Carter.

Nineteen Eighty-Four. 1956, film. John Croydon, producer; Michael Anderson, director. Starring Edmond O'Brien as Winston Smith and Jan Sterling as Julia; omitted much of the literary complexity of the original.

Nineteen Eighty-Four. 1984, film. Simon Perry, producer; Michael Radford, director; Roger Deakins, cinematographer; starring John Hurt as Winston Smith, Richard Burton, Suzanna Hamilton, and Cyril Cusack. See Stanley Kauffmann, "Future Tense," *The New Republic* (4 February 1985): 26–28, and Susan Barraclough, "*1984* The Film: Past, Present or Future?," *History Today* 34 (December 1984): 59–60.

Nineteen Eighty-Four. 1963, play. Adapted and produced by Dramatic Publishing.

BIOGRAPHICAL/AUTOBIOGRAPHICAL STUDIES BY OR ABOUT ORWELL'S CONTEMPORARIES

Bright-Holmes, John. *Like It Was: The Diaries of Malcolm Muggeridge*. London: Collins, 1981.

Buddicom, Jacintha. *Eric and Us: A Remembrance of George Orwell.* London: Frewin, 1974.

Connolly, Cyril. *Enemies of Promise.* London: Routledge, 1938; Boston: Little, Brown, and Company, 1939.

Fyvel, T. R. *George Orwell: A Personal Memoir.* London: Weidenfield and Nicolson, 1982; New York: Macmillan, 1982.

Ogilvy, David. *Blood, Brains and Beer.* New York: Atheneum, 1978.

Plante, David. *Difficult Women: A Memoir of Three.* London: Gollancz, 1983; New York: Atheneum, 1983.

Rosenthal, Tom. "Putting on Her Orwell's Widow Act," *Daily Telegraph.* http://www.telegraph.co.uk/et/ac.

Thompson, John. *Orwell's London.* London: Fourth Estate, 1984; New York: Schocken Books, 1985.

Topp, Sylvia. "In Search of Orwell's Scottish Retreat," *North American Review* March–April 1994: 11–13.

Wadhams, Stephen, compiler. *Remembering Orwell.* Markham, Ontario: Penguin Books Canada, 1984.

Warburg, Fredric. *All Authors Are Equal.* London: Hutchinson, 1973.

Wolfe, Gregory. *Malcolm Muggeridge: A Biography.* Grand Rapids, MI: Eerdmans, 1997.

HISTORICAL AND LITERARY REFERENCES

Antonov-Ovseyenko, Anton. *The Time of Stalin: Portrait of a Tyranny.* New York: Harper and Row. 1981.

Arnstein, Walter L. *Britain Yesterday and Today: 1830 to the Present*, 5th ed. Lexington, MA: Heath, 1988.

Bentley, Michael. "Social Change: Appearance and Reality," in *The Cambridge Historical Encyclopedia of Great Britain and Ireland.* Ed. Christopher Haigh. Cambridge: Cambridge University Press, 1985.

Berthoud, Jacques. *"Literature and Drama," Early Twentieth Century Britan,* in *The Cambridge Cultural History of Britain.* Ed. Boris Ford. Cambridge: Cambridge University Press, 1989.

Brabazon, James. *Dorothy L. Sayers.* New York: Scribners, 1981.

Briggs, Asa. *A Social History of England.* New York: Viking, 1983.

Chaffee, Ellen Earle and Lawrence A. Sherr. *Quality: Transforming Postsecondary Education.* Washington, DC: George Washington University, 1992.

Churchill, R. S. and Martin Gilbert. *Winston S. Churchill.* 5 vols. London: Heinemann, 1966.

Cooper, Frederic Taber. "Arnold Bennett," in *Some English Story Tellers: A Book of the Younger Novelists.* New York: Holt, 1912.

Eckert, Charles W. "Initiatory Motifs in the Story of Telemachus," in *Myth and Literature.* Ed. John B. Vickery. Lincoln: University of Nebraska Press, 1966.

Eckstein, Arthur. Review of *Orwell, Masculinity and Feminist Criticism* by Daphne Patai (Amherst, MA: Univeristy of Massachusetts Press, 1984), *The Intercollegiate Review* (Fall 1985), 52–53.

Edwards, Bob. "George Orwell: A Programme of Recorded Reminiscences." Broadcast by the BBC 2 November 1960. BBC Archives, Red. No. TLO 24177.

Eliade, Mircea. *Myths, Dreams, and Mysteries.* Princeton, NJ: Princeton University Press, 1957; New York: HarperCollins, 1975.

Ford, Ford Madox. "H. G. Wells," in *Portraits from Life.* Boston: Houghton Mifflin, 1937.

Gilman, Richard. "Salvation, Damnation, and the Religious Novel," *New York Times* 2 December 1984, late city ed.: G1.

Goldberg, Paul. "Survival Course," review of *Man Is Wolf to Man: Surviving The Gulag* (Berkeley: University of California Press, 1998); *New York Times Book Review* 9 August 1998: 17.

Johnson, Paul. *Modern Times,* rev. ed. New York: HarperCollins, 1991.

Joravsky, David. Introduction to *Let History Judge: The Origins and Consequences of Stalinism* by Roy A. Medvedev. Ed. David Joravsky and Georges Haupt. New York: Knopf, 1971.

Karl, Frederick R. *A Reader's Guide to Joseph Conrad.* New York: Farrar, Straus and Giroux, 1960.

Koestler, Arthur. *The Invisible Writing.* London: Gollancz, 1954.

Leo, John. "True Lies vs. Total Recall," *U.S. News and World Report* 7 August 1995: 16.

Lyons, Eugene. *Assignment in Utopia.* London: Heinemann, 1937.

Mellers, Wilfrid and Rupert Hildyard. "The Cultural and Social Setting," in *Early Twentieth Century Britain.* Ed. Boris Ford. Cambridge: Cambridge University Press, 1989.

Progoff, Ira. "Waking Dream and Living Myth," in *Myths, Dreams and Religion.* Ed. Joseph Campbell. New York: Dutton, 1970.

Robbins, Keith. "From Imperial Power to European Partner 1901–1975: Overview," in *The Cambridge Historical Encyclopedia of Great Britain and Ireland.* Ed. Charles Haigh. Cambridge: Cambridge University Press, 1985.

Rose, Michael E. "Society: The Emergence of Urban Britain," in *The Cambridge Historical Encyclopedia of Great Britain and Ireland.* Ed. Christopher Haigh. Cambridge: Cambridge University Press, 1985.

Roszak, Theodore. *The Cult of Information,* 2nd ed. Berkeley: University of California Press, 1994.

Sayers, Dorothy L. "The English War," *Times Literary Supplement* 2014 (7 September 1940): 445.

———. "The Meaning of Heaven and Hell," in *Introductory Papers on Dante.* New York: Harper, 1956.

Seymour-Smith, Martin. *The New Guide to Modern World Literature,* 3rd ed. New York: Peter Bedrick, 1985.

Shapiro, Leonard and Peter Reddaway, eds. *Lenin: The Man, the Theorist, the Leader: A Reappraisal.* New York: Basic Books, 1967.

Shentalinsky, Vitaly. *Arrested Voices: Resurrecting the Disappeared Writers of the Soviet Regime.* Trans. John Crowfoot. New York: Martin Kessler Books, Free Press, 1996.

Solzhenitsyn. Aleksandr. "Nobel Lecture," trans. Alexis Klimoff. In *Aleksandr Solzhenitsyn: Critical Essays and Documentary Materials.* Ed. John B. Dunlop, Richard Hugh, and Alexis Klimoff. New York: Macmillan, 1973.

Supple, Barry. "The Economy: Adjustment, Affluence, Decline," in *The Cambridge Encyclopedia of Great Britain and Ireland.* Ed. Christopher Haigh. Cambridge: Cambridge University Press, 1985.

Sutherland, John. *The Stanford Companion to Victorian Fiction.* Stanford, CA: Stanford University Press, 1989.

Tertz, Abram (pseud. Andrei Sinyavski). *On Socialist Realism.* New York: Pantheon, 1960.

Tolstoy, Nikolai. *Stalin's Secret War.* New York: Holt, Rinehart and Winston, 1981.

Twigg, Carol A. and Diana C. Oblinger. "The Virtual University." Report from a Joint Educom/IBM Roundtable, Washington, DC, 5–6 November 1996.

Walker, Ronald G. "D. H. Lawrence," in *Critical Survey of Long Fiction.* Ed. Frank Magill. Englewood Cliffs, NJ: Salem Press, 1983.

Watson, Bruce. "Jack London Followed His Muse into the Wild." *Smithsonian* (February 1998): 105–13.

Whitaker, Reg. *The End of Privacy.* New York: New Press, 1999.

Index

About the Author

MITZI M. BRUNSDALE is professor of English at Mayville State University in North Dakota and Chair of the Division of Communication Arts.

4/00

ML